THE GREAT TRIBULATION

PAST OR FUTURE?

Two Evangelicals Debate the Question

Thomas Ice
Kenneth L. Gentry Jr.

kregel
PUBLICATIONS
Grand Rapids, MI 49501

*The Great Tribulation: Past or Future? Two Evangelicals
Debate the Question*

Copyright © 1999 by Thomas Ice and the Gentry Family
Trust

Published by Kregel Publications, a division of Kregel, Inc.,
P.O. Box 2607, Grand Rapids, MI 49501. Kregel Publications
provides trusted, biblical publications for Christian growth and
service. Your comments and suggestions are valued.

For more information about Kregel Publications, visit our
web site at www.kregel.com.

Cover design: Frank Gutbrod
Book design: Nicholas G. Richardson

Library of Congress Cataloging-in-Publication Data
Ice, Thomas.
    The great tribulation, past or future? / Thomas Ice,
Kenneth L. Gentry Jr.
        p.   cm.
    Includes bibliographical references and indexes.
    1. Tribulation (Christian eschatology). I. Gentry,
Kenneth L. II. Title.
BT888.I25   1999   236'.9—dc21   99-19010
                                                          CIP
ISBN 0-8254-2901-3

Printed in the United States of America

1 2 3 4 5 / 03 02 01 00 99

CONTENTS

INTRODUCTION

S ince the Bible is the Word of the Living God, it claims to prophetically "declare the end from the beginning" (Isa. 46:10).[1] So it does!
But all Christians do not agree as to when certain aspects of God's
prophetic Word are to be fulfilled in history. This is no small matter. If
large segments of prophecy have already been fulfilled, the future will
be quite different than many believers expecting a future consummation suppose. The opposite is also true. You can imagine the surprise
if certain events are still future for one who believes that they are past.
This would require a major adjustment in the thinking of many about
the past, present, and future. It is important to know what the Bible
teaches about the timing of the fulfillment of prophecy. And of para-
mount importance in Bible prophecy is determining whether the Tribulation—including the Great Tribulation—is a past, present, or future
event. That is the focus of this book.

When it comes to the fulfillment of biblical prophecy and the timing
of the Tribulation in history, there are four possibilities. The four views
are simple in the sense that they reflect the only four possible ways that
one can relate to time: past, present, future, and timeless. When speaking about the fulfillment of Bible prophecy, these four timing possibilities are called preterism, historicism, futurism, and idealism.

The *preterist* (Latin for "past") believes that most, if not all prophecy,
has already been fulfilled, usually in relation to the destruction of
Jerusalem in A.D. 70. The *historicist* (present) sees much of the current
church age as equal to the Tribulation period. Thus, prophecy has been
and will be fulfilled during the current church age. *Futurists* (future)
usually believe that almost no prophetic events are occurring in the
current church age, but will take place in the following future episodes:
the Tribulation of seven years, the Second Coming, the 1,000-year
millennium, and the eternal state. The *idealist* (timeless) does not

5

believe either that the Bible indicates the timing of events or that we can determine their timing in advance. Therefore, idealists see prophetic passages as teaching great truths about God to be applied to our present lives.

As we approach the historically significant prophetic year of A.D. 2000, a debate is developing within American evangelical Christianity over the timing of prophetic fulfillment. This represents somewhat of a shift in focus, for eschatological debate among conservatives has traditionally revolved around hermeneutics and millennial issues. This continues, but with the added factor of a new consciousness relating to the timing of prophetic fulfillment. The debate is shaping up as a showdown between preterism and futurism.

Idealism, as an approach to Bible prophecy, is rarely followed outside of liberal scholarship and thus is not a significant factor in the mainstream of current evangelical debate over when prophecy will be fulfilled. Historicism, once the dominant view of Protestants from the Reformation until the middle of the last century, appears to exert little attraction as a system of prophetic interpretation to conservative Christians (outside of Seventh-Day Adventist circles). However, it must be noted that most historicists take a preterist view of the Olivet discourse, disassociating it from the Tribulation as found in Revelation and some New Testament epistles. Within evangelicalism during the last one hundred fifty years, futurism has grown to dominate and overcome historicism. At the turn of the millennium, we see arising from evangelical preterism an attempt to challenge futurism. We must await the next millennium to see where this development will lead.

D. H. Kromminga has noted that "the preterist and the futurist methods, or approaches, stand at opposite extremes."[2] Perhaps this explains why the historicist and idealist approaches have receded into the background, while the futurist and preterist views are in the forefront. Until recently, futurism has enjoyed an unobstructed field. Preterism, the polar opposite of futurism, has arisen at least to provide a challenge to the futurist dominance within evangelicalism. This is why only futurism and preterism are considered in this book.

I have noted that American evangelical interpretation of Bible prophecy is still overwhelmingly dominated by the futurist approach, usually expressed in some form of dispensationalism. Around the 1970s, preterism began its current resurgence. Before its recent upswing, contemporary forms of preterism tended to be found only within academic circles, providing an occasional commentary here or there. The preterist rise to a more popular visibility likely began simultaneously within the ranks of the Church of Christ as it received renewed attention within evangelical consciousness through those within the Reformed tradition by the publishing of Jay Adams's *The Time Is at Hand* (1966) and J. Marcellus Kik's *An Eschatology of Victory* (1971). However, the most significant impetus to the resurgence of preterism has to be its widespread adoption and propagation by those within the Christian Reconstruction movement. Reconstructionist attraction to preterism appears to have been adopted by the late Dr. Greg Bahnsen and spread through him to many of his disciples who, in turn, helped it to expand.

It is important to realize that there are three kinds of preterism that I have labeled as (1) mild; (2) moderate; and (3) extreme. Mild preterism holds that the Tribulation was fulfilled within the first three hundred years of Christianity as God judged two enemies: the Jews in A.D. 70 and Rome by A.D. 313; but adherents still look for a future Second Coming. Moderate preterism, which is the position of Dr. Kenneth L. Gentry Jr., sees the Tribulation and the bulk of Bible prophecy as fulfilled in events surrounding the destruction of Jerusalem and the temple in A.D. 70; but they still hold to a future Second Coming, a physical resurrection of the dead, an end to temporal history, and the establishing of the consummate new heaven and new earth. Extreme or consistent (as they like to call themselves) preterism believes that the Second Coming, and thus the resurrection of believers, is all past. For all practical purposes all Bible prophecy has been fulfilled, and we are beyond the millennium and even now in the new heaven and new earth. They believe that if there is an end of current history it is not recorded in the Bible. Both Dr. Gentry and I believe that such a position is heretical, for it denies a bodily resurrection of believers and a future second coming of Christ.

It would be an overstatement to characterize the popularity of preterism as even approaching the dominance of futurism within American evangelicalism at the close of the twentieth century. On the other hand, preterism has seen significant growth from hundreds of advocates to thousands. Therefore, it seems appropriate at this time that a presentation and interchange of futurism and preterism be made to the public to help facilitate this discussion between Christians interested in understanding the timing of prophetic fulfillment.

Though futurism is currently the dominant view, it is doubtful that most who hold the position have thought through why they are futurists. This is likely for most evangelicals, since futurism has become so dominant. Also, in the absence of any perception of a challenger, the system has been taken for granted, so that effort has been spent expounding futurism, not defending it. Of course, a biblical case can be made for futurism, as I hope to show in my portion of the book.

An interchange between futurism and preterism with respect to the Tribulation is needed because that event is the focus of fulfillment for each system. The place of the Tribulation, or the Great Tribulation, in each system is determinative of the validity or failure of each approach. If the Tribulation is a past event, then preterism would be vindicated. If it is future, then futurism is the scriptural intent.

I am appreciative of Dr. Kenneth L. Gentry Jr., whom I consider to be a brother in Christ, a friend, and one of the top spokespersons and defenders of evangelical preterism, for his willingness to champion the moderate preterist cause. We also extend thanks to Dennis Hillman and Kregel Publications for providing us with this opportunity. It is Ken's prayer and mine that anyone reading this discussion will, like the Bereans of old, be driven to search Scripture to see whether these things are true (Acts 17:11).

THOMAS ICE
July 4, 1998

THE GREAT TRIBULATION
IS PAST

1

THE GREAT TRIBULATION IS PAST:

FOUNDATION

Kenneth L. Gentry Jr.

Introduction

Two thousand years ago, the greatest prophecies ever uttered were nearing fulfillment. Within just a few short years, God the Son would take upon Himself a human body and soul, entering history to provide Himself as a ransom for our sins. In the events of the Incarnation "the fulness of time" had come (Gal. 4:4). Angels would sing. Saints would utter the praise of God. Mighty men would bring gifts and worship.

Now, two thousand years later, as we approach the year 2000, many believe another prophetic "fulness of time" has come. This prophetic time, though, will result in judgment and chaos, rather than song, praise, and worship. Growing numbers of Christian books are sounding the alarm: *Planet Earth—2000: Will Mankind Survive?; Earth's Final Days; Prophecy 2000: Rushing to Armageddon;* and *Is This the Last Century?*[1]

One popular prophecy writer expresses well the sentiments of untold millions of Christians:

> Do you believe that at any instant you could find yourself hurtling through the skies to meet your Lord face-to-face? Are you confident that God will spare you and your loved ones the horrifying judgment of the Tribulation. . . . Christians today have more evidence that Christ could come in our lifetime than any generation that has come before.[2]
>
> The Day is coming when the worst traumas in history will be eclipsed by a seven-year period that will be far more terrifying than anything man can imagine.[3]

These words of Tim LaHaye reflect the viewpoint of the majority of American evangelicals today: at any instant the Lord Jesus could rapture all Christians from this world, signaling the outbreak of the Tribulation with all of its attendant horrors. LaHaye, in a book edited by Thomas Ice, contributes a chapter entitled: "Twelve Reasons Why This Could Be the Terminal Generation," which profusely references Matthew 24, the main focus of my presentation below.[4] I myself held this belief during my early Christian life, through my Christian college days at Tennessee Temple College, and into the first part of my graduate studies during my two-year enrollment at Grace Theological Seminary. I no longer hold this view, for I do not believe that the Bible teaches such.[5]

Exegetical Purpose

In this book, my friend Dr. Thomas Ice (an associate of LaHaye cited above) and I debate particularly the matter of the *chronology* of the Tribulation. Hence our title: *The Great Tribulation: Past or Future?* In defending our positions, however, we will also show our differing perspectives on the *nature* and *purpose* of the Tribulation. Our views differ radically on each of these questions:

- *Regarding tribulational chronology:* I hold that the Tribulation occurs in our distant past in the first century; Dr. Ice holds that it is impending in our fast-approaching future.
- *Regarding tribulational nature:* I hold that the Tribulation is a series of dramatic providential events; he holds that it also involves numerous direct, supernatural phenomena.
- *Regarding tribulational purpose:* I hold that the Tribulation closes out the Jewish-based, old covenant order, and establishes the new covenant (Christian) order as the conclusive redemptive-historical reality; he holds that it sets the stage for reestablishing a Jewish-based, millennial order complete with a rebuilt temple and reinstituted sacrificial system.

Both Dr. Ice and I are conservative, evangelical, born-again Christians who hold firmly to the Bible as the inspired, inerrant, and authoritative Word of God. Nevertheless, as our book title suggests, our tribulational positions are polar opposites. In fact, we represent two different evangelical theological systems that undergird our views on prophecy. My theology is covenantal; his is dispensational.

Furthermore, our exegetical differences regarding the Tribulation can create many practical differences of great consequence: differences regarding Christian living and the Christian worldview, especially with reference to our Christian labor, financial planning, raising children—

indeed, all our hopes regarding the future. A future that threatens impending, catastrophic, and global chaos, "when the worst traumas in history will be eclipsed by a seven-year period that will be far more terrifying than anything man can imagine"[6] will produce a practical orientation quite different from a view that holds the foreordained, prophetically determined judgments of the Tribulation are in our past.

Our debate is ultimately over the relative merits of two schools of prophetic thought: preterism and futurism.[7] The word "preterist" is based on the Latin term *praeteritus,* which means "gone by," or *past.* Preterism holds that the tribulation prophecies occur in the *first century,* thus in our past. Futurism, on the other hand, holds that the tribulation prophecies loom in our future.

Though presently enjoying strong growth, preterism is a decidedly minority viewpoint among evangelicals. Nevertheless, the view of a first-century Great Tribulation is not a newcomer to the prophetic debate. In fact, it has enjoyed a powerful influence in the last few centuries, as we may discover from the writings of such influential Christian scholars as John Calvin (1509–1564), John Lightfoot (1601–1675), John Owen (1616–1683), Matthew Henry (1662–1714), John Gill (1697–1771), Thomas Scott (1747–1821), Adam Clarke (1762–1832), Moses Stuart (1780–1852), J. A. Alexander (1809–1860), Albert Barnes (1798–1870), Philip Schaff (1819–1893), David Brown (1803–1897), F. W. Farrar (1831–1903), Milton Terry (1840–1914), Benjamin B. Warfield (1851–1921), J. Marcellus Kik (1903–1965), and Loraine Boettner (1903–1989), to name but a few.

Nor does the preterist principle arise in these relatively recent centuries. In fact, a preteristic understanding of the Great Tribulation appears among early church writers. For instance, Origen (A.D. 185–254) and Eusebius (A.D. 260–340) clearly hold this position.[8] When speaking about the Great Tribulation passage in Matthew 24, Eusebius points to "the infallible forecast of our Savior in which He prophetically expounded these very things" (*Eccl. Hist.* 3:7:1)—after citing many paragraphs "from the history written by Josephus" (*Eccl. Hist.* 3:5:4) to document the A.D. 70 fulfillment of this discourse.[9]

Due to the enormous present popularity and presumed contemporary relevance of the futurist position, I have a mammoth task before me. I am contradicting the commonly received expectation. Nevertheless, I am convinced that if the reader will lay aside his preconceptions and carefully reflect on Scripture *in its original literary and historical context,* he or she will be quite surprised at the strength of the preterist position. Come, let us reason together!

Before I engage the debate particulars, I must make two procedural comments, one regarding my focus and the other my method.

Exegetical Focus

I will focus on the tribulation passage in Matthew 24:1–34, which is the opening portion of our Lord's famous Olivet discourse. This is not the only place where we find a reference to the "Great Tribulation": not only do we find parallel accounts of the discourse in Mark 13 and Luke 21, but also the phrase "Great Tribulation" appears in Revelation 7. Matthew's account, however, contains the most familiar, concentrated, sustained, and structured treatment of the Great Tribulation in Scripture. And both its focus and structure are important for a coherent understanding of this vital prophetic issue. In fact, my disputant, Dr. Ice, titles one of the chapters in an earlier work of his: "The Olivet Discourse as the *Key to Eschatology*."[10] There he complains about another author who "goes to other unrelated passages" to interpret the Olivet discourse. My concentrating on the Olivet discourse in Matthew should rein in a potentially unmanageable subject by narrowing the field of survey, as well as focusing on the passage Dr. Ice admits is a "key to eschatology."

Regarding the familiarity of the discourse, who has not heard about the various foreboding elements of this great prophetic discourse: "wars and rumors of wars" (Matt. 24:6), "earthquakes in various places" (v. 5), "the abomination of desolation" (v. 15), "Great Tribulation" (v. 21), and "the powers of the heavens shaken" (v. 29)? And who is not touched by the dread in the calls to "endure to the end" (v. 13), to "flee to the mountains" (vv. 16–18), to not believe "if anyone says to you, 'Behold, here is the Christ'" (vv. 23, 26)?

I agree with Dr. Ice's earlier work: too many prophecy enthusiasts fail to focus on this concentrated passage, preferring rather to pluck verses from a wide assortment of contexts. I will concentrate on this one "key" section of Scripture (with occasional reference to corollary Scriptures, of course) in order to reduce the confusion resulting from the random proof texting method.[11] Any reasonable tribulational theology should be able to make its case here in Matthew 24.

What is more, this remarkable passage arises out of the context of the disciples' questions to Christ (24:2–3) regarding His dramatic, abrupt, and final departure from the temple (23:37–24:1). As another of Ice's associates notes: "The questions of the disciples are completely Jewish" and "the fact remains that the passage is directed towards Jews!"[12] And in that these "completely Jewish" questions occur at the close of Christ's ministry among the Jews, we must not only focus on their *immediate* context, but we must also seek their *wider* contextual setting. In this section of my presentation, then, I will provide a brief survey of the flow of Matthew, illustrating the sociocultural and redemptive-historical setting of this terrifying discourse.

Exegetical Method

I will state here at the outset that my interpretive methodology is the widely held, evangelical grammatical-historical method, as expounded in Milton S. Terry's classic *Biblical Hermeneutics*.[13] Terry, a preterist,[14] presents an able case for the proper method of biblical interpretation. The page constraints of this book forbid a thorough analysis of interpretive principles, which are much more complex and involved than popular prophecy writers imply. But since others ably establish these principles, I will simply refer the reader to them.[15] The following exposition will *illustrate* a proper application of the grammatical-historical method for the discerning reader.

Nevertheless, I must make three hermeneutical assertions that the reader should bear in mind: (1) The alleged "consistent literalism" of my debater is not the functional equivalent of "grammatical-historical" exegesis. The literalism principle is a subspecies of the grammatical-historical method, as even more recent dispensational theologians are beginning to admit. See works by Craig A. Blaising and Darrell L. Bock, as well as other noted dispensationalists, such as Robert L. Saucy and John S. Feinberg. For example, Blaising and Bock show that the claim to consistent literalism was never attainable in dispensationalism, but was really more or less a *goal*. Literalism is, in fact, an *aberration* of otherwise fundamentally sound principles.[16]

As Carson observes in his exposition of Matthew 24: "Untutored Christians are prone to think of prophecy and fulfillment as something not very different from straightforward propositional prediction and fulfillment. A close reading of the NT reveals that prophecy is more complex than that."[17] In his comments on Matthew 24, renowned Baptist Greek scholar A. T. Robertson agrees that "literalism is not appropriate in this apocalyptic eschatology."[18] Moody Bible Institute dispensationalist scholars Pate and Haines warn: "It is in the failure to grasp the interplay between prose and poetry that doomsday prophets make a major mistake, overemphasizing the literal meaning to the neglect of the symbolic."[19]

(2) We must be careful to distinguish between a "figurative" use of language (a legitimate function of the grammatical-historical method) and a "spiritual" interpretive methodology. Figurative expressions portray *historical events* by means of colorful, dramatic, and overdrawn descriptions. Spiritual interpretation, however, is a system of hermeneutics that evacuates all historical sense from a text in order to replace it with an abstract spiritual reality. Charges of "spiritualization," though common in debates such as ours, are far afield when one is merely interpreting figurative language. As premillennialist commentator Robert Mounce notes: "That the language of prophecy is highly

figurative has nothing to do with the reality of the events predicted. Symbolism is not a denial of historicity but a matter of literary genre."[20] (3) We must be alert to the Old Testament warrant for occasional figurative interpretation. New Testament commentator William Lane notes of the Olivet discourse: "The OT plays an essential part in the structure and imagery of the prophetic discourse."[21] I will show below that the Old Testament prophets frequently use figurative language dramatically to portray future events. I will also show that Christ, who is "the prophet" par excellence, employs their method in His Olivet discourse.

Preparation

Let me now begin the interpretive process. In this chapter I will lay the groundwork first by considering Israel's sociospiritual crisis in Matthew's gospel, and second by observing Christ's own chronological assertion regarding the time of the Great Tribulation. Though this preparatory study might seem a bit laborious, it is essential for understanding Christ's discourse in its biblical and historical setting. Much of the problem plaguing modern prophetic studies is the tendency to adopt a jigsaw puzzle approach to random prooftexts. I want to avoid such.

Cultural Decline

Spiritual Setting: Rejecting Christ

Matthew is an artist, and his scroll is a canvas. Indeed, the subtitle of Gundry's commentary on Matthew is most apropos: "A Commentary on His Literary and Theological Art." Matthew's artistic majesty combined with his gospel's structural coherence lead Goodspeed to declare it "the most successful book ever written."[22] Truly Matthew has an "astonishingly orderly mind."[23] Let me then offer a brief survey tracing Matthew's well-crafted dramatic development leading up to the Olivet discourse.[24] This famous discourse—the final one of the five major discourses that structure his gospel—appears when and where it does in the gospel for a reason. And that reason is helpful to the evangelical preterist interpretation.

Jewish orientation. Most commentators concur that Matthew's gospel is one of the most Jewish-oriented writings of the New Testament, third perhaps only to Revelation and Hebrews. Charles Ryrie, a major dispensational theologian and an associate of Dr. Ice, speaks strongly of "the dispensationalist's idea of the Jewish character of Matthew's gospel."[25] Not only do we see this in Matthew's untranslated Aramaic terms (for example, Matt. 5:22; 27:6) and his assuming a knowledge of Jewish customs (23:5; compare 15:2 with Mark 7:3–4), but also in the available ancient evidence from tradition, which suggests that Matthew wrote the original in Hebrew or Aramaic.[26]

Matthew's opening words provide clear evidence of his Jewish concern: "The book of the genealogy of Jesus Christ, the son of David, the son of Abraham" (Matt. 1:1). Here he immediately attracts the Jew's attention by tracing Christ's descent through King David back to father Abraham. (By contrast, the Gentile Luke traces the Lord's genealogy back to Adam, the father of the human race; Luke 3:38.)

Furthermore, a distinguishing feature of Matthew's gospel is its fulfillment motif, proving Jesus' messiahship time and again from the Jewish Scriptures.[27] In fact, Matthew is so Jewish that his is the only gospel mentioning Christ's restricting His earthly ministry to Israel: "These twelve Jesus sent out after instructing them, saying, 'Do not go in the way of the Gentiles, and do not enter any city of the Samaritans; but rather go to the lost sheep of the house of Israel'" (Matt. 10:5–6). "But He answered and said, 'I was sent only to the lost sheep of the house of Israel'" (15:24).

Judgment concern. Having noted all of this, we now come upon a surprising fact: Matthew's tone is so remarkably judgmental in respect to Israel that evangelical commentators have to defend him from charges of anti-Semitism! For instance, Carson asks: "But is Matthew's polemic so harsh that he must be considered anti-Semitic?"[28] Peter Walker observes: "One of the frequently observed paradoxes in Matthaen studies is that this Gospel, which at one level can rightly be seen as the most Jewish one, is at another level the most severely '*anti*-Jewish.'"[29] Anthony J. Saldarini postulates that Christ's "vitriolic" words are really not Christ's, but Matthew's.[30] Obviously, Matthew is not anti-Semitic, for he himself is a Jew. Furthermore, his alleged anti-Semitic statements are actually those of our sinless Lord Jesus Christ Himself.[31] Nor is Matthew's purpose to show the wholesale, permanent rejection of Israel by God, for Scripture elsewhere teaches that God will graciously call her back to Himself before the end of history (Rom. 11:11–25).[32]

Nevertheless, early on in his gospel, Matthew forecasts a gathering storm drifting toward Israel. Matthew's warning of Israel's demise ultimately culminates in his notice of the impending absolute devastation of her temple and its levitical worship system (Matt. 24) and in the including of "all nations" in the blessings of God (28:18–20). Let me briefly show how this is so.

After we read Matthew's opening reference to the genealogy and birth of Jesus, we begin uncovering in the infancy narrative early hints of Israel's spiritual crisis and approaching judgment. In chapter 2 of this strongly Jewish gospel, we witness the arrival of *Gentile* magi to worship Christ (2:1–2). But among the Jews all we see is the troubled spirit of Israel's King Herod "and all Jerusalem with him" (v. 3).[33] Luke mentions the joy of the Jewish shepherds and those in the temple (Luke 2); Matthew does not.

Matthew then skips ahead to the ministry of John the Baptist. John appears on the scene calling Israel to repentance for her sin (Matt. 3:1–2, 6). He scathingly rebukes her religious leaders (vv. 7–9), calling them a "brood of vipers" (v. 7; compare Matt. 12:34; 23:33), despite their claim to be the children of Abraham (v. 9). This preaching against the "brood of vipers" reminds us of the curse on the seed of the serpent in Eden, for indeed, they are of their "father the devil" (John 8:44).

John urgently preaches to Israel because of her grave situation; a spiritual crisis is upon her: "Repent, for the kingdom of heaven is *at hand*" (Matt. 3:2, emphasis mine; compare Jesus' preaching in 4:17). Her unbelieving response to God's kingdom offer will lead inexorably to judgment. "But when he saw many of the Pharisees and Sadducees coming for baptism, he said to them, 'You brood of vipers, who warned you to flee from *the wrath to come?*'" (v. 7, emphasis mine). The wrath about which John speaks "came down upon Jews of Palestine in an unparalleled manner in A.D. 70,"[34] when the Romans furiously destroyed Jerusalem, the temple, and untold thousands of Jews.

Matthew records John's warning that "the axe is *already* laid at the root of the trees; every tree therefore that does not bear good fruit is cut down and thrown into the fire" (3:10).[35] Here John draws his imagery from God's judgment against Assyria (Isa. 10:33–34): that sort of judgment soon will break out upon Israel. Indeed, "his winnowing fork is in his hand" *already* (Matt. 3:12).

Kingdom removal. Moving a little further into Matthew's record, we discover Jesus' amazement at a *Gentile's* faith—amazement prompting His warning to Israel: "'Truly I say to you, I have not found such great faith with *anyone in Israel*. And I say to you, that many shall come *from east and west,* and recline at the table with Abraham, and Isaac, and Jacob, in the kingdom of heaven; but *the sons of the kingdom shall be cast out* into the outer darkness; in that place there shall be weeping and gnashing of teeth'" (8:10–13, emphasis mine). The clouds are darkening; the rumble of thunder may be heard in the distance.

Frustrated with the recalcitrance of His contemporaries to both His and John's preaching, the Lord compares Israel with pagan cities of old, threatening her with judgment:

But to what shall I compare this generation? It is like children sitting in the market places, who call out to the other children, and say, "We played the flute for you, and you did not dance; we sang a dirge, and you did not mourn." For John came neither eating nor drinking, and they say, "He has a demon!" The Son of Man came eating and drinking, and they say, "Behold, a gluttonous man and a drunkard, a friend of tax-gatherers and sinners!" Yet wisdom is vindicated by her deeds. Then He began to reproach the cities in which most of His miracles were done, because they did not repent. "Woe to you, Chorazin! Woe to you, Bethsaida! For if the miracles had occurred in Tyre and Sidon which occurred in you, they would have repented long ago in sackcloth and ashes. Nevertheless I say to you, it shall be more tolerable for Tyre and Sidon in the day of judgment, than for you. And you, Capernaum, will not be exalted to heaven, will you? You shall descend to Hades; for if the miracles had occurred in Sodom which occurred in you, it would have remained to this day. Nevertheless I say to you that it shall be more tolerable for the land of Sodom in the day of judgment, than for you" (11:16–24).

Shortly thereafter Matthew records the Lord's charge that the "men of Nineveh" and the "Queen of the South shall stand up with this generation at the judgment, and shall condemn it" (12:38–45). In His sorrow over Israel's spiritual lethargy, Jesus informs His disciples: "Therefore I speak to them in parables; because while seeing they do not see, and while hearing they do not hear, nor do they understand. And in their case the prophecy of Isaiah is being fulfilled, which says, 'You will keep on hearing, but will not understand; and you will keep on seeing, but will not perceive'" (13:13–14). Indeed, Jesus castigates Israel's rulers with Isaiah's words: "This people honors me with their lips, but their heart is far away from me" (15:8). Certainly His is "an evil and adulterous generation" (12:39; 16:4), "a wicked generation" (12:45), "a faithless and perverse generation" (17:17).

Tribulation preparation. Of course, matters worsen as Jesus' ministry continues. Beginning in chapter 21, Matthew starts piling up judgment material through Jesus' private instruction, public proclamation, and symbolic action. In 21:12–16, the Lord cleanses the temple of its corrupting influences, stirring the indignation of the temple authorities. Within a space of but two verses, Matthew shows Jesus departing Jerusalem and then returning, whereupon He sees a fig tree in full leaf but lacking fruit. He curses the fig tree, withering it immediately (21:19–20). Given its contextual setting, this barren fig tree obviously represents Israel (compare Jer. 8:13; Mic. 7:1), as most commentators agree.[36] This remarkable episode suggests not only Israel's inner spiritual barrenness despite her ostentatious show of religiosity, but also her imminent withering under God's judgment (compare Matt. 21:42–45).

The Lord's parable of the two sons exhibits the failure of Israel's religious authorities, exposing a low-level spirituality beneath that of the tax gatherers and harlots (Matt. 21:28–32). This leads directly into His parable of the landowner, in which the vineyard represents Israel (compare Isa. 5:1–2). Jesus here castigates Israel's rulers for their long-standing opposition to God's prophets (Matt. 21:33–36), warning that *now,* since the Son has come and they are rejecting Him (vv. 37–39), God will "rent out the vineyard to other vine-growers" (v. 41). God will withdraw His kingdom from Israel and bestow it upon "a nation producing the fruit of it" (v. 43). The church is that "nation" (1 Peter 2:9). This results in God's crushing judgment upon Israel in A.D. 70 (Matt. 21:44). Interestingly, the curse on the fig tree earlier (v. 19) is due to its not bearing fruit; now the parabolic vineyard owner is also frustrated with a lack of fruit.

Immediately thereafter (in Matthew's scenario) Jesus proclaims the parable of the marriage feast, which recounts the resistance of Israel to God's call (22:1–6). Once more He teaches that this will result in Israel's judgment: "The king was enraged and sent his armies, and destroyed those murderers, and set their city on fire" (v. 7). This so clearly warns of the A.D. 70 destruction of Jerusalem that critical scholars claim it is *ex eventu* prophecy. God then sends His messengers to gather other guests (the Gentiles) to the feast (vv. 8–14).

We now enter chapter 23, which sets up the Olivet discourse by calling down seven woes upon the religious leaders in Israel. Whereas Luke's gospel places Jesus' woes against the leaders in Luke 11:37–54, far separated from the Olivet discourse (21:5–38), Matthew brings the woes and the discourse together. Carson discusses the relationship of chapters 23 and 24, then observes that "Matthew's material is remarkably coherent,"[37] suggesting the following:

> The literary context of the chapter is extremely important. Not only does Matthew 23 climax a series of controversies with the Jewish religious authorities (21:23–22:46), but it immediately follows the christologically crucial confrontation of 22:41–46. The question "What do you think about Christ?" raised by Jesus (v. 42) "was not simply a theological curiosity which could be thrashed out in the seminar room," as Garland (p. 24) puts it; it stands at the heart of the gospel. The failure

of the Pharisees to recognize Jesus as the Messiah prophesied in Scripture is itself already an indictment, the more so since they "sit in Moses' seat" (see on v. 2), and the woes that follow are therefore judicial and go some way toward explaining the prophesied destruction of Jerusalem in the Olivet Discourse (24:1–25:46).[38]

Carson continues: "Thus Jesus' strong language in this chapter ('fools,' 'hypocrites,' 'blind guides,' 'son of hell') is . . . the language of divine warning (cf. vv. 37–39) and condemnation."[39]

The seventh woe (23:29–32) and the expository material following it are particularly relevant in the transition to the Olivet discourse and its description of "the Great Tribulation" (24:21). Now we see graphically how dire Israel's circumstances are:

> *Woe to you, scribes and Pharisees, hypocrites! Because you build the tombs of the prophets and adorn the monuments of the righteous, and say, "If we had lived in the days of our fathers, we would not have been partakers with them in the blood of the prophets." Therefore you are witnesses against yourselves that you are sons of those who murdered the prophets. Fill up, then, the measure of your fathers' guilt. Serpents, brood of vipers! How can you escape the condemnation of hell? Therefore, indeed, I send you prophets, wise men, and scribes: some of them you will kill and crucify, and some of them you will scourge in your synagogues and persecute from city to city, that on you may come all the righteous blood shed on the earth, from the blood of righteous Abel to the blood of Zechariah, son of Berechiah, whom you murdered between the temple and the altar. Assuredly, I say to you, all these things will come upon this generation. (23:29–36)*

Here Jesus paints in bold relief Israel's moral and spiritual turpitude. Interestingly, He chooses the first and last martyrs of the Old Testament: Abel and Zechariah (23:35). Not only are these the first and last martyrs in the Hebrew canon, well representing all righteous martyrs in between, but both accounts record calls for vengeance (Gen. 4:10 and 2 Chron. 24:22). This is quite appropriate for Jesus' point: God's vengeance against all those who shed innocent blood will crash down upon first-century Israel (Matt. 23:36).

In his exposition of Daniel 9, church father Eusebius observes regarding Matthew 23 and the Jews:

For while their sins were not fulfilled, the patience and long-
suffering of God bore with them, calling them many times to
repentance by the prophets. But when, as our Savior said, they
had filled up the measure of their fathers, then the whole collected weight worked their destruction at one time, as our Lord
taught again when He said: "All the blood poured forth from
the foundation of the world, from the blood of righteous Abel
to the blood of Zacharias, shall come upon this generation."
For presuming last of all to lay their hands on the Son of God
they completed their disobedience and completed their sins.[40]

France notes of Jesus' surprising command to "fill up, then, the
measure of your fathers' guilt" (Matt. 23:32): an "ironic imperative
introduces the idea . . . that Jesus' own generation is the one in which
Jewish rebellion against God reaches its climax and will incur its ultimate punishment."[41] And why not? Israel intensifies her guilt in demanding Christ's death *and calling down God's judgment upon herself:*
"When Pilate saw that he could not prevail at all, but rather that a tumult was rising, he took water and washed his hands before the multitude, saying, 'I am innocent of the blood of this just Person. You see
to it.' And all the people answered and said, 'His blood be on us and
on our children'" (27:24–25). Jesus expressly declares to the Roman
procurator Pontius Pilate that the "greater sin" is upon Caiaphas the
high priest (and those whom he represents before God) for delivering
Jesus to him (John 19:11).

The early, post-apostolic church reads the events of A.D. 70 as a divine vindication of Christ—and Christianity. For instance, referring
to the historical account of Jerusalem's destruction by eyewitness Jewish historian Josephus, Eusebius comments: "The same writer [Jose-
phus] shows that besides this, innumerable other revolts were started
in Jerusalem itself, affirming that from that time risings and war and
the mutual contrivance of evil never ceased in the city and throughout
Judea, until the time when the siege under Vespasian came upon them
as the last scene of all. Thus the penalty of God pursued the Jews for
their crimes against Christ" (*Eccl. Hist.* 2:6:8). In fact, Eusebius's
massive *The Proof of the Gospel* repeatedly and forcefully drives home
God's judgment on Israel as a sign of God's favor to Christianity, usually while explaining Old Testament prophecies.[42]

Symbolic Action: Departing the Temple

As I show above, "Jesus' condemnation of 'this generation' is a
prominent theme in Matthew,"[43] virtually serving as a vindication of
Christ's ministry and a warning of God's forthcoming judgment upon

Israel: "That the Gentiles were to be included in the people of God because the original Israel had for the most part rejected Jesus the Messiah, is a dominant theme of the Gospel of Matthew."[44] After all, Jesus "came to His own, and His own did not receive Him" (John 1:11). Israel's moral guilt is so great because her spiritual opportunity is so grand: "O Jerusalem, Jerusalem, the one who kills the prophets and stones those who are sent to her! How often I wanted to gather your children together, as a hen gathers her chicks under her wings, but you were not willing!" (Matt. 23:37). Eventually, Paul shakes the dust from his feet and turns to the Gentiles, setting the pattern for Christian expansion in the world (Acts 13:46–48).

Temple desolation. In response to her callous unwillingness, the Lord seals Israel's doom with these final words: "See! Your house is left to you desolate" (Matt. 23:38). Earlier, when the Lord cleanses the temple, He cites an Old Testament reference to it as "my house" (in other words, the house of God; 21:13). In the very context before us, He deems the temple the place wherein "God dwells" (23:21). But with His dramatic departure from the temple, it becomes "*your* house." Mark's account of Jesus' trial records the charges against the Lord as saying He will destroy the temple "made with hands" (Gk., *cheiropoiētos;* Mark 14:58). This is the Old Testament way of referring to idols (compare Deut. 4:28; 2 Kings 19:18; Pss. 115:4; 135:15; Isa. 37:19; 44:10; 46:6; Acts 17:24). This suggests the idolatrous nature of the Jewish view of the temple. Hebrews 12:27 warns that the "things that are made" (i.e., the temple and its physical implements; 9:11, 24) will soon be shaken, so that that "which cannot be shaken" (i.e., Christianity) may remain. Jesus is the temple made "without hands" (Mark 14:58).

Though practically invisible in English versions, the shifting of number from singular to plural in Matthew 23:37–38 is significant: "O Jerusalem, Jerusalem, the one [sg.] who kills the prophets and stones those who are sent to her [sg.]! How often I wanted to gather your [sg.] children together, as a hen gathers her chicks under her wings, but you were not willing! See! Your [pl.] house is left to you [pl.] desolate." Jesus shifts the number in His lament to show Israel's problem is both corporate-national and personal-individual, that is, both the government (singular) and the people (plural) are guilty. Though Jesus is finishing His seven woes upon "the scribes and Pharisees," we must remember that "*all the people* [Gk., *pas ho laos*] answered and said, 'His blood be on us and on our children'" (27:25, emphasis mine). Israel's sin is not confined to her leadership.

In verse 38, the Greek word *erēmos* ("desolate") anticipates the related word *erēmōseōs* ("desolation") in 24:15, which speaks about "the abomination of desolation." This makes "the implied destruction explicit,"[45] and, as we will see, demands a first-century fulfillment of the Great Tribulation and abomination of desolation prophecy. Surely Jesus does not denounce the first-century temple in which He is standing (24:1) by declaring it "desolate" (23:38), prophesying its total destruction (24:2), then answering the question "when shall these things be?" (v. 3), and warning about the temple's "abomination of desolation" (v. 15) only to speak about the destruction of a totally different temple some two thousand years (or more) later!

Christ's lament over Jerusalem's sanctuary is charged with religious significance: Israel's temple serves as a sign and seal of her relationship to God; when God abandons the holy house, He breaks the relationship with Israel[46] —as we see very plainly in 1 Kings 9:6–9:

> *But if you or your sons at all turn from following Me, and do not keep My commandments and My statutes which I have set before you, but go and serve other gods and worship them, then I will cut off Israel from the land which I have given them; and this house which I have consecrated for My name I will cast out of My sight. Israel will be a proverb and a byword among all peoples. And as for this house, which is exalted, everyone who passes by it will be astonished and will hiss, and say, '"Why has the LORD done thus to this land and to this house?" Then they will answer, "Because they forsook the LORD their God, who brought their fathers out of the land of Egypt, and have embraced other gods, and worshiped them and served them; therefore the LORD has brought all this calamity on them."*

Messianic Departure. Immediately after declaring the sanctuary desolate, "Jesus went out and departed from the temple, and His disciples came up to show Him the buildings of the temple" (Matt. 24:1). As Robertson observes: "Now Jesus leaves [the temple] for good after the powerful denunciation of the scribes and Pharisees in chapter 23. His public teaching is over. It was a tragic moment."[47]

Interestingly, after Jesus declares the temple "desolate" (23:38), He dramatically departs it (24:1) and heads to the Mount of Olives (v. 3). Jesus' departure follows the pattern of God's Shechinah glory departing the Old Testament temple: "So the cherubim lifted up their wings, with the wheels beside them, and the glory of the God of Israel was high above them. And the glory of the LORD went up from the midst of the city and stood on the mountain, which is on the east side of the city," in other words, the Mount of Olives (Ezek. 11:22–23). In that the Mount is "opposite" (Gk., *katenanti*, Mark 13:3) the temple, this action also illustrates the Lord's opposition to it.[48]

Surprised at Jesus' denouncing and vacating the temple, the disciples ask Him the questions that spark the Olivet discourse:

> *His disciples came up to show Him the buildings of the temple. And Jesus said to them, "Do you not see all these things? Assuredly, I say to you, not one stone shall be left here upon another, that shall not be thrown down." Now as He sat on the Mount of Olives, the disciples came to Him privately, saying, "Tell us, when will these things be? And what will be the sign of Your coming, and of the end of the age?" (Matthew 24:1b–3)*

The incongruity between the beautiful majesty of the temple and the scathing denunciation of the Lord sparks the disciples' bewilderment; their feelings "still clung with the loving pride of their nationality to that sacred and memorable spot"[49] in their holy and beloved city.[50] In effect, they are asking: Is not the majestic temple of God a fitting testimony to His glory? Will You not reconsider Your abandoning of such an exalted place? Could we not gloriously serve God here? Later, "when they then reflected further on Jesus' prophetic statements in the Gospels about the city and His claims in relation to the temple, it became clear that their attitudes towards Jerusalem had to be reevaluated."[51] The ancient Jewish love for the temple is such that Stephen is accused of hating the sanctuary for declaring its coming destruction (Acts 6:14). Sanders well observes: "It is impossible to make too much of the temple in first-century Jewish Palestine"[52] for it is "the central heartbeat of Jerusalem."[53]

Ancient accounts of the temple portray its imposing beauty, accounts such as those we find in Josephus and the Jewish Mishnah.[54] The first-century Jewish philosopher Philo (25 B.C.–A.D. 40) says its was "beautiful beyond all possible description," and that "the buildings of it are of most exceeding beauty and magnificence, so as to be universal objects of admiration to all who behold them, and especially to all foreigners who travel to those parts, and who comparing them with their own public edifices, marvel both at the beauty and sumptuousness of this one."[55] The ancient Jewish rabbis exult in the temple: "He that never saw the temple of Herod never saw a fine building" *(Baba Bathra).* Consequently, according to the Roman historian Tacitus, the Jewish temple "was famous beyond all other works of men," a "temple of immense wealth."[56]

Josephus marvels over the temple's striking beauty:

> Now the outward face of the temple in its front wanted nothing that was likely to surprise either men's minds or their eyes, for it was covered all over the plates of gold of great weight, and, at

the first rising of the sun, reflected back a very fiery splendor, and made those who forced themselves to look upon it to turn their eyes away, just as they would have done at the sun's own rays. But this temple appeared to strangers, when they were at a distance, like a mountain covered with snow (*Wars* 5:5:6).

I will consider the disciples' question later. But I now conclude my introductory survey of Matthew's flow, which illustrates the enormous guilt of first-century Israel before God. All of this is extremely important for understanding the Olivet discourse and its reference to the Great Tribulation. The Great Tribulation crashes down upon a generation most deserving of the wrath of God. As Christianity's first martyr, Stephen, challenges the Jewish leaders just a few years after Christ's death: "Which of the prophets did your fathers not persecute? And they killed those who foretold the coming of the Just One, of whom you now have become the betrayers and murderers" (Acts 7:52).

Now let us focus on the all-important:

Chronological Indicator

Matthew's protracted exposition of Jewish guilt leads inexorably to Jesus' abrupt departure from the temple and His warning of its impending doom, prompting the disciples' surprised query: "Tell us, when will these things be, and what will be the sign of Your coming, and of the end of the age?" (Matt. 24:3b).

In these questions we sense once again the bewilderment among the disciples at Jesus' teaching—a bewilderment such as is seen elsewhere in Matthew, as in their confusion about the "leaven of the Pharisees" (16:6–12), Christ's death (vv. 21–23), the purpose of the Transfiguration (17:4–5), Christ's interest in children (19:13–15), and the nature of kingdom service (20:20–25). Quite clearly Christ divides their question into two episodes in His answer: (1) He speaks about the coming Great Tribulation resulting in the destruction of Jerusalem and the temple in A.D. 70 (24:4–34, which is in "this generation," v. 34); and (2) His distant future second coming at the end of history (24:36–25:46, which is after a "long time," 25:19). In that our discussion revolves around whether the Great Tribulation is past or future, I will not deal with the question related to the second advent of Christ, that Dr. Ice and I agree is still future.

Christ's Emphasis

We find the key to locating the Great Tribulation in history in Matthew 24:34: "Truly I say to you, this generation will not pass away until all these things take place." This statement of Christ is indisputably clear—and absolutely demanding of a first-century fulfillment of the events in the preceding verses, including the Great Tribulation (v. 21). In the next chapter I will give a seriatim exposition of the text to show *how* this is so. Now, though, I will secure the Tribulation's place in history by focusing on this important assertion by Christ.

The Lord here is quite insistent; the declaration before us is solemn and emphatic. Christ is not in the least irresolute when He begins a statement with "truly" (Gk., *amēn*). Hendriksen notes concerning the Greek word *amēn:* "In every case . . . in which this word occurs in the New Testament it introduces a statement which not only expresses a truth or fact . . . but an *important,* a *solemn* fact, one that in many cases is at variance with popular opinion or expectation or at least causes some surprise."[57] Thus, Christ emphatically draws the disciples' attention to what He is saying—just as He does in 24:2, where He "assuredly" (Gk., *amēn*) prophesies the destruction of the temple, which prophecy leads to the extended discourse.

In addition, the literal rendering of the Greek reads: "Truly I tell you that *by no means* passes away generation this until all these things happen."[58] The "by no means" is a strong, double negative (Gk., *ou mē*). By itself it carries great emphasis, but here Jesus also places it first in His statement, which in antiquity was a means for adding emphasis. He is staking His credibility on the absolute certainty of this prophetic pronouncement. Indeed, "heaven and earth will pass away, but My words will by no means pass away" (24:35).

But what does Jesus so clearly and forcefully declare? Whatever the difficult apocalyptic imagery in verses 29–31 may indicate (I will get to that in the next chapter), Jesus strongly asserts that "*all* these things" about which He has just spoken (in other words, vv. 4–33) will occur *before* "this generation" passes away: "When you see *all these things,* recognize that He is near, right at the door. Truly I say to you, *this generation* will not pass away until *all these things* take place" (vv. 33–34, emphasis mine).

Linguist A. T. Robertson comments on this passage: "In the Old Testament a generation was reckoned as forty years. This is the natural way to take verse 34 as of 33 . . . , 'all things' meaning the same in both verses."[59] Remember that Israel's forty years wandering in the wilderness was for the purpose of killing off that sinful "generation" (Num. 32:13; Ps. 95:10). Since Jesus is speaking sometime around A.D. 30, He is referring to a time about forty years into the future, that is, to A.D. 70 when the Roman legions will destroy the temple in Jerusalem. The "Great Tribulation" of verse 21, then, characterizes the events that must occur in "this generation" (Gk., *genea*).

Surprisingly, by a number of contrived stratagems, futurists vigorously challenge the dramatic force of this simple, unambiguous statement. But let us see how clearly Jesus ties the events of the Tribulation passage—including the "Great Tribulation" (24:21)—to His own generation, to "this generation" to whom He originally ministers.

As we begin I would urge the reader to reflect upon the foregoing survey of Matthew. It fits perfectly with such a conclusion: *judgment must fall upon first-century Israel.* The Jews in the first century live at history's critical point: they live in "the fullness of times" when the kingdom of God had "drawn near" (Gk., perfect tense; Mark 1:15). They see and hear things that "many prophets and righteous men desired to see and . . . hear" (Matt. 13:17). Though they see all of Jesus' glorious miracles and hear His authoritative instruction, Jesus "came to His own" but they "did not receive Him" (John 1:11). In not recognizing the time of their "visitation," Israel squanders her opportunity, thereby sealing her doom: "And when He approached, He saw the city and wept over it, saying, 'If you had known in this day, even you, the things which make for peace! But now they have been hidden from your eyes. For the days shall come upon you when your enemies will throw up a bank before you, and surround you, and hem you in on every side, and will level you to the ground and your children within you, and they will not leave in you one stone upon another, because you did not recognize the time of your visitation'" (Luke 19:41–43). As France puts it: "Jesus' condemnation of 'this generation' is a prominent theme in Matthew; see . . . 11:16–19; 16:4; 17:17; 24:34, and especially 23:29–36, which shows that it refers to His contemporaries, not just Jews or men in general, as those in whom Israel's age-long rebellion has culminated, and on whom judgment must therefore fall."[60]

Generation Proven

I will offer a seven-point argument for interpreting the phrase "this generation" at face value. We must understand Jesus' statement in Matthew 24:34 as a nonapocalyptic, nonpoetic, unambiguous, didactic assertion.

First, *the first-century temple is the focus of the disciples' question.* Notice the introduction to the discourse: "And Jesus came out from the temple and was going away when His disciples came up to *point out the temple buildings to Him.* And He answered and said to them, 'Do you not see *all these things?*'" (vv. 1–2a, emphasis mine). His discourse cannot refer to events associated with some other rebuilt temple hundreds and hundreds of years in the future. Jesus' dramatic denunciation of and departure from the first-century Herodian temple spark the question in the disciples, whose question He answers by His famous discourse. The events He prophesies in such a setting must relate to that first-century temple. And understanding "generation" as referring to Jesus' own era fits perfectly. "Truly I say to you, this generation will not pass away until all these things take place" (v. 34). Strangely, Dr. Ice understands that Matthew records the disciples' question regarding the destruction of the temple, but then he says Matthew does not record the answer:

> The three questions in Matthew 24:3 are:
>
> • When will the temple be destroyed?
> • What will be the sign of Christ's coming?
> • What will be the sign of the end of the age?
>
> The first question is answered in Luke 21:20–24, since Luke is the one who specializes in the A.D. 70 aspects. Luke records Jesus' warning about the soon-to-come destruction of Jerusalem—the days of vengeance. The second and third questions are answered in Matthew 24.[61]

This is an extremely anticontextual assertion that seems forced by nothing other than Ice's predisposition. Matthew 24:34 fits quite perfectly with the historical and literary context. Remarkably, Dr. Ice recognizes that the disciples ask the question "when"—it is the first question in Ice's listing—but does not allow that Matthew records the answer *despite the fact that he does give a time indicator:* "all these things" will occur "in this generation."

Second, *the first-century temple is, in fact, destroyed in Jesus' generation.* Historical and archaeological evidence prove that the Romans destroy that same temple forty years later. Christ boldly asserts: "Do you not see *all these things?* Truly I say to you, *not one stone here shall be left upon another, which will not be torn down*" (v. 2). The Greek structure of Jesus' statement quite emphatically declares the temple's absolute devastation: He opens with His emphatic "truly I say to you"; He employs the double negative, powerfully asserting "not [Gk., *ou mē*] one stone shall be left on another." (Mark 13:2 even records the emphatic double negative *twice* in the statement.)

The Jewish historian Josephus is an eyewitness to the A.D. 70 holocaust, one of the most horrible episodes of war in history. He watches as the Romans tear apart the temple stone-by-stone:

> Now, as soon as the army had no more people to slay or to plunder, because there remained none to be objects of their fury (for they would not have spared any, had there remained any

other such work to be done) Caesar [namely, Titus] gave orders
that they should now demolish the entire city and temple. . . .
But for all the rest of the wall, it was so thoroughly laid even
with the ground by those that dug it up to the foundation, that
there was left nothing to make those that came thither believe it
had ever been inhabited. This was the end which Jerusalem came
to by the madness of those that were for innovations; a city
otherwise of great magnificence (*Wars* 7:1:1).

The archaeological and historical evidence so strongly supports the
validity of Christ's prophecy that higher critical theologians declare
Matthew 24 an *ex eventu* prophecy read back into the mouth of Christ
after the events.[62] It so stunningly confirms the authority of Christ and
the integrity of Christianity that several early church fathers cite Matthew 24 and the destruction of the temple as proof that God has turned
from the Jews and is now favoring the Christians. Eusebius speaks
forcefully about this:

Such was the reward of the iniquity of the Jews and of their
impiety against the Christ of God, but it is worth appending to
it the infallible forecast of our Savior in which He prophetically expounded these very things. . . . If anyone compares
the words of our Savior with the other narratives of the historian concerning the whole war, how can he avoid surprise and
a confession of the truly divine and supernaturally wonderful
character both of the foreknowledge and of the foretelling of
our Savior? (*Ecclesiastical History* 3:7:5–6).

Elsewhere Eusebius writes:

On the [Jews] also Scripture foretells an extreme curse, adding
a lamentation for the Jewish race, which actually overtook them
immediately after their impiety against our Lord and Savior
Jesus Christ. For of a truth from that day to this the House of
Israel has fallen, and the vision once shewn by God and the
rejection have been brought to pass, concerning the falling of
their house in Jerusalem, and against their whole state. . . . For
since they did not accept the Christ of God when He came,
perforce He left them and turned to all the Gentiles, telling the
cause of His turning, when He said with tears, as if almost apolo-
gizing: "Jerusalem, Jerusalem, which killeth the prophets, and
stonest them which are sent unto her, how often would I have
gathered thy children together" (*Proof of the Gospel* 4:16).

Third, *the warning embedded in the prophecy indicates the primary focus of the events.* In Matthew 24:16 we read: "then let those who are in Judea flee to the mountains." Not only does Jesus refer exclusively to the inhabitants of Judea (the region surrounding Jerusalem wherein stands the temple), but also He urges His followers to escape this judgment by flight to the nearby mountains. This local coloring fits well with the temporally confined assertion that "all these things" will happen in "this generation" (vv. 33–34).

Fourth, *the same time designate indisputably applies to the scribes and Pharisees.* In Matthew 23 the Lord scathingly chastises the "scribes and Pharisees" (vv. 2, 13–15, 23, 25, 27, 29, 34), concluding with a phrase parallel to 24:34: "Truly I say to you, all these things shall come upon this generation" (23:36). Thus, the literary context of chapter 24 demands "this generation" refer to Christ's contemporaries in the first century—those who reject Him and demand His crucifixion.

Fifth, *the first mention of "generation" in Matthew uses the Greek term in the sense of a life span.* After listing the genealogy of Christ, Matthew says: "Therefore all the *generations* from Abraham to David are fourteen generations; and from David to the deportation to Babylon fourteen generations; and from the deportation to Babylon to the time of Christ fourteen generations" (Matt. 1:17; compare Luke 1:48, 50). The generations here are specifically associated with the life spans of particular individuals.

Sixth, *"generation" is used elsewhere in Matthew (and the other gospels) of those living in Christ's day.* "Then some of the scribes and Pharisees answered Him, saying, 'Teacher, we want to see a sign from You.' But He answered and said to them, 'An evil and adulterous *generation* craves for a sign; and yet no sign shall be given to it but the sign of Jonah the prophet'" (Matt. 12:38–39, emphasis mine; compare Luke 11:29). Here the scribes and Pharisees of the first century ask for a sign proving the identity of the incarnate Lord. He says the only sign it—that *generation*—will receive is that of the prophet Jonah, that is, Christ's resurrection. In Matthew 17:17, Jesus wearies of the unbelieving response of His contemporaries: "O unbelieving and perverted *generation,* how long shall I be with you? How long shall I put up with you?" (emphasis mine; compare Mark 9:19; Luke 9:41).

Seventh, *the phrase "this generation" elsewhere in Matthew points to the contemporary generation of Christ's own day.* Matthew 11:16 reads: "But to what shall I liken *this generation?* It is like children sitting in the marketplaces and calling to their companions" (emphasis mine). The context clearly speaks about first-century Israel's refusal to hear John the Baptist and Christ. John and Jesus live at the same time and in the same generation. This reference indicates a heightened judgment for that particular era. They see, yet refuse to believe Christ's miracles.

In Matthew 12:40–45, Jesus compares His generation to earlier generations and warns that "this generation" will suffer for their spiritual failure:

> *For as Jonah was three days and three nights in the belly of the great fish, so will the Son of Man be three days and three nights in the heart of the earth. The men of Nineveh will rise up in the judgment with this generation and condemn it, because they repented at the preaching of Jonah; and indeed a greater than Jonah is here. The queen of the South will rise up in the judgment with this generation and condemn it, for she came from the ends of the earth to hear the wisdom of Solomon; and indeed a greater than Solomon is here. When an unclean spirit goes out of a man, he goes through dry places, seeking rest, and finds none. Then he says, "I will return to my house from which I came." And when he comes, he finds it empty, swept, and put in order. Then he goes and takes with him seven other spirits more wicked than himself, and they enter and dwell there; and the last state of that man is worse than the first. So shall it also be with this wicked generation.*

Jesus must mean the Ninevites of Jonah's day, not *all* Ninevites of *all* time! Likewise does "this generation" mean those of Christ's day.

As I note above, though Dr. Ice denies that Matthew 24 applies to the A.D. 70 events, he states that Luke 21 deals with A.D. 70. Interestingly, we find the same time designation in Luke 21 as we do in Matthew 24: "Truly I say to you, this *generation* will not pass away until all things take place" (Luke 21:32, emphasis mine). Why should we not understand Matthew 24:34 in the same way?

Due to her spiritual recalcitrance in the face of her redemptive opportunity, first-century Israel stands on a prophetic fault line. After tenderly calling her to repentance for over three years, her Messiah warns of "the Great Tribulation" that will shake her self-confidence in "this generation." This tribulation will shake down the temple then existing. As we shall see in the next chapter, the particulars of his prophecy fit the first-century events.

2

THE GREAT TRIBULATION IS PAST:

EXPOSITION

Kenneth L. Gentry Jr.

In the previous chapter I traced Matthew's thematic development up to Matthew 24 and highlighted Jesus' temporal expectation in 24:34. I believe this material alone is sufficient to locate the Great Tribulation in the first century. I will now offer a seriatim exposition of the text, further illustrating, explaining, and defending the A.D. 70 perspective. Most of the verses in 24:4–34 virtually demand the preterist position to the unbiased reader, though a few *initially* appear contradictory to it. I trust that the preterist position already appears plausible—and even quite alluring. Upon surveying the text in the light of the preceding, I hope, of course, that the reader finds the preterist view exegetically coherent and theologically compelling.

In 24:3 the disciples ask "*when* shall these things be," in response to the Lord's statement that one stone shall not be left on another (v. 2, emphasis mine). In verses 4 through 14, Jesus provides them with anticipatory signs of the temple's coming destruction; in verses 15 through 31, He focuses on threshold events and the actual destruction of the temple itself. After the transition in verses 32 through 36, Jesus looks to the distant Second Coming. Let us begin first with the anticipatory phenomena.

Anticipation: Cautionary Instruction

In Matthew 24:4, Matthew records Christ's initial response to the disciples' query: "And Jesus answered and said to them, 'See to it that no one misleads you.'" First-century Israel is rife with apocalyptic expectation; it is "an apocalyptically charged tinderbox in the process of being ignited."[1] From that era we have an enormous body of apocalyptic literature illustrating the popular infatuation with and expectation of catastrophic divine events.[2] We also have historical records of a strong and violent zealot movement whose radical Zionism eventually ignites the Jewish War, resulting in the destruction of the temple and the devastation of Jerusalem.[3]

Consequently, an attempt to force a political kingship upon Jesus should not surprise us: "Jesus therefore perceiving that they were intending to come and take Him by force, to make Him king, withdrew again to the mountain by Himself alone" (John 6:15).[4] Given this first-century religious backdrop, His death disheartens many of His own followers caught up in the militaristic hope: "But we were hoping that it was He who was going to redeem Israel. Indeed, besides all this, it is the third day since these things happened" (Luke 24:21).

False Christs

The Lord's warning in the next verse is quite relevant to His immediate hearers. He warns that though the events He prophesies are close ("this generation"), His apostles and their converts need to be cautious and not jump the gun: "For many will come in My name, saying, 'I am the Christ,' and will mislead many" (Matt. 24:5). The Lord here warns about messianic pretenders ("I am the Christ"). Those coming in His name are "arrogating to themselves the title and authority which properly belongs to" Christ.[5]

In John's first epistle we find a warning that "many antichrists have arisen" (1 John 2:18b). The Greek word *anti* in "antichrist" is instructive. The *Theological Dictionary of the New Testament* defines the significance of the preposition *anti:* "In its basic meaning of 'over against' it does not occur in the NT, but is mostly used in the sense of: a. 'in place of' . . . , b. 'on behalf of' . . . , and also c. 'for the sake of.'"[6] Seemingly, in the term "antichrist," *anti* should imply "over against." Greek scholar A. T. Robertson, though, argues that "antichrist" entails both substitution (instead of Christ) and opposition (against Christ).[7] Obviously, one who substitutes himself for Christ opposes the true Christ. Thus, John's warning of "many" (Gk., *polloi*) substitutes for Christ in his day (1 John 2:18), fulfills Christ's prophecy that "many" (Gk., *polloi*) false Christs would arise (Matt. 24:5).

In Acts 5:36–37, we hear about the same real historical dangers of religious pretenders in the first century:

> *Men of Israel, take care what you propose to do with these men. For some time ago Theudas rose up, claiming to be some-body; and a group of about four hundred men joined up with him. And he was slain; and all who followed him were dis-*

persed and came to nothing. After this man Judas of Galilee rose up in the days of the census, and drew away some people after him, he too perished, and all those who followed him were scattered.

In 8:9–10, another claimant to divine authorization arises:

Now there was a certain man named Simon, who formerly was practicing magic in the city, and astonishing the people of Samaria, claiming to be someone great; and they all, from smallest to greatest, were giving attention to him, saying, "This man is what is called the Great Power of God."

Jewish historian Josephus bemoans Judea's first-century plight: "In Judea matters were constantly going from bad to worse. For the country was again infested with bands of brigands and impostors who deceived the mob" (*Antiquities* 20:5:5). "Moreover, impostors and deceivers called upon the mob to follow them into the desert. For they said that they would show them unmistakable marvels and signs that would be wrought in harmony with God's design" (*Antiquities* 20:5:6). "Deceivers and impostors, under the pretense of divine inspiration fostering revolutionary changes, they persuaded the multitude to act like madmen, and led them out into the desert under the belief that God would there give them tokens of deliverance" (*Wars* 2:13:4).

Jesus' prophetic warning is most apropos to "this *generation.*"

Wars and Rumors of Wars

Matthew 24:6–7a says, "And you will be hearing of wars and rumors of wars; see that you are not frightened, for those things must take place, but that is not yet the end. For nation will rise against nation, and kingdom against kingdom." In a book edited by Dr. Ice, Tim LaHaye states that this prophecy is foreshadowed in World War I: "The sign was not wars, but a most significant war, which was World War I, with its accompanying phenomena of famines, pestilences, and earthquakes. Out of the fulfillment of this sign, Israel started going back into the land, leading many prophecy scholars to conclude that God's prophetic clock began ticking again. Personally, I look on that period, 1917–1948, as God winding His clock."[8]

The alarm of war often excites anxiety among God's people (Isa. 13:6–22; 17:14; Jer. 4:19–31; 6:29–30; Joel 2:1–11; Nah. 2:11). War is an instrument of God's vengeance upon evildoers (Deut. 28:15, 25; Isa. 13:9; 14:30; 19:2; Jer. 4:27; Mic. 3:8–12). Of course, Jesus says these should *not* alarm His followers, for when these (and the following few signs) arise, it "is not yet the end" (Matt. 24:6). Indeed, these are but the "beginning of birth pangs" (v. 8). He designs these delay-sayings to brace His people for lingering historical turbulence. Warfare as a sign, however, seems too general to be useful—when have there not been "wars and rumors of wars"?

Some commentators go too far when they argue that this and the following signs "stretch over the period between the advents."[9] Or as Walvoord expresses it: "In the predictions that Christ made almost two thousand years ago, He accurately portrayed the progress in the present age. In verses 4–14, He predicted at least nine distinctive features of the period. . . . All of these situations have been fulfilled in history."[10] Though "wars and rumors of wars" clearly are not *immediate* indicators of "the end," surely they are somehow predecessory to and must, therefore, erupt in the general vicinity of, "the end" (i.e., of the temple; Matt. 24:2–3). I agree with my disputant, Dr. Ice, that these compose "a description of the Tribulation years."[11] However, I believe the Tribulation occured in the first century.

But how, then, may these nebulous "wars and rumors of wars" function as *signs?* Here a little refresher course in ancient history will prove helpful. Julius Caesar plants the seeds for the Roman empire when he defeats Pompey and Mark Antony, thereby becoming dictator of Rome. After his death a brief civil war results in the formal establishment of the empire by Augustus Caesar. One important result of Augustus's administrative and military prowess is his enforcing peace throughout the empire. This time of peace, the famous *Pax Romana* ("peace of Rome"), begins with Augustus's establishment of the "Age of Peace" in 17 B.C.

Historians inform us that "the peace of the Roman Empire that Augustus established was purchased by monarchy, but it was a real and enduring peace. It embraced the entire Mediterranean world as no constitutional dispensations had ever done before."[12] The prominent church father Origen (A.D. 185–254) speaks about the "abundance of peace that began at the birth of Christ" (*Against Celsus* 2:30).

Remarkably for our study, "in the Roman Empire proper, this period of peace remained comparatively undisturbed *until the time of Nero*."[13] Nero is the emperor who in February of A.D. 67 commissions Roman general Flavius Vespasian to put down the revolt in Israel, which results in the destruction of the temple three-and-one-half years later (August, A.D. 70).[14] Vespasian's military strategy in the Jewish War was to "first overthrow what remained elsewhere [for example, in Galilee and Judea] and to leave nothing outside of Jerusalem behind him that might interrupt in the siege" (*Wars* 4:7:3). Josephus records for us that Vespasian "went and burnt Galilee and the neighboring parts" (*Wars*

6:6:2) as he makes his way toward Jerusalem. This means there would be numerous battles in Israel prior to the siege of Jerusalem and the temple (resulting in "the end" of the temple system; Matt. 24:6b).

What is more, during the Jewish War (A.D. 67–70) Rome erupts in civil war, almost destroying both city and empire. Introducing the weeks following Nero's death in the middle of the Jewish War, Tacitus writes: "The history on which I am entering is that of a period rich in disasters, terrible with battles, torn by civil struggles, horrible even in peace. Four emperors failed by the sword; there were three civil wars, more foreign wars and often both at the same time" (*Histories* 1:2). Josephus notes concerning these events:

> Now at the time when this great concussion of affairs happened [namely, the Jewish War], the affairs of the Romans themselves were in great disorder. Those Jews also, who were for innovations, then arose when the times were disturbed; they were also in a flourishing condition for strength and riches, insomuch that the affairs of the east were then exceeding tumultuous, while some hoped for gain, and others were afraid of loss in such troubles; for the Jews hoped that all of their nation which were beyond Euphrates would have raised an insurrection together with them. The Gauls also, in the neighborhood of the Romans, were in motion, and the Celtae were not quiet; but all was in disorder after the death of Nero (*Wars* 1:1:2).

These upheavals would strike both the subjects and the enemies of the vast empire as being the *very death throes of Rome*. Indeed, in Tacitus' estimation it very nearly is so: "This was the condition of the Roman state when Serius Galba, chosen consul for the second time, and his colleague Titus Vinius entered upon the year that was to be for Galba his last and *for the state almost the end*" (*Histories* 1:11).

And this historical survey does not even take into account local riots and battles prior to the mid-sixties. Bruce relates the history of the "increase in militant messianism in the period following A.D. 44. This is indicated especially by the number of insurgent movements based in the wilderness of Judea. . . . Under Felix in particular a succession of 'deceivers and impostors' (as Josephus calls them) 'fomented revolutionary changes under the pretext of divine inspiration.'"[15] Josephus relates numerous instances of brigandage within Israel and battles between the Jews and others—for example, with the Samaritans (*Antiquities* 20:6:1), the Syrians (*Wars* 2:18:1), the Askelonians (*Wars* 2:18:5), and the Alexandrians (*Wars* 2:18:7).[16] Many ancient historians relate the arising of nation against nation in the first century just prior to the Jewish War.[17]

Consequently, the unrest just prior to Nero's reign (A.D. 44 and following) and under it (A.D. 55–68) are historically significant *in that they occur during a time of great peace.* Perhaps the key "rumor of war" is the remarkable victory of the Jews in November, A.D. 66, against Cestius Gallus and the Roman Twelfth Legion (*Wars* 2:19:2–9). This victory inflames the passions of the Jews to arm themselves for a war for independence from Rome—which action seals the doom of A.D. 70 (*Wars* 2:18–19).

Famines and Earthquakes

Jesus said in Matthew 24:7, "and in various places there will be famines and earthquakes." These second and third features of the "birth pangs" (v. 8) also speak about first-century events in a remarkable and relevant way. In the same text of Scripture itself we read about the New Testament prophet Agabus, who "stood up and began to indicate by the Spirit that there would certainly be a great famine all over the world. And this took place in the reign of Claudius" (Acts 11:28). This seems to be the famine that strikes Jerusalem. According to Josephus, "a famine did oppress them at that time, and many people died for want of what was necessary to procure food withal" (*Antiquities* 20:2:5). He later calls it "the great famine" (*Antiquities* 20:5:2). He mentions others (*Antiquities* 20:2:6; 20:4:2; *Wars* 6:3:3).

Of these events in A.D. 51, Tacitus (ca. A.D. 55–117) writes: "This year witnessed many prodigies. . . . Further portents were seen in a shortage of corn, resulting in famine. . . . It was established that there was no more than fifteen days' supply of food in the city [Rome]."[18] Tacitus mentions earthquakes in Crete, Rome, Apamea, Phrygia, Campania, Laodicea (of Revelation fame), and Pompeii during the time just before Jerusalem's destruction.[19] Of one series of quakes under Claudius's rule Tacitus comments: "Houses were flattened by repeated earthquakes, and as terror spread the weak were trampled to death by the panic-stricken" (*Annals* 12:58). Severe earthquakes plague the reigns of the Emperors Caligula (A.D. 37–41) and Claudius (A.D. 41–54).[20] According to Seneca (ca. 4 B.C.–A.D. 65), others occur in Asia, Achaia, Syria, and Macedonia (Seneca, *Epistles* 91). Concerning this era, Ellicott's commentary observes: "Perhaps no period in the world's history has ever been so marked by these convulsions as that which intervenes between the Crucifixion and the destruction of Jerusalem."[21]

In that Israel's "world comes apart" in the Jewish War, we should not be surprised that a massive earthquake strikes Jerusalem during the first phase of the Jewish War with Rome. Josephus informs us: "There broke out a prodigious storm in the night, with the utmost violence, and very strong winds, with the largest showers of rain, and continual lightnings, terrible thunderings, and amazing concussions and bellowings of the earth, that was in an earthquake." Josephus, at least, can read the signs of the times, for he provides editorial commentary on these phenomena: "These things were a manifest indication that some destruction was coming upon men, when the system of the world was put into this disorder; and anyone would guess that these wonders foreshadowed some grand calamities that were coming" (*Wars* 4:4:5).

Birth Pangs

In Matthew 24:8 Christ said, "But all these things are merely the beginning of birth pangs." Ironically, though Jesus is speaking about issues regarding "the end" (vv. 3, 6), He employs the Greek term rendered "birth pangs," which suggests a beginning. These birth pangs point to the *end* of the temple system and ceremonial era (23:38–24:2), which is brought about by the *beginning* of the new covenant era, the establishing of the kingdom of heaven.[22] On another occasion Jesus affirms: "Truly I say to you, there are some of those who are standing here who shall not taste death until they see the kingdom of God after it has come with power" (Mark 9:1; compare Heb. 12:18–28). The judgment and destruction of the old order serve as a powerful confirmation, vindication, and establishment of the new. For the disciples, then, these troubles are the birth pangs of the kingdom. *Because of these coming birth pangs, the future is bright with hope, even if sore with the pain of labor.* As the temple goes up in smoke, Christ's kingdom enters into its own life, separating from its "mother" (Israel).

Jesus is careful to brace His disciples for the tumultuous future that they themselves will face. The disciples will witness "wars and rumors of wars" (Matt. 24:6). The enemy "will deliver [them] to tribulation" (v. 9). Many will "fall away" and "deliver up one another" (v. 10). Lawlessness will be "increased" (v. 12). And all of this will ultimately issue forth in "the abomination of desolation" (v. 15) and "the Great Tribulation" (v. 21).

Jesus, however, is not a Jewish apocalyptist, spouting only gloom and doom. Indeed, the parenetic framework of the discourse is crucial to its interpretation: Jesus' dire warnings are tempered with sure encouragements, and His display of apocalyptic events is interspersed with moral admonitions. In the discourse, exhortation and consolation play off each other. He even expresses compassion for the difficulties imposed upon pregnant and nursing mothers (v. 19). Through it all God is in control, promising that "the one who endures to the end, he shall be saved" (v. 13) and that "the gospel of the kingdom shall be preached in the whole world for a witness" (v. 14). Those horrible days will "be cut short" for the sake of His people (v. 22). In all of this, they must remember "I have told you in advance" (v. 25). The disciple must re-alize that the hand of God is at work plowing the soil with a view to a fruitful harvest.

Persecution and Martyrdom

Matthew 24:9 says, "Then they will deliver you to tribulation, and will kill you, and you will be hated by all nations on account of My name." In this verse the Lord warns His disciples that they will be per-secuted. This is a continuation and expansion of 23:34–36, which ap-plies easily to the first century (see my preceding chapter). The fulfillment of this prophecy by Jewish opposition appears in Acts, which covers virtually the entire apostolic period up to the very de-cade of the Jewish War.[23] Mark's parallel account points clearly to Jew-ish persecution in the first century: "But watch out for yourselves, for they will deliver you up to *councils,* and you will be beaten in the *syna-gogues.* You will be brought before rulers and kings for My sake, for a testimony to them" (Mark 13:9; compare Matt. 10:17–18, emphasis mine).

For evidence of the massive first-century Jewish persecution, note the following sample passages:

> On that day a great persecution arose against the church in Jerusalem; and they were all scattered throughout the regions of Judea and Samaria, except the apostles. (Acts 8:1)

> For you, brethren, became imitators of the churches of God in Christ Jesus that are in Judea, for you also endured the same sufferings at the hands of your own countrymen, even as they did from the Jews, who both killed the Lord Jesus and the prophets, and drove us out. They are not pleasing to God, but hostile to all men, hindering us from speaking to the Gentiles that they might be saved; with the result that they always fill up the measure of their sins. But wrath has come upon them to the utmost. (1 Thess. 2:14–16)

> But remember the former days, when, after being enlightened, you endured a great conflict of sufferings, partly, by being made a public spectacle through reproaches and Tribulations, and partly by becoming sharers with those who were so treated. For you showed sympathy to the prisoners, and accepted joy-fully the seizure of your property, knowing that you have for yourselves a better possession and an abiding one. (Heb. 10:32–34)

This persecution is but a continuation of Israel's persecution of Christ. In fact, Luke traces the history of the apostolic church, showing that the persecution of Christians *is* the persecution of Christ. Luke introduces Acts by saying it is a record of the things Jesus "began to do" (Acts 1:1), which "suggests that the 'acts of the apostles' must be seen as the action of *Jesus*. . . . To reject Jesus' followers is thus to reject Jesus Himself a second time."[24] So to persecute Christians is to "persecute me," says Jesus to Paul (Acts 9:4). When the Jews reject Paul, Luke records the Jews crying out the same words as at Jesus' trial: "away with this fellow" (Acts 22:22; compare Luke 23:18).

The *Jewish* persecution of Christians breaks out early in church history (about A.D. 33, Acts 8:1) and continues up to the Jewish War (A.D. 67–70). Toward the end of the apostolic era, the first Roman onslaught erupts, just preceding the temple's destruction (A.D. 64–68).[25] The Roman historian Tacitus records the horror of the Neronic persecution: Nero "inflicted unheard-of punishments on those who, detested for their abominable crimes, were vulgarly called Christians" so that eventually "an immense number were involved in the same fate" (*Annals* 15:44). Church father Orosius (A.D. 390–?) speaks about this persecution when he writes that Nero "was the first at Rome to torture and inflict the penalty of death upon Christians, and he ordered them throughout all the provinces to be afflicted with like persecution; and in his attempt to wipe out the very name, he killed the most blessed apostles of Christ, Peter and Paul."[26] (Significantly, evidence suggests "that the promptings of the orthodox Jews in the capital had something to do with it."[27] Earlier the Jews cause riots over Christianity, leading the emperor Claudius to banish them from Rome for awhile: "As the Jews were indulging in constant riots at the instigation of Chrestus, he banished them from Rome."[28])

Betrayal and Apostasy

Matthew 24:10 says, "And at that time many will fall away and will deliver up one another and hate one another." Here Jesus reveals a sad consequence of this horrendous persecution: defection and betrayal among the early Christians. We may easily document this in the apostolic era also. Paul laments "that all those in Asia have turned away from me" (2 Tim. 1:15); "Demas has forsaken me, having loved this present world" (4:10); "at my first defense no one stood with me, but all forsook me" (2 Tim. 4:16; compare Gal. 3:1–4; 2 Thess. 3:1).

John reports such apostasy under his ministry: "They *went out from us,* but they were not of us; for if they had been of us, they would have continued with us; but they went out that they might be made manifest, that none of them were of us" (1 John 2:19, emphasis mine; compare

2 and 3 John). The epistle to the Hebrews indicates a sizable apostasy from among Jewish converts to Christianity (see 2:1–4; 6:1–6; 10:26–31). Tacitus even reports the apostasy and betrayal arising during the Neronic persecution: "First, Nero had self-acknowledged Christians arrested. Then, *on their information,* large numbers of others were condemned" (*Annals* 15). The New Testament abounds with examples of heresy and apostasy.[29]

False Prophets

Matthew 24:11 says, "And many false prophets will arise, and will mislead many." Just as religious figures taking the place of Christ arise in the first century (v. 5), so do false prophets. Paul warns the Ephesians about "wolves" who will "draw away the disciples after them" when he leaves (Acts 20:29–30), about men with "smooth and flattering speech" who "deceive the hearts of the unsuspecting" (Rom. 16:17–18), about "false apostles, deceitful works, disguising themselves as apostles of Christ" (2 Cor. 11:13), and about "false brethren" who cause trouble (Gal. 2:4).

Peter cautions about "false prophets" who will "secretly introduce destructive heresies" among his followers (2 Peter 4:1). John clearly alerts those under his ministry of "many false prophets [who] have gone out into the world" (1 John 4:1). Luke records the name of one of these false prophets: "Now when they had gone through the island to Paphos, they found a certain sorcerer, a false prophet, a Jew whose name was Bar-Jesus" (Acts 13:6).

Especially relevant, though, is Josephus' record of false prophets arising among the Jews in Israel: "Now it came to pass, while Fadus was procurator of Judea, that a certain magician, whose name was Theudas, persuaded a great part of the people to take their effects with them, and follow him to the river Jordan; for he told them he was a prophet, and that he would, by his own command, divide the river, and afford them an easy passage over it; and many were deluded by his words." In fact, the false prophets in Jerusalem help aggravate the destruction of the city by buoying up the hopes of the zealots:

> A false prophet was the occasion of these people's destruction, who had made a public proclamation in the city that very day, that God commanded them to get up upon the temple, and that there they should receive miraculous signs of their deliverance. Now, there was then a great number of false prophets suborned by the tyrants to impose upon the people, who denounced this upon the people, who denounced this to them, that they should wait for deliverance from God: and this was

in order to keep them from deserting, and that they might be buoyed up above fear and care by such hopes (*Wars* 6:5:2).

Lawlessness and Enduring

Matthew 24:12 says, "And because lawlessness will abound, the love of many will grow cold." The persecution of believers in Christ by first-century Jews is a clear and relevant example of lawlessness before God. And as I show above, such persecution abounds in the New Testament era.

What is more, Josephus records the horrible "lawlessness" associated with the Jewish condition around the era of the destruction of the temple. He reports that the Jewish Zealots act "as though they had covenanted to annul the laws of nature along with those of their country," because "every human ordinance was trampled under foot" (*Wars* 4:6:3). He notes that "in the first place, all the people of every place betook themselves to rapine; after which they got together in bodies, in order to rob the people of the country, insomuch that for the barbarity and iniquity those of the same nation did no way differ from the Romans; nay, it seemed to be a much lighter thing to be ruined by the Romans than by themselves" (*Wars* 4:2:2). Furthermore, Josephus writes, "it is therefore impossible to go distinctly over every instance of these men's iniquity I shall therefore speak my mind here at once briefly: That neither did any other city ever suffer such miseries, nor did any age ever breed a generation more fruitful in wickedness than this was, from the beginning of the world" (*Wars* 5:10:5; see also: 7:8:1).

Matthew 24:13 says, "But the one who endures to the end, he shall be saved." Here the Lord reminds His faithful followers about the ultimate issues involved. Though lawless people will deliver up His followers before their courts to be scrutinized by their judgments, His disciples must remember to stand firm in the faith knowing their vindication will be before the bar of God. The one who endures the persecution, resists the false prophets, and defies the lawless—that is, the one who "endures to the end," to the conclusion of the tribulation period—will be saved. On an earlier occasion Jesus teaches His disciples to "not fear those who kill the body, but are unable to kill the soul; but rather fear Him who is able to destroy both soul and body in hell" (Matt. 10:28). He, therefore, urges them to persevere in the faith in light of the eternal consequences for their souls.

Worldwide Witness

Matthew 24:14 says, "And this gospel of the kingdom shall be preached in the whole world for a witness to all the nations, and then the end shall come." Oftentimes futurists cite this verse as evidence of the impossibility of a first-century Great Tribulation. Certainly a cursory glance at this statement appears to pose difficulties for the preterist. But looks are deceiving. We must read this statement in the light of the New Testament record itself. How *does* the preterist account for this?

Fundamental principles of interpretation lead us to bear in mind contextual clues: the time indicator ("this generation"), the audience (the disciples who ask about the temple), the specific concern (the destruction of the temple), and the harmony of the preceding signs with the first-century experience. All of these should dispose us to seek a first-century fulfillment of this verse. And Scripture clearly allows this.

First, the term rendered "world" here is the Greek noun *oikoumenē* (from which we derive "economy"). It often speaks about the Roman Empire, as in a number of verses: "And it came to pass in those days that a decree went out from Caesar Augustus that all the *world* should be registered" (Luke 2:1, emphasis mine). "One of them, named Agabus, stood up and showed by the Spirit that there was going to be a great famine throughout all the *world,* which also happened in the days of Claudius Caesar" (Acts 11:28, emphasis mine). Acts 24:5 is quite relevant to our point: "For we have found this man [Paul] a plague, a creator of dissension among all the Jews throughout the *world,* and a ringleader of the sect of the Nazarenes" (compare 17:6). A surface reading of these texts suggests global events. Yet we know these "world" events happen within the Roman empire of the first century.

Second, we should remember that both John the Baptist and Christ preach to the first-century Jews that "the kingdom of heaven is at hand" (Matt. 3:1ff.; Mark 1:15). Indeed, the gospel of Christ's redemptive kingdom is "to the Jew first" (Matt. 10:5–6; Rom. 1:16; 2:9–10). Here in Matthew 24 the King, Jesus Christ (compare Acts 17:7; Rev. 1:5), promises a universal testimony of the gospel of the kingdom to the "world-wide" Jewish presence. According to Acts, the disciples teach "all the Jews throughout the nations" (Acts 21:21) and cause dissension "among all the Jews throughout the world (Gk., *oikoumenē*)" (24:5).

Third, the parallel in Mark 13:8–10 further strengthens this interpretation, providing additional insight into Christ's meaning: "These are the beginnings of sorrows. But watch out for yourselves, for they will deliver you up to councils, and you will be beaten in the synagogues. And you will be brought before rulers and kings for My sake, for a testimony to them. And the gospel must first be preached to all the nations." The Lord is referring to the Jewish opposition to the disciples by "councils" and "synagogues"; the book of Acts demonstrates this actually happens in the first century.

Fourth, we find several clear references to events fulfilling the same conditions of Christ's prophecy. In Romans 1:8 Paul writes: "First, I thank my God through Jesus Christ for you all, that your faith is spoken of throughout the whole world." Their faith is the Christian faith; Paul says it is being spoken of throughout the "whole world." Christians are being a witness (see also, Rom. 10:18; 16:19). Elsewhere Paul speaks about "the gospel which has come to you, as it has also in all the world" (Col. 1:6). He remarks that "the gospel which you heard . . . was preached to every creature under heaven" (Col. 1:23).

Thus, Matthew 24:14 is no hindrance at all to the preteristic viewpoint. In fact, it harmonizes beautifully with the many other lines of evidence.

Realization

At this juncture in the discourse, the Lord begins dealing directly with the Great Tribulation, rather than its precursory signs. Some of the more difficult verses in the Olivet discourse occur in this section— verses modern evangelicals too easily distort due to a deficient understanding of the Old Testament background.

Abomination of Desolation

Matthew 24:15–20 reads as follows:

> *Therefore when you see the* abomination of desolation *which was spoken of through Daniel the prophet, standing in the holy place (let the reader understand), then let those who are in Judea flee to the mountains; let him who is on the housetop not go down to get the things out that are in his house; and let him who is in the field not turn back to get his cloak. But woe to those who are with child and to those who nurse babes in those days! But pray that your flight may not be in the winter, or on a Sabbath.*

Contextual Setting

Here the Lord borrows a famous but obscure phrase from Daniel's prophecy (Dan. 9:26–27; 11:31; 12:11). But what does Jesus mean by this "abomination of desolation"? We know from the Old Testament that "abomination" often relates to some abuse of worship (Lev. 7:18; Deut. 7:25; 17:11; 27:15). Indeed, in Matthew 24:15 "the abomination of desolation" involves "the holy place," just as in Daniel 9:24–27.

This prophecy of our Lord must refer to the A.D. 70 events. After all, the first-century temple is standing in a "holy city" (Matt. 4:5; 27:53; Josephus, *Wars* 4:4:3). Jesus' disciples could imagine no other

referent for this "abomination" in "the holy place," especially given
the circumstances of Jesus' prophecy: this prediction is part of Christ's
response to the disciples' query regarding that same temple (Matt.
23:38–24:1). Even the prayer that their flight not be "on the Sabbath"
is relevant to the first century while Jerusalem's walls are standing:
Jewish authorities close the gates on the Sabbath (Neh. 13:19, 22),
which would prevent escape. To assume some other referent in some
other time (see Matt. 24:3) would be an incredible, anticontextual leap
of logic.

Furthermore, Christ expressly points to that historical temple—"see
ye not all these things"—while warning about its coming destruction:
"not one stone shall be left on another that shall not be thrown down"
(Matt. 24:2). In fact, He has just stated its approaching "desolation":
"Behold, your house is being left to you desolate!" (23:38). The A.D.
70 stone-by-stone dismantling of the temple surely involves its "desolation." And, as I will show, it includes abominable acts. Interestingly,
when speaking about Jerusalem's destruction, Josephus uses the word
erēmōthē (*Wars* 6:10:1), which is the verbal form of the Greek term
rendered "desolation" that Christ uses (*erēmōseōs*, Matt. 24:21). In fact,
Josephus, like Christ, applies Daniel's prophecy to this event: "In the
very same manner Daniel also wrote concerning the Roman government, and that our country should be made desolate by them" (*Antiquities* 10:11:7), an obvious allusion to Daniel 9:24–27.

The Gentile Luke's parallel account in Luke 21:21 greatly assists
in interpreting Matthew's Jewish account.[30] Luke often uses language
more easily understood by the Gentile. Rather than employing the
obscure Old Testament phrase "abomination of desolation" (from Dan.
9:27, as recorded in Matt. 24:15), Luke interprets it for the Gentile
reader: "But when you see Jerusalem *surrounded by armies, then know
that its desolation* is near" (Luke 21:20). I strongly urge the reader to
lay Matthew 24:15–21 and Luke 21:20–24 side-by-side. Such quickly
reveals that the *same* events must be in view, despite Dr. Ice's contrary assertion.

Jerusalem's Destruction

The "abomination of desolation" is so dreadful that it will prompt
desperate flight from the area, a forsaking of home and property (Matt.
24:17). This horrible episode will occur "in the holy place." Though
the phrase "the holy place" might seem to refer to the temple alone,
several indicators suggest the reference involves both the temple *and*
the city: Jerusalem itself is a holy place,[31] being the capital of the "holy
land" (Zech. 2:12).[32] Luke clearly interprets the phrase as the surrounding of the city of Jerusalem (Luke 21:21). What is more, the prophecy

urges flight from *all of Judea,* not just the temple (Matt. 24:16, emphasis mine). This is why Christ weeps over the city of Jerusalem just before uttering this prophecy (23:37). Christ is warning of Jerusalem's devastation by military assault, not just the temple's desecration by profane actions. The rising storm of war, not the spread of ritual heresy, prompts flight from the region.[33]

This becomes even more evident when we consider that the backdrop in Daniel's original prophecy mentions both "the city and the sanctuary" (Dan. 9:26). Verse 25 even calls Jerusalem "the holy city" (whereas Matthew speaks about "the holy place"). In fact, the original prophecy pivots on the rebuilding of the *city* (Dan. 9:25), which the Jews consider a "holy city."[34] We better understand Matthew's record of the Lord's statement, then, as agreeing with Daniel in involving *both* the *city* and the *temple* (Matt. 23:37–38).

Well then, what *is* this "abomination of desolation" that befalls the city and temple? The holy city *and* the temple are both desecrated and desolated in the Jewish War. During the Roman siege, the Zealots hole up in Jerusalem, and stir up factional infighting between the parties of John of Gischala, Eleazar, and Simon. Even while Jerusalem's mighty walls resist the Romans, this internal strife brings war into the holy temple itself: "the outer temple was all of it overflowed with blood; and that day, as it came on, saw eight thousand five hundred dead bodies there" (*Wars* 4:5:1). The inner strife is so bad that Josephus calls it "a sedition begotten by another sedition"; he says that Jerusalem is "like a wild beast grown mad, which for the want of food from abroad, fell now upon eating its own flesh" (*Wars* 5:1:1). Hence, Christ's dire warning to flee without turning back (Matt. 24:16–18).

As Titus begins his final march toward Jerusalem in A.D. 70, the Zealots "seize upon the inner court of the temple, and lay their arms upon the holy gates, and over the holy fronts of that court." They even partake of the "the great abundance of what was consecrated to sacred uses," causing such an uproar that the "temple was defiled everywhere with murders" (*Wars* 5:1:2). They "went over all the buildings, and the temple itself, and fell upon the priests, and those that were about the sacred offices" (*Wars* 5:1:3). John of Gischala "emptied the vessels of that sacred wine and oil which the priests kept to be poured on the burnt offerings, and which lay in the inner court of the temple, and distributed it among the multitude, who, in their anointing themselves and drinking, used each of them above a hin of them" (*Wars* 5:13:6). They commit crimes of great enormity even in the Holy of Holies (*Wars* 4:3:10; 5:4). They invest Phanni as high priest, which prompts the former (and legitimate) high priest Ananus to lament: "It would have been far better for me to have died before I had seen the house of God

laden with such abominations and its unapproachable and hallowed
places crowded with the feet of murderers" (*Wars* 4:3:10). Surely these
events are abominations in the holy temple in the holy city of the holy
nation!

Though these abominations are consequences of Jesus' prophecy,
He cannot be referring to these actions *solely*. After all, He warns His
followers: "when you see the abomination of desolation . . . then let
those who are in Judea flee" (Matt. 24:15–16). This warning must
somehow be relevant not just to those at the temple or in Jerusalem,
but in all of *Judea*.

This is where Luke helps us. Remember that Luke records Jesus'
reference to the "abomination of desolation" with these words: "But
when you see Jerusalem surrounded by armies, then recognize that her
desolation is at hand. Then let those who are in Judea flee to the mountains, and let those who are in the midst of the city depart, and let not
those who are in the country enter the city" (Luke 21:20–21). The
Roman armies themselves must be involved. Josephus notes that Titus
literally builds "a wall round about the whole city" before the final siege
(*Wars* 5:12:1).

The Jews consider the Roman soldiers with their ensigns to be
abominable, not only due to the Jewish avoidance of images, but also
because these standards hold a religious significance for the Romans.[35]
The images carried by the Romans are, thus, forbidden in Jerusalem.
Pontius Pilate tries on one occasion to garrison troops in Jerusalem.
But because of their ensigns, the Jews force him to withdraw the troops
(Josephus, *Antiquities* 18:3:1). On another occasion the Jews implore
the Roman general Vitellius to avoid marching troops through Israel
because of the insignia (*Antiquities* 18:5:3). The presence of Roman
soldiers in military regalia would then be an abomination; and their
presence surrounding the city in a time of war would be an abomination leading to desolation.

Flight Opportunities

But how could Jesus' followers heed His warning to leave at this
stage? Titus seals off Jerusalem for good; no hope of escape remains.
A history lesson will resolve this problem. Jerusalem is encircled
several times during her investiture and before she is finally destroyed.
In the events leading up to full-scale imperial engagement, the Roman
governor Cestius Gallus marches toward Jerusalem during the Feast
of Tabernacles in A.D. 66 in order to put down growing Jewish unrest:
"But as for the Jews, when they saw the war approaching to their
metropolis, they left the feast, and betook themselves to their arms;
and taking courage greatly from their multitude, went in a sudden and

disorderly manner to the fight, with a great noise, and without any consideration had of the rest of the seventh day, although the Sabbath was the day to which they had the greatest regard" (*Wars* 2:19:2).

Cestius pursues the Jewish forces into the outer city up to the walls of the inner city. Then "he sent out a great many of his soldiers into neighboring villages, to seize upon their corn" (*Wars* 2:19:4), thus surrounding the city "on all sides" (Gk., *pantothen*), allowing him to besiege her walls for five days (*Wars* 2:19:5). Yet, remarkably "without having received any disgrace, he retired from the city, without any reason in the world" (*Wars* 2:19:7).

This unexpected retreat of Cestius serves a twofold providential purpose: it buoys up the (vain) Jewish hopes, thereby furthering the war[36] and provides an opportunity of escape for the Christians who were alert to the Lord's warning: "But when you see Jerusalem surrounded by armies, then recognize that her desolation is at hand" (Luke 21:20). Josephus informs us that after Cestius's siege and retreat, Jews left Jerusalem like swimmers from a sinking ship (*Wars* 2:20:1). Josephus's best known English translator, William Whiston (1737), astutely observes concerning these affairs (*Wars* 2.19.6.b):

> There may another very important, and very providential, reason be here assigned for this strange and foolish retreat of Cestius; which, if Josephus had been now a Christian, he might probably have taken notice of also; and that is, the affording the Jewish Christians in the city an opportunity of calling to mind the prediction and caution given them by Christ about thirty-three years and a half before, that 'when they should see the abomination of desolation' [the idolatrous Roman armies, with the images of their idols in their ensigns, ready to lay Jerusalem desolate,] 'stand where it ought not;' or, 'in the holy place;' or, 'when they should see Jerusalem encompassed with armies,' they should then 'flee to the mountains.' By complying with which those Jewish Christians fled to the mountains of Perea, and escaped of Cestius, this destruction.[37]

Later during the full-scale imperial assault of Jerusalem under General Vespasian (A.D. 68), the city is once again encompassed: "And now Vespasian had fortified all the places round about Jerusalem." Josephus records the results of Vespasian's efforts: "And now the war having gone through all the mountainous country, and all the plain country also, those that were at Jerusalem were deprived of the liberty of going out of the city; for as to such as had a mind to desert, they were watched by the zealots; and as to such as were not yet on the side of the Romans, their army kept them in, by encompassing the city round about on all sides" (*Wars* 4:9:1). But Nero's suicide causes the cessation of Roman hostilities and the withdrawal of their forces, providing yet another opportunity for escape (*Wars* 4:9:1–2; 4:10:2). Then another encompassment occurs while the Romans withdraw: civil war erupts once again within Jerusalem, leading Simon "to encompass the wall all round again" (*Wars* 4:9:10).

Finally, after the Roman upheaval relating to Nero's death and the Roman Civil Wars (A.D. 68–69), Vespasian becomes emperor and commissions his son Titus to complete the Jewish War. Titus soon builds "a wall round about the whole city" of Jerusalem (*Wars* 5:12:1), sealing her doom (A.D. 70). Titus's victory is complete: "the Romans upon the flight of the seditious into the city, and upon the burning of the holy house itself, and of all the buildings lying round about it, brought their ensigns to the temple, and set them over against its eastern gate; and there did they offer sacrifices to them, and there did they make Titus imperator, with the greatest acclamations of joy" (*Wars* 6:6:1). Though the "abomination of desolation" involves the destruction of Jerusalem (beginning with its several encirclings by Cestius, Vespasian, Simon, and Titus), it culminates in this final abominable act within the temple itself.[38]

Remarkably this same conclusion seems to be in Christ's mind when He states: "For wherever the carcass is, there the *eagles* [Gk., *aetoi*] will be gathered together" (Matt. 24:28 NKJV). Josephus describes the marching order of the Roman troops, mentioning the prominence of their eagle ensigns: "Then came the ensigns encompassing the *eagle* [Gk., *aeton*], which is at the head of every Roman legion, the king, and the strongest of all birds, which seems to them a signal of dominion, and an omen that they shall conquer all against whom they march; these sacred ensigns are followed by the trumpeters" (*Wars* 3:6:2; cf. 5:2:1). The Roman ensigns—to which Titus's soldiers offer sacrifices in the temple of God—are *eagles*.[39] Certainly this gathering of these eagles is a grievous abomination, one that indicates the death of Jerusalem. In A.D. 70, the Roman "eagles" gather over the corpse of Jerusalem to pick it clean: "The army now having no victims either for slaughter or plunder, through lack of all objects on which to vent their rage" (*Wars* 7:1:1). According to Josephus, "the soldiers had such vast quantities of the spoils which they had gotten by plunder, that in Syria a pound weight of gold was sold for half its former value" (*Wars* 6:6:1).

Great Tribulation

Matthew 24:21–22 says, "For then there will be a Great Tribulation, such as has not occurred since the beginning of the world until now, nor ever shall. And unless those days had been cut short, no life would have been saved; but for the sake of the elect those days shall be cut short." We now come to the text giving rise to our book's title and which seems to preclude a Great Tribulation in A.D. 70. How may we claim that the A.D. 70 holocaust is the greatest catastrophe in world history? Surely here the preterist ship runs aground! But once again a careful analysis of the text *in the light of biblical and cultural information available from the first century* reinforces preterism in a remarkable way.

Here again we must remember Jesus' time delimiter just twelve verses after His reference to the "Great Tribulation." Christ dogmatically asserts that "all these things" will happen to "this generation" (v. 34). Christ utters this in a context dealing with the destruction of the same temple then standing (23:36–24:3). We know as a matter of indisputable historical record that Titus destroys the temple in August/September, A.D. 70.[40] This evidence alone, I believe, is sufficient to demand a first-century occurrence.

Yet the troubling question remains: Is the destruction of first-century Jerusalem a disaster "such as has not occurred since the beginning of the world until now, nor ever shall"? Surely World Wars I and II far outstrip the Jewish War in terms of international dimensions, cultural upheaval, social chaos, and loss of lives! Hitler cruelly destroys far more Jews in World War II than the Romans in the Jewish War.

To answer such a surprised query, we must transport ourselves back into the first-century Jewish context—and think in terms of biblical categories, as would the original hearers of Christ. The Jewish War with Rome from A.D. 67–70 results in the deaths of tens of thousands of the Jews in Judea and enslaves untold thousands more (*Wars* 6:9:2). Josephus, an eyewitness to the Jewish War, reports that 1,100,000 Jews perished in the siege of Jerusalem (*Wars* 6:9:3). Not only do an enormous number perish, but we witness the absolute destruction of the temple and the permanent cessation of the sacrificial system, a matter of immense spiritual, religious, and cultural significance to the Jews. Since that time the Jewish people have never been able to worship God, as prescribed in their own Scriptures, at a temple in Jerusalem.

Interestingly, Josephus mourns the devastation of Jerusalem in several places by employing words virtually identical to that of our Lord: "Whereas the war which the Jews made with the Romans hath been the greatest of all those, not only that have been in our times, but, in a manner, of those that ever were heard of" (*Wars,* Preface, 1). "The misfortunes of all men, from the beginning of the world, if they be compared to these of the Jews, are not considerable as they were" (*Wars,* Preface, 4). "Neither did any other city ever suffer such miseries . . . from the beginning of the world" (*Wars* 5:10:5).

Furthermore, we must properly interpret the apocalyptic language of Christ. According to biblical scholars, "it is characteristic for oracles of judgment to be couched in language that is universal and radical."[41] Such judgment is often framed in terms of prophetic hyperbole, a common apocalyptic device used by the writers of Scripture. For instance, concerning the tenth plague upon Egypt, we read: "Then there shall be a great cry throughout all the land of Egypt, *such as was not like it before, nor shall be like it again*" (Exod. 11:6, emphasis mine). Who would dare say that *literally* there was not as great a lamentation during World War II as there was during this one plague upon this one ancient nation? In addition, this verse states that Egypt will *never again* experience such a terrible event, which occurs hundreds of years before Christ. Yet the future Great Tribulation is supposed to be the worst ever for everyone—including Egyptians.

In a prophecy regarding the Babylonian captivity and the destruction of Jerusalem, God employs language reminiscent of Christ's: "And I will do among you what *I have never done, and the like of which I will never do again*, because of all your abominations" (Ezek. 5:9, emphasis mine). Even dispensationalists such as Walvoord, Pentecost, and Dyer admit this prophecy concerns the Babylonian captivity of the distant past.[42] And yet, though this is specifically about Old Testament Jerusalem, Jesus warns about *another* such judgment on Jerusalem in the Matthew 24 passage. Ezekiel 7:5–6 even speaks about the Old Testament catastrophe as a "unique disaster" that is "an end" of Jerusalem: "An end is coming; the end has come! It has awakened against you; behold, it has come!" If "the end" of Jerusalem "has come," why then does Jerusalem continue even into Christ's time? This is prophetic hyperbole.

Daniel speaks about the Babylonian captivity in similar language: "And He has confirmed His words, which He spoke against us and against our judges who judged us, by bringing upon us a great disaster; for *under the whole heaven such never has been done as what has been done to Jerusalem*" (Dan. 9:12, emphasis mine). Clearly, the unique-event language is common parlance in prophetic literature. We must not interpret it in a woodenly literal manner.

Furthermore, just a few verses after His "Great Tribulation" statement, the Lord mentions Noah's Flood (Matt. 24:38–39). The Genesis record clearly teaches that the Flood covered "all the high mountains" (Gen. 7:19–20; 8:4) and remained at that depth for a period of one hundred and fifty days (7:24; 8:3). God sent the Flood to "destroy all air breathing animal life" (6:13, 17), and especially the entire human race, except for Noah and his family (Gen. 6:13; 7:21; Heb. 11:7; 1 Peter 3:20; 2 Peter 2:5). Thus, the Noahic Flood destroyed the *entire* world except one family (2 Peter 2:5). Not even Dr. Ice's future Great Tribulation continues until only one family remains.

Obviously, we should not interpret Christ's language literally after all. It is dramatic hyperbole, well justified by the gravity of the situation. Not every Jew dies in the Jewish War, but the devastation is such that only an act of God in behalf of His "elect" prevents the destruction of *all* of Israel (compare Matt. 24:22).[43] The Lord is not referring to His Second Advent, or else we should wonder why His disciples should pray about fleeing from Judea (v. 16): what good would running to the hills be at the return of Christ? And why should "winter" be a concern at that time (v. 20)?

Due to space constraints and to avoid repetition, I will not discuss Matthew 24:23–26, for the warning is similar to verses 4 and 5. The Lord's repetition of His warning about false Messiahs is not wasteful redundancy, though. His earlier reference is in the section on slightly distant predecessory signs; this one is in the same context of the horrible Great Tribulation itself. This warning bears repeating due to the extreme conditions that might lead some early Christians to follow a false Messiah.

Coming as Lightning

Matthew 24:27 says, "For just as the lightning comes from the east, and flashes even to the west, so shall the coming of the Son of Man be." Jesus warns His followers that He will *not* appear bodily in the first-century judgment (vv. 23, 25–26). Nevertheless, He will "come" in judgment like a destructive lightning bolt against Jerusalem (v. 27). This coming, however, is a providential *judgment coming,* a Christ-directed judgment, rather than a miraculous, visible, bodily coming.

Oftentimes in Scripture the Lord (whether the Father or the Son) "comes" in judgment against evildoers. I will deal with this prophetic phenomenon in a little more detail at Matthew 24:30. For the moment, however, we should observe what Christ says to the high priest at His trial: "The high priest answered and said to Him, 'I adjure You by the living God that You tell us if You are the Christ, the Son of God.' Jesus said *to him,* 'It is as *you* said. Nevertheless, I say *to you,* hereafter *you will see* the Son of Man sitting at the right hand of the Power, and *coming* on the clouds of heaven'" (26:63–64, emphasis mine). Here the Lord informs the high priest and the other members of the Jewish Sanhedrin that *they* will "see" His coming. Obviously, they are not still alive today! Jesus must be referring to an event in their first-century life spans.

The *coming* the Sanhedrin will witness is like that Isaiah attributes to Yahweh against Egypt: "The burden against Egypt. Behold, the Lord rides on a swift cloud, and will *come* into Egypt" (Isa. 19:1, emphasis mine). The Lord did not physically and visibly ride down into Egypt on a cloud. In fact, according to Dallas Theological Seminary's *The Bible Knowledge Commentary,* this coming on a swift cloud to Egypt is an apocalyptic picture of Egypt's conquering by the Assyrian king Esaharddon in 671 B.C.[44]

Nor is the coming as lightning in Matthew 24:27 a publicly visible, physical coming. Rather, it is a judgment coming against those who call down Jesus' blood upon them and their children (v. 25). The Lord here speaks about His judgment coming against Jerusalem (see 23:37–24:2) as analogous to "the lightning [that] comes from the east, and flashes even to the west." As I begin to interpret the passage, remember that the local context demands this coming occur in "this generation" (24:34), having reference to the destruction of the temple (v. 2).

First, notice the fuller statement of Christ with its specific contextual addendum: lightning "comes from the east and flashes even to the west." Elsewhere when Christ says that Satan falls from heaven "like lightning" (Luke 10:18), the *direction* is clearly in view (given the spatial imagery of Scripture, with heaven being up and hell being down). Satan's fall from heaven is neither rapid nor visible to the physical eye, being similar to a flash of lightning. The direction of this judgment coming of Christ in Matthew 24:27 apparently reflects the Roman armies marching toward Jerusalem from an easterly direction. Josephus's record of the march of the Roman armies through Israel shows they wreak havoc on Jerusalem by approaching it from the east.[45]

Second, in the wider biblical context, lightning is that which terrifies (Ezek. 19:16; 20:18), for it is so violently destructive (Ps. 78:48–49). Scripture records numerous examples of such lightning imagery;[46] lightning is a nerve-shattering feature of a violent storm. Frequently the Scripture speaks about catastrophic wars as storms (for example, Isa. 28:2; 29:6; Ezek. 38:9).

Matthew 24 surely involves the idea of terrifying desolation, in that the Lord warns of destruction (v. 2), war (vv. 6–7), sorrow (v. 8), desolation (v. 15), flight from danger (vv. 16–20), Great Tribulation (v. 21), and death (v. 28). Obviously, the calamitous storm that befalls Israel during the Jewish War and under Christ's prophetic governance is historical and visible. Yet it is not *Christ Himself* who is *corporally present.* Rather, He directs the Roman armies by His providence, just as God directs Cyrus as a bird of prey under His sovereign providence (Isa. 46:10–11)—or any other army (Deut. 28:49–50; Isa. 5:26–30; 7:18–20; 45:7; Dan. 4:35; Amos 3:6). Jesus provides a parabolic description of the destruction of Jerusalem in Matthew 22:2–15, where "the king" represents God the Father: "But when the king heard about it, he was furious. And he sent out *his* armies, destroyed those murderers, and burned up their city" (v. 7, emphasis mine). The Roman armies during the Jewish War are the Lord's armies—"his armies"—to do His will (compare Dan. 2:21; 4:35), just as were the armies of Assyria against Israel of old (Isa. 10:5–6).

Cosmic Disturbances

Matthew 24:29 says, "But immediately after the tribulation of those days 'the sun will be darkened, and the moon will not give its light, and the stars will fall' from the sky, and the powers of the heavens will be shaken." Here we encounter remarkable cosmic disturbances that seem too catastrophic for applying to A.D. 70. But as with the previous apocalyptic verses, so here this portrays historical divine judgment under the dramatic imagery of a universal catastrophe. Remember that just five verses after this statement Jesus says: "Truly I say to you, this generation will not pass away until all these things take place" (v. 34). What then does verse 29 mean? To understand it properly, we must interpret it *covenantally,* which is to say *biblically,* rather than according to a presupposed simple literalism. Allow me to explain.

Apocalyptic language is a dramatic way of expressing national calamity or victory in battle. The sun, moon, and stars appear to be unmovable—"not one of them fails" (Isa. 40:26; compare Job 9:7–8; Isa. 48:13; Jer. 31:35). So when Deborah defeats Jabin, king of Canaan (Judg. 4), she celebrates her military victory in battle by means of poetic song (5:1): "LORD, when Thou didst go out from Seir, when Thou didst march from the field of Edom, the earth quaked, the heavens also dripped, even the clouds dripped water. The mountains quaked at the presence of the LORD, this Sinai, at the presence of the LORD, the God of Israel" (vv. 4–5). Today when faced with a catastrophe, we might cry out: "My world is coming apart!" or "My whole world is crashing down upon me!"

In Scripture, prophets often express *national catastrophes* in terms of *cosmic destruction.* The famed twelfth-century Jewish theologian Maimonides notes that such language "is a proverbial expression, importing the destruction and utter ruin of a nation" (*More Nev.* 2). For instance, Isaiah prophesies Babylon's Old Testament era judgment using language similar to Christ's: "For the stars of heaven and their constellations will not give their light; the sun will be darkened in its going forth, and the moon will not cause its light to shine. . . . Therefore I will shake the heavens, and the earth will move out of her place" (Isa. 13:10, 13). Nevertheless, Isaiah clearly has the fall of Babylon in view, for he introduces this prophecy with these words: "The burden *against Babylon* which Isaiah the son of Amoz saw" (v. 1, emphasis mine); "Behold, I will stir up *the Medes* against them. . . . And Babylon, the glory of kingdoms, the beauty of the Chaldeans' pride, will be as when God overthrew Sodom and Gomorrah" (vv. 17, 19, emphasis mine). Yet Isaiah describes Babylon's fall *as cosmic destruction.* And in a figurative sense it is, for Babylon's world is coming apart.

Later, Isaiah similarly pictures Edom's fall: "Their slain shall be thrown out; their stench shall rise from their corpses, and the mountains shall be melted with their blood. All the host of heaven shall be dissolved, and the heavens shall be rolled up like a scroll; all their host shall fall down as the leaf falls from the vine. . . . For My sword shall be bathed in heaven; indeed it shall come down on Edom" (vv. 3–5). Mark's rendering of Christ's prophecy shows that the Savior draws from this passage in Isaiah: "But in those days, after that tribulation, 'the sun will be darkened, and the moon will not give its light, and the stars will be falling from heaven,' and the powers that are in the heavens will be shaken" (Mark 13:24–25).

Elsewhere Ezekiel describes the fall of Egypt in the Old Testament: "'Son of man, take up a lamentation for Pharaoh king of Egypt, and say to him. . . . When I put out your light, I will cover the heavens, and make its stars dark; I will cover the sun with a cloud, and the moon shall not give her light. All the bright lights of the heavens I will make dark over you'" (Ezek. 32:2, 7–8).

Such imagery, then, indicates that the God of the heavens (the Creator of the sun, moon, and stars) is moving in judgment against a nation (blotting out their light). According to Dallas Seminary's Charles H. Dyer (a collaborator with Dr. Ice), when a national government collapses in war and upheaval, the Bible often portrays it poetically "as a cosmic catastrophe—an undoing of Creation."[47]

In fact, Jeremiah portrays the destruction of Jerusalem by the Babylonians in similar terms: "At that time it will be said to this people and to Jerusalem, 'A dry wind of the desolate heights blows in the wilderness toward the daughter of My people. . . . I beheld the earth, and indeed it was without form, and void; and the heavens, they had no light. I beheld the mountains, and indeed they trembled, and all the hills moved back and forth. . . . For this shall the earth mourn, and the heavens above be black, because I have spoken" (Jer. 4:11, 23–24, 29). Similarly the prophet Joel threatens Israel's Old Testament judgment: "Blow the trumpet in Zion, and sound an alarm in My holy mountain. . . . The earth quakes before them, the heavens tremble; the sun and moon grow dark, and the stars diminish their brightness" (Joel 2:1, 10).

Consequently, we may legitimately apply Matthew 24:29 to the destruction of Jerusalem in A.D. 70. Christ draws upon the imagery from Old Testament judgment passages that sound as if they are world-ending events. And in a sense it is "the end of the world" for those nations God judges. So is it with Israel in A.D. 70: her time of God's favor ends, and her temple system vanishes from history (Heb. 8:5, 13–9:25). The Jewish Mishnah bemoans A.D. 70: "Since the day that the temple was destroyed there has been no day without its curse; and the dew has not fallen in blessing and the fruits have lost their savor" (*Sotah* 9:12). After spending his whole epistle showing the superiority of Christ over all elements of old covenant persons, rituals, and experiences, in catastrophic terms, the writer of Hebrews explains the demise of the tabernacle-temple system with all its implements "made with hands" (Heb. 9:11, 24; compare Mark 14:58; 2 Cor. 5:1):

> And his voice shook the earth then, but now He has promised, saying, "yet once more I will shake not only the earth, but also the heaven." And this expression, "Yet once more," denotes the removing of those things which can be shaken, as of created things, in order that those things which cannot be shaken may remain. Therefore, since we receive a kingdom which cannot be shaken, let us show gratitude, by which we may offer to God an acceptable service with reverence and awe" (Heb. 12:26–28).

The Sign of the Son of Man

Matthew 24:30 says, "And then the sign of the Son of Man will appear in the sky, and then all the tribes of the earth will mourn, and they will see the 'Son of Man coming on the clouds of the sky' with power and great glory." As I have been showing, "coming with the clouds" language is common prophetic parlance for historical divine judgments upon nations. Again, recall Isaiah 19:1, where God's coming judgment against Egypt appears in similar terms: "See, the Lord rides on a swift cloud and is coming to Egypt. The idols of Egypt tremble before him, and the hearts of the Egyptians melt within them" (Isa. 19:1). God "comes" upon Israel's enemies in general (Pss. 18:7–15; 68:4; 104:3; Nah. 1:1–3), upon Babylon (Isa. 13:1, 9–13), upon disobedient Israel in the Old Testament (Joel 2:1–2), upon Samaria and Jerusalem (Mic. 1:1–4), and so forth. This type of statement is called "apocalyptic metaphor," according to hermeneutics scholar Milton Terry.[48] Even Dallas Theological Seminary's *The Bible Knowledge Commentary* recognizes this phenomenon in some of these Old Testament texts.[49]

As I begin to explain this text, I must depart from the New American Standard Bible due to its inaccurate, interpretive translation. I prefer the Authorized Version (KJV), for it follows the Greek word order more closely and translates the passage more accurately. I will cite several more acceptable translations of Matthew 24:30 as I begin:

- "Then shall appear the sign of the Son of Man in heaven" (King James Version).
- "And then shall appear the sign of the Son of man in heaven" (American Standard Version).
- "Then will appear the sign of the Son of man in heaven" (Revised Standard Version).
- "And then shall appear the sign of the Son of Man in the heaven" (Young's *Literal Translation*).
- "And then will appear the sign of the Son of man in heaven" (Marshall's *Interlinear Greek-English New Testament*).
- "The sign of the Son of Man in heaven" (Robertson, *Word Pictures in the New Testament.* vol. 1)

Lexically we may translate the Greek word *ouranos* to mean either "sky" or "heaven." Yet it is quite misleading here to translate the phrase in question as "then shall appear the Son of Man in the *sky*." This requires a restructuring of the text (as I will show), is patently anticontextual (as I am showing), and totally destroys Jesus' citation of Daniel 7:13–14 (where God's heavenly throne room is clearly intended). Matthew frequently uses *ouranos* to refer to God's heavenly abode (Matt. 5:34; 6:10, 20; 11:25; 14:19; 16:1; 18:18; 21:25; 22:30; 23:22; 28:2). Significantly, the "sign" is what "shall appear": "then will appear[50] *the sign*." The Son of Man does not appear; rather, the *sign* appears. Then Christ defines what the sign signifies: it is the sign "of the Son of Man in heaven."

Christ's teaching here is extremely important to redemptive history. He is responding to the question of His disciples regarding *when* the end of the "age" (Gk., *aiōn*) will occur (24:3). In essence, His full answer is: when the Romans lay waste the temple (vv. 6 and 15 anticipate this) and pick apart Jerusalem (v. 28). That is, when the government of Israel utterly collapses (v. 29), then it will be evident that the one who prophesies her destruction is "in heaven." The "sign" is not a visible token in the sky. Rather, the sign is that the "Son of Man" rejected by the first-century Jews is *in heaven*.[51] The destruction of Israel vindicates Christ.

But what is "the sign"? The temple's final destruction (which is the main point of the discourse; 23:38–24:3) serves as *the* sign that the Son of Man is in heaven. His curse upon "these things" (24:2) insures this woe; His wrath as the Son of Man in heaven effects the judgment: "Daughters of Jerusalem, do not weep for Me, but weep for yourselves and for your children. For indeed the days are coming in which they will say, 'Blessed are the barren, the wombs that never bore, and the breasts which never nursed!' Then they will begin to say to the mountains, 'Fall on us!' and to the hills, 'Cover us!' For if they do these things in the green wood, what will be done in the dry?" (Luke 23:28–31). Jesus prophesies it; the first-century Jews experience it.

The idea of Matthew 24:30 parallels in sentiment Acts 2:19: "I will show wonders in heaven above and signs in the earth beneath: blood and fire and vapor of smoke." Blood, fire, and smoke mark the total collapse of Jerusalem and Israel, serving as the sign the Son of Man is at God's right hand—the same one whom Israel crucifies (Acts 2:23). He is in God's heaven above, despite Israel's rejecting Him (Matt. 27:22–24), calling down His blood upon them (27:25), and condemning Him for declaring the truth that He is the Son of Man (26:64–67).

The era of racial focus (Jewish race), geographical delimitation (the promised land), and typological ministry (the temple and its services) is fading away (John 4:21–23; Eph. 2:11–21; Heb. 8:13; 12:27–28). The destruction of the temple is the final, conclusive sign: the Son of Man is in heaven so that He might be Lord of all nations (Matt. 28:19–20; Acts 2:21; Eph. 1:19–22; Rev. 1:5).

The Mourning of the Tribes

Matthew 24:30 says, "then all the tribes of the earth will mourn." Here again we come upon a word with two possible meanings. The Greek noun *ge* ("earth") may have either a general referent: *the tangible ground, the earth.* Or it may have a specific referent: *a particular land area, a nation.* But which will we choose?

The context of Matthew 24—involving the scribes and the Pharisees (23:1ff.), the temple (24:2), Judea (24:16), and "this generation" (24:34)—strongly suggests the proper translation of verse 30 is "the tribes of *the land*," in other words, the land of Israel. In fact, the New Testament commonly uses this term of Palestine (Matt. 2:6, 20; 27:45; Mark 15:33; Luke 4:25; Luke 21:23; John 3:22; Acts 7:3). So does the history of the era: the rabbis are particularly careful in their description of "the land" *(hē gē)*. Edersheim notes that "Palestine was to the Rabbis simply 'the land,' all other countries being summed up under the designation of 'outside the land.'"[52] Elsewhere he comments:

> The pilgrim who, leaving other countries, entered Palestine, must have felt as if he had crossed the threshold to another world. Manners, customs, institutions, law, life, nay, the very intercourse between man and man, were quite different. All was dominated by the one all-absorbing idea of religion. It penetrated every relation of life. Moreover, it was inseparably connected with the soil, as well as the people of Palestine, at least so long as the temple stood. Nowhere else could the

Shekinah . . . dwell or manifest itself; nor could, unless under
exceptional circumstances, and for 'the merit of the fathers,'
the spirit of prophecy be granted outside its bounds. To the
orthodox Jew the mental and spiritual horizon was bounded
by Palestine. It was 'the land'; all the rest of the world, except
Babylonia, was 'outside the land.' No need to designate it especially as 'holy'; for all here bore the impress of sanctity, as
he understood it.[53]

The reference to "the tribes" (Gk., *phulē*) reinforces this view, in
that it commonly designates the twelve tribes of Israel.[54] The Septuagint "with few exceptions . . . has *phulē* [tribe], so that this becomes
a fixed term for the tribal system of Israel."[55] Indeed, the Old Testament text from which Christ draws this wording shows that the tribes
of Israel are in view (see Zech. 12:10–14).

So then, the mourning will befall the first-century Jewish tribes in
Israel; they will endure the brunt of God's wrath and judgment for rejecting Christ. They must flee the area, if they are to preserve their lives
(Matt. 24:16). After this fearful flight, they will mourn the loss of their
beloved land, government, homes, friends, and temple.

Coming on the Clouds

Matthew 24:30 (KJV) says, "They will see the Son of Man coming
on the clouds of heaven with power and great glory." We must again
recall Christ's interchange with the Sanhedrin at His ecclesiastical trial
before His crucifixion: "The high priest said to Him, 'I adjure You by
the living God, that You tell us whether You are the Christ, the Son of
God.' Jesus said to him, 'You have said it yourself; nevertheless I tell
you, hereafter you shall see the son of man sitting at the right hand of
power, and coming on the clouds of heaven'" (26:63–64).

Here Christ informs the Sanhedrin that *they* will see His coming.
As I argue above, this is not a physical, visible coming, but a judgment-
coming upon Jerusalem. They "see" it in the sense that we "see" how
a math problem works: with the "eye of understanding" rather than
the organ of vision. Robert Thomas, dispensationalist commentator and
friend of Dr. Ice, notes concerning John's own "beholding" in
Revelation 4:1: "This action should not be equated with the physical
eye. Rather, it is sight with the eye of ecstatic vision as throughout the
Apocalypse."[56] Yet both of these are types of "seeing." Thus, those who
actually condemn Jesus will "see" (perceive) His judgment wrath
against the land.

In fact, Scripture often mentions "seeing" in a nonliteral sense. To
have "unseeing eyes" is to be spiritually dull or morally insensitive—

not physically handicapped (Jer. 5:21; Ezek. 12:2; Matt. 13:15–16; Mark 8:18; Luke 6:42; John 12:40; Acts 28:27; Rom. 11:8, 10). Paul teaches that "since the creation of the world His *invisible attributes, His eternal power and divine nature, have been clearly seen*, being understood through what has been made, so that they are without excuse" (Rom. 1:20, emphasis mine). The writer of Hebrews says that "by faith" Moses was "seeing Him who is unseen" (Heb. 11:27).

The Old Testament background to Jesus' statement here is Daniel 7:13–14 (emphasis mine): "Behold, with the clouds of heaven one like the Son of Man was coming, and He came *up to* the Ancient of Days and was presented before Him. And to Him was given dominion, glory and a kingdom." This actually refers to Jesus' ascension. In the destruction of the temple, the rejected Christ is vindicated as the ascended Lord and shown to possess great power and glory.

The Great Jubilee

Matthew 24:31 says, "And He will send forth His angels with a great trumpet and they will gather together His elect from the four winds, from one end of the sky to the other." This verse continues the poetic imagery: the destruction of the temple trumpets in the *ultimate* Jubilee Year. As I will show, this interpretation is both covenantally reasonable and contextually justified. The demise of the temple and the Jewish-focused, land-confined, typologically based blessings of God open to the world the time of the forgiveness of man's ultimate debt before God. The new era of Christianity in "the fulness of times" (Gal. 4:4) brings in the "day of salvation" (2 Cor. 6:2), which fulfills the Old Testament redemptive hope. By employing imagery drawn from the typological Year of Jubilee in Leviticus 25, the Lord here speaks about the final stage of redemption, which is finally secured as the temple vanishes from history. Let us refresh our understanding of this Old Testament ceremonial law and then apply this information to the situation at hand.

Under the Old Testament ceremonial system, the "Sabbath year" serves as a God-ordained year of rest for the Lord's Old Testament people, and is held every seventh year. According to God's law in Deuteronomy 15:1–2: "At the end of every seven years you shall grant a remission of debts. And this is the manner of remission: every creditor shall release what he has loaned to his neighbor; he shall not exact it of his neighbor and his brother, because the LORD's remission has been proclaimed."

After seven consecutive Sabbath-year cycles comes the Year of Jubilee. The Jubilee every fifty years culminates all of the sabbatical tokens of rest (seven times seven years being completed).[57] In the Year of Jubilee Israel experiences release from bondage and debt:

And you shall consecrate the fiftieth year, and proclaim liberty
throughout all the land to all its inhabitants. It shall be a Jubi-
lee for you; and each of you shall return to his possession, and
each of you shall return to his family. That fiftieth year shall be
a Jubilee to you; in it you shall neither sow nor reap what grows
of its own accord, nor gather the grapes of your untended vine.
For it is the Jubilee; it shall be holy to you; you shall eat its
produce from the field. In this Year of Jubilee, each of you shall
return to his possession. And if you sell anything to your neigh-
bor or buy from your neighbor's hand, you shall not oppress
one another (Leviticus 25:10–14 NKJV).

This Jubilee legislation beautifully typifies God's gracious, full redemption. Isaiah employs Jubilee imagery to prophesy the coming
ultimate, final Jubilee in Christ: "The Spirit of the Lord GOD is upon
Me, because the LORD has anointed Me to preach good tidings to the
poor; He has sent Me to heal the brokenhearted, to proclaim liberty to
the captives, and the opening of the prison to those who are bound; to
proclaim the acceptable year of the LORD, and the day of vengeance of
our God" (Isa. 61:1–2). Evangelical Christians recognize this prophecy refers to Christ.

The Lord Jesus Himself introduces the fulfillment of the Jubilee law
in His ministry, when He preaches from Isaiah 61 at the temple:

And He was handed the book of the prophet Isaiah. And when
He had opened the book, He found the place where it was
written: "The Spirit of the LORD is upon Me, because He has
anointed Me to preach the gospel to the poor. He has sent Me
to heal the brokenhearted, to preach deliverance to the cap-
tives and recovery of sight to the blind, to set at liberty those
who are oppressed, to preach the acceptable year of the LORD."
Then He closed the book, and gave it back to the attendant
and sat down. And the eyes of all who were in the synagogue
were fixed on Him. And He began to say to them, "Today this
Scripture is fulfilled in your hearing" (Luke 4:17–21 NKJV).

Thus, Christ's ministry introduces God's day of "visitation" (Luke
1:68), "the acceptable year of the Lord" (4:19), "the day of salvation"
(2 Cor. 6:6), "the fulness of times" (Gal. 4:4), which the Old Testament saints longed to see (Matt. 13:17; John 8:56; Heb. 11:13; 1 Peter
1:10–12). The Old Testament economy provides ceremonial instruction regarding coming future redemption (Gal. 3:23–4:4; Heb. 9:8–10,
23–24). And that redemption involves all nations (Matt. 28:19; Acts

1:8; 13:46–47; 15:14–17; compare Pss. 2:1–12; 22:27–31; Isa. 2:2–4; 25:6–10; 56:6–8; Mic. 4:1–4; Zech. 8:20–23).

This redemptive culmination begins in Jesus' earthly ministry, as we may surmise from such passages as Mark 1:15: "The time is fulfilled, and the kingdom of God is at hand. Repent, and believe in the gospel." And Matthew 11:13–15: "For all the prophets and the law prophesied until John. And if you are willing to receive it, he is Elijah who is to come. He who has ears to hear, let him hear!"

The change of the age is finalized and sealed at the destruction of Jerusalem; allusions to the A.D. 70 transition abound: "Assuredly, I say to you that there are some standing here who will not taste death till they see the kingdom of God present with power" (Mark 9:1).[58] "Jesus said to her, 'Woman, believe Me, the hour is coming when you will neither on this mountain, nor in Jerusalem, worship the Father'" (John 4:21). Because "the present Jerusalem . . . is in slavery" and the "Jerusalem above" is free, historical Jerusalem will be "cast out" (Gal. 4:25–31). God will soon shake the old covenant system to establish the new covenant order (Heb. 12:18–29).[59] The levitical Jubilee law symbolizes the coming of full forgiveness in the Messiah and the incorporation of the nations into the one people of God (see Matt. 8:11–12; Luke 24:47; John 10:16; Acts 15:14–19; Rom. 11:11–25; 16:25–26; Eph. 2:12–3:5).

This is why the Lord mentions the sounding of the "trumpet" in Matthew 24: such is the means for announcing the Jubilee. The background of Jesus' imagery is Leviticus 25:9: "Then you shall cause the trumpet of the Jubilee to sound on the tenth day of the seventh month; on the Day of Atonement you shall make the trumpet to sound throughout all your land."[60] According to Matthew 24:31, when the temple order collapses, Christ's "angels" will go forth to all nations joyfully trumpeting the gospel of salvific liberation: "And He will send his angels with a great sound of a trumpet, and they will gather together his elect from the four winds, from one end of heaven to the other."

The word "angels" here is *angeloi* in Greek. We can translate it "messengers," signifying *human* messengers, as in several places in Scripture (Matt. 11:10; Mark 1:2; Luke 7:24, 27; 9:52; James 2:25).[61] The term does not seem to refer to the supernatural heavenly beings here, but to those who now proclaim the message of full salvation, the removal of humanity's sin debt to God. Even if we apply this to angels, however, it would then refer "to the supernatural power which lies behind such preaching."[62] Then it would teach that the angels of God attend our faithful proclamation of God's Word. The Olivet discourse, then, has as a major point the breaking of the centripetal dynamic within Israel (a self-focus tied to the temple) by the centrifugal force of world missions.

The fall of Jerusalem dramatically frees the church from its bond-age to Judaism. This occurs so that she might become a truly *universal* church, rather than a racially focused, geographically confined people. A major problem plaguing the pre-A.D. 70 church is Zionism: the early Jewish Christians tend to avoid the Gentiles (Acts 11:1–3; Gal. 2:11–16), require circumcision for salvation (Acts 15:1–2; Gal. 5:1–2), observe Jewish ceremonial law (Gal. 3:1–3; 4:9–10; Rom. 14:1–5), gravitate to Jerusalem (Acts 8:1), and apostatize back into Judaism (Heb. 2:1–4; 6:1–6).[63] This represents a serious threat to the integrity, universality, and advance of the Christian message.

Through Christ-commissioned gospel preaching by faithful messengers, God gathers the elect into His kingdom from the four corners of the world (Matt. 28:19; Luke 24:47; Acts 1:8; 13:47; 17:30). The phrase "from one end of the sky to the other" does not indicate that the place of the action is in the sky (or heaven) above. The phraseology often signifies nothing more than "horizon to horizon" (Deut. 30:4; Neh. 1:9; compare Matt. 8:11; Luke 13:28–29). Thus, it speaks about evangelistic activity spreading throughout the earth. In fact, it parallels "from the four winds," that is, the four points of the compass. This, of course, Jesus promises in His ministry, despite the failure of His own people: "And I say to you that many will come from east and west, and sit down with Abraham, Isaac, and Jacob in the kingdom of heaven. But the sons of the kingdom will be cast out into outer darkness" (Matt. 8:11–12; Luke 13:29 speaks about all four points of the compass).

The "gathering together" (Gk., *episunaxousin*) of the elect involves both the gathering of the saints into local assemblies or churches (Heb. 10:25; James 2:2) and the universal assembling of the saints into the body of Christ, the church universal (compare Matt. 22:7–13).[64] The proclamation of the gospel will be worldwide, as confidently expected in the Old Testament (Ps. 22:27; Isa. 2:2–3; 45:22; Mic. 5:4) and the New Testament (Matt. 28:19–20; Luke 13:29; Acts 13:39).

This view seems much more reasonable to me than that of Dr. Ice. He holds that Matthew 24:31 speaks about thousands of angels coming down from heaven and bodily lifting up thousands of individual Jews and taking them to Israel during the future tribulation period. One of Dr. Ice's seminary professors, J. Dwight Pentecost, comments: "During the Tribulation, Israel will be scattered out of the land by military invasions (Rev. 12:14–16), and the Israelites will flee and find refuge among the Gentile nations. Supernaturally God will bring the people back to the land through the instrumentality of angels."[65]

The significance of the collapse of Jerusalem and the destruction of the temple in A.D. 70 is little appreciated by modern Christians. But A.D. 70 effectively closes out the old, typological era and removes a major hindrance to the spread of the Christian faith. We see this particularly in two respects: (1) The Jewish ceremonial laws confuse many early Christians. Circumcision is genuinely troublesome, in that some require it for salvation (Acts 15; Gal. 5:1–6; Phil. 3:1–3). The growing danger exists that Christianity will be a mere sect of Judaism, as the Romans originally assume. With the temple's destruction, this tendency will subside. (2) The first persecutors of the faith are the Jews (Acts 8:1ff.; 1 Thess. 2:14–16). With the A.D. 70 demise of the Jews' strength and the dissipation of their energy, Christianity receives much less resistance from them. Jewish persecution of Christians does not cease entirely, but it does decline significantly.

Conclusion: The Key Text Revisited

In this conclusion to the exposition of Matthew 24, I remind the reader about the verse I deal with in my introduction. Matthew 24:32–36 includes the all-important *key* text for the understanding of this section of the Olivet discourse:

> *And He will send his angels with a great sound of a trumpet, and they will gather together his elect from the four winds, from one end of heaven to the other. Now learn this parable from the fig tree: When its branch has already become tender and puts forth leaves, you know that summer is near. So you also, when you see all these things, know that it is near, at the very doors.* Assuredly, I say to you, this generation will by no means pass away till all these things are fulfilled. *Heaven and earth will pass away, but My words will by no means pass away. But of that day and hour no one knows, no, not even the angels of heaven, but My Father only.*

A simple reading of Matthew 24:34 lucidly reveals that *all* of the things Christ the Great Prophet mentions up to this point—that is, everything in verses 4 through 34—will occur *in the same generation of the original disciples:* "Assuredly, I say to you, *this* generation will by no means pass away till *all* these things are fulfilled." Here "this generation" is identical to "this generation" of Matthew 23:36. In chapter 23, the Lord rebukes the scribes and Pharisees of His own day (vv. 13–16, 23, 25, 27, 29), then assures them: "I say to you, all these things will come upon *this generation*" (v. 36). These woes upon the scribes and Pharisees may not be catapulted two thousand years (or more!) into the future without violence to the text.

Neither may we project the events of 24:4–34 into the distant future. In fact, as I show above the whole impetus to this discourse is

Christ's reference to the destruction of the historical temple to which the disciples point (23:38–24:1–3). Here we must remind ourselves that a series of divinely ordained signs will precede the approaching destruction of the temple (24:4ff.). The first few signs are general indicators of the final judgment on the temple: "All these are the beginning of sorrows" (24:8). All of these signs do, in fact, come to pass in the era before A.D. 70. Just as surely as fig leaves indicate approaching summer (v. 32), so the events of verses 4–32 signify the looming destruction of the temple. Thus, the Great Tribulation and all of its attendant signs belong to the first century—to the generation that cries out, "Crucify him! Crucify him!" (John 19:6) and "We have no king but Caesar!" (v. 15). This is the same generation that tragically demands: "His blood be on us and on our children!" (Matt. 27:25).

THE GREAT TRIBULATION IS FUTURE

3

THE GREAT TRIBULATION IS FUTURE:

THE OLD TESTAMENT

Thomas Ice

I believe it is important for any Christian to know whether the Tribulation is past or future. This issue is not just an academic exercise, for if the Tribulation is past, then there are many implications that should practically follow. If the Tribulation is a past event, then the rapture of the church is impossible, premillennialism cannot be true, Israel does not have a future national blessing, the current nation of Israel is not prophetically significant, and our current state of existence would have to be the millennial kingdom or new heaven and new earth. There would be no future Antichrist and false prophet, and there would be none of the Tribulation events (such as the two witnesses). In short, the present perspective of Christianity for millions of believers would be quite different than now perceived, for our view of the future would be significantly changed.

However, I do not believe the Bible teaches that the Tribulation is in any way *past*. Instead, Scripture tells us that it is a *future* event that could commence very soon. I believe the correct teaching of Scripture includes a future time period of seven years in length that will commence with the signing of a covenant between the nation Israel and the European Antichrist, who will have reconstituted his version of a revived Roman empire. At the midpoint of the seven years, the Antichrist (also known as the Beast) will defile a rebuilt Jewish temple in Jerusalem and set himself up as god, demanding that all the world show allegiance to him by receiving his mark (666) on their right hand or forehead. At this point, the Antichrist will turn against the Jews. Those in Jerusalem will flee to the wilderness, where they will experience divine protection for the second three-and-a-half years. Toward

69

the end of the Tribulation the Antichrist will gather the armies of the world to surround Jerusalem in an effort to destroy the Jews. This will lead to the conversion of all Israel to Jesus as its Messiah. Now converted, the Jews will plead for their Savior to rescue them from sure destruction by the surrounding armies. Jesus will hear their plea and return from heaven to earth with His entourage of angels and saints to rescue now-submissive Israel. Upon His return, Jesus will prepare the world for His thousand-year reign on earth from Jerusalem.

Does the above scenario have a basis in future reality, or is all of this just the product of an overactive imagination? Is it just great for novels and science fiction movies, but not really based in Scripture? Or has the Tribulation already taken place? Did it occur *symbolically* through the destruction of Jerusalem in A.D. 70?

How can we resolve the differences between preterists, who say that these events have already been fulfilled, and futurists, who contend that the prophecies are unfulfilled events that will take place in the future? I believe it can be shown from Scripture that the world can expect a future time that the Bible calls the Tribulation or Great Tribulation, which has yet to occur on the stage of history.

The Old Testament

The ancient philosopher Archimedes said, "Give me a place to stand and I can move the Universe." Applied philosophically, if the starting point of one's position can be established, then it provides a base upon which to develop further thought. The starting point for any Christian should be God's revelation as found in the Bible. But how do we go about establishing an Archimedean starting point in order to resolve an interpretive difference over whether the Tribulation is past or future? I will explain the various reasons why the Tribulation—as revealed by God in the Bible—is a future event. Once a biblical foundation for this issue is established, it will be clear that the Tribulation has not yet taken place in history, but that it is certain to occur in the future. Both God's reputation in the area of clearness of speech and His veracity are at stake.

The Abrahamic Covenant

Instead of starting with the Olivet discourse, where preterists like to begin, we will begin in Genesis, where the Bible begins. Following the dictum that "Scripture interprets Scripture," we need to also let the Bible itself teach us about the Tribulation and God's timing for this great future event. When speaking on Matthew 24:29 and the Great Tribulation, the late Dr. Greg Bahnsen, a preterist, said,

The difficulty, however, is that dispensational and modern interpreters have come to these words without an appreciation for, in many cases, even a knowledge of the literature of the Old Testament. Scripture is its own best interpreter.[1]

In pursuit of letting Scripture provide the questions as well as the answers, we will start in the Old Testament with the fountainhead of Bible prophecy—the Abrahamic covenant (Gen. 12:1–3, 7; 13:14–17; 15:1–21; 17:1–21; 22:15–18). It is the "mother of all redemptive covenants," and God's blessings springing forth from it extend to all humankind and planet earth.

The Abrahamic covenant is an unconditional agreement or pact in which God's sovereign election of Abraham and his descendants is revealed and God's decrees for them are declared. Dr. Arnold Fruchtenbaum explains:

> An unconditional covenant can be defined as a sovereign act of God whereby God unconditionally obligates Himself to bring to pass definite promises, blessings, and conditions for the covenanted people. It is a unilateral covenant. This type of covenant is characterized by the formula "I will," which declares God's determination to do exactly as He promised. The blessings are secured by the grace of God.[2]

The unconditional nature of the Abrahamic covenant is reinforced by understanding the covenant or treaty formats of the second millennium B.C. within which the biblical covenants were cast. There are three kinds of covenants in the Bible: (1) the royal grant treaty; (2) the suzerain-vassal treaty; and, (3) the parity treaty. They may be described as follows:

- *The royal grant treaty (unconditional)*—a promissory covenant that arose out of a king's desire to reward a loyal servant.
  Examples:
  The Abrahamic covenant
  The Davidic covenant
  The Palestinian covenant

- *The suzerain-vassal treaty (conditional)*—bound an inferior vassal to a superior suzerain and was obligatory only for the one who swore.
  Examples:
  The Adamic covenant

> The Noahic covenant
> Chedorlaomer (Genesis 14)
> The Mosaic covenant (book of Deuteronomy)
> Jabesh-Gilead serving Nahash (1 Sam. 11:1)

- *The parity treaty*—bound two equal parties in a relationship and provided conditions as stipulated by the participants.
  Examples:
  > Abraham and Abimelech (Gen. 21:25–32)
  > Jacob and Laban (Gen. 31:44–50)
  > David and Jonathan (1 Sam. 18:1–4; see 2 Sam. 9:1–13)

The Abrahamic covenant is classified as a royal grant treaty, thus underscoring its *unconditional* nature. Confirmation of the covenant is given in Genesis 15 when God sealed the treaty through a unique procedure whereby He put Abraham into a deep sleep and bound Himself to keep the covenant regardless of the patriarch's response. Since God is the only one who swore to keep the covenant, then it is clearly an unconditional covenant, based solely on what God alone does. Thus, we can be absolutely confident that He will keep it and bring to pass in history every stipulation of the agreement.

There are three major provisions of the Abrahamic covenant (Gen. 12:1–3). They are usually summarized as (1) land to Abram and Israel; (2) a seed; and (3) a worldwide blessing. A more complete breakdown of the covenant can be seen in its fourteen provisions, which are gleaned from the five major passages containing the treaty and its reconfirmations. Dr. Fruchtenbaum lists them as follows:

a. A great nation will come out of Abraham, namely, the nation of Israel (Gen. 12:2; 13:16; 15:5; 17:1–2, 7; 22:17b).
b. The Lord promises Abraham a land, namely, the land of Canaan (12:1, 7; 13:14–15, 17; 15:17–21; 17:18).
c. Abraham himself will be greatly blessed (12:2b; 15:6; 22:15–17a).
d. Abraham's name will be great (12:2c).
e. Abraham will be a blessing to others (12:2d).
f. Those who bless Abraham and his descendants will be blessed (12:3a).
g. Those who curse Abraham and his descendants will be cursed (12:3b).
h. In Abraham all will ultimately be blessed; this is a promise of Gentile blessing (12:3c; 22:18).
i. Abraham will receive a son through his wife Sarah (15:1–4; 17:16–21).

j. Abraham's descendants through this son will undergo bondage in Egypt (15:13–14).
k. Other nations as well as Israel will come forth from Abraham (17:3–4, 6; the Arab states are some of these nations).
l. The patriarch's name will be changed from Abram to Abraham (17:5).
m. Sarai's name will be changed to Sarah (17:15).
n. Circumcision will be a token of the covenant (17:9–14); and so, according to the Abrahamic covenant, circumcision will be a sign of Jewishness.[3]

The above breakdown of the Abrahamic covenant exhibits a wide variety of promises that will prove to give direction to an interesting history for Israel and the world. Dr. Fruchtenbaum notes that fulfillment of these fourteen promises is distributed and fulfilled among the following three parties:

a. *Abraham*—The following promises are made to Abraham: a, b, c, d, e, f, i, k, l, m.
b. *Israel, the Seed*—The following promises are made to Israel: a, b, e, f, g, j, n.
c. *Gentiles*—The following promises include Gentiles: f, g, h, k.[4]

Dr. John Walvoord summarizes the importance of the Abrahamic covenant as foundational to the study of Bible prophecy:

> The Abrahamic covenant contributes to the eschatology of Israel by detailing the broad program of God as it affects Abraham's seed. . . . It is not too much to say that the exegesis of the Abrahamic covenant and its resulting interpretation is the foundation for the study of prophecy as a whole, not only as relating to Israel, but also for the Gentiles and the church. It is here that the true basis for premillennial interpretation of the Scriptures is found.[5]

The Abrahamic covenant is important to a discussion of the Tribulation, for it expresses many unconditional decrees that will be expanded upon in subsequent revelation and thus surely fulfilled in history. This expansion of a biblical theme in the later revelation of Scripture has been called "progressive revelation." Progressive revelation is clearly at work in relation to the subject of the Tribulation. As we pass through the pages of Holy Writ, we will see greater detail about God's program for the Tribulation.

A great deal of the Abrahamic covenant is implemented through God's dealings with national Israel. A significant period of history that will occur as part of this outworking with Israel includes the time known as the Tribulation.

The Mosaic Covenant

As noted above, the Mosaic or Sinaitic covenant is in the form of a suzerain-vassal treaty format of the second millennium B.C. The book of Deuteronomy is generally recognized to have been set within the following structure of a suzerain-vassal treaty:

> Suzerain-Vassal Treaty Format of Deuteronomy
> • Preamble (1:1–5)
> • Historical Prologue (1:6–4:49)
> • Main Provisions (5:1–26:19)
> • Blessing and Curses (27:1–30:20)
> • Covenant Continuity (31:1–33:29)

Suzerain-vassal treaties or covenants are conditional. This is important, for it is within this framework that the Tribulation is first mentioned in the Bible as an event in Israel's history that will occur in "the latter days" and will lead to the people's repentance and conversion to Jesus as their Messiah (Deut. 4:30). An interesting aspect of Deuteronomy is that its covenantal structure provides the framework for Israel's history. In the historical prologue section (1:6–4:49) the Lord does not merely provide the customary history of the two contractual parties' dealings up to the time of the treaty, but He also goes one step further and provides a prophetic overview of Israel's entire future history. This is a significant observation for discussing when the Tribulation will occur in history, for Deuteronomy provides a prophetic road map of Israel's history.

Covenantal Relationships

Perhaps it would be helpful at this point to stop and contemplate the relationship of an unconditional covenant, such as the Abrahamic covenant, to that of a conditional covenant, such as the Mosaic covenant. The unconditional covenants provide humanity with God's sovereign decrees of where He is taking history, while the conditional covenants provide us with the means that He will use to get us there. God has said in the Abrahamic covenant that He will do certain things for the descendants of Abraham, and the Mosaic covenant provides conditional stipulations that must be met before something can take place. God decreed that Israel would receive certain blessings within the land of Israel, but that they would only enjoy them if the people were obedient. When the Israelites disobeyed, they would be cursed. That cursing would eventually lead to the people's obedience and finally result in the ultimate blessing promised.

"The primary purpose of the Sinaitic covenant," explains Dr. George Harton, "was to instruct the newly redeemed nation how they were to live for YHWH."[6] He then concludes:

> The covenant program revealed in the Pentateuch rests squarely on the twin pillars of the Abrahamic and Sinaitic covenants. This covenant program contains unconditional elements, which reveal some things that God has bound himself to do for the nation Israel. It also contains some conditional elements, which define the conditions upon which any individual Israelite may receive the benefits of the covenant. The Jews in Christ's day felt that the unconditional covenant guaranteed their participation in the promised kingdom. They had forgotten that an unconditional covenant may have conditional blessings. The Sinaitic covenant is essentially an amplification of these promises and covenant on which they rested.[7]

Just such a covenantal relationship is displayed in Deuteronomy, providing a masterful underscoring of the certainty of Israel's destiny, while at the same time insisting that the Israelites would receive their blessing by traveling God's road and not one of their own choice. Thus, Deuteronomy provides a prophetic road map covering the whole of history of the nation before Israel started down the road. This map includes a stop in the Tribulation, as well as other judgments along the way.

A Prophetic Road Map

As the nation of Israel sat perched on the banks of the Jordan River, before she ever set one foot upon the promised land, the Lord gave an outline of her entire history through Moses, His mouthpiece. Deuteronomy is this revelation, and it is like a road map of where history is headed before the trip ever gets underway. Disclosure of an event called the Tribulation is included by God as part of the original itinerary. While different segments of the historical journey have been updated, with more details being added along the way, not a single adjustment from the earlier course has ever been made. Part of that journey includes the Great Tribulation. In fact, it appears that there is more information in Scripture relating to the time of the Tribulation than to any other period of history, with the possible exception of our Lord's first coming.

Before we look at God's prophetic road map, it is important that we see the purpose of all the books in the Pentateuch. This will help us to better understand the contribution that Deuteronomy makes in explaining the relationship of the Tribulation to human history. Dr. Harton will prove helpful once again by providing the following overviews:

- The purpose of Genesis is to reveal to Israel at the time of the exodus her place as God's chosen instrument to minister to His fallen world.[8]
- The purpose of Exodus is the revelation of the deliverance of Israel to independent status as a nation.[9]
- The purpose of Leviticus is to show how Israel could maintain fellowship with her holy Redeemer.[10]
- The purpose of Numbers is to reveal God's response to Israel's disobedience.[11] Numbers does this by removing from the Israelites conditional blessings and by reassuring them of God's unconditional promise.[12]
- The purpose of Deuteronomy is to call for new commitment to the covenants by new generations in Israel. The point of the book is not primarily *legal* (namely, to recite a corpus of law), nor *historical* (namely, to recount a series of events), but rather it is *hortatory* (namely, to preach so as to move Israel to faith and obedience).[13]

In the process of Moses' exhortation to the nation of Israel, he provides in Deuteronomy 4:25–31 an outline of what will happen to the people of this elect nation once they cross over the Jordan River and settle the promised land.

> When you become the father of children and children's children and **have remained long in the land, and act corruptly**, and make an idol in the form of anything, and do that which is evil in the sight of the LORD your God so as to provoke Him to anger, I call heaven and earth to witness against you today, that **you shall surely perish quickly from the land** where you are going over the Jordan to possess it. You shall not live long on it, but shall be utterly destroyed. And **the LORD will scatter you among the peoples**, and you shall be left few in number among the nations, where the LORD shall drive you. And there you will serve gods, the work of man's hands, wood and stone, which neither see nor hear nor eat nor smell. **But from there you will seek the LORD your God**, and you will

find Him if you search for Him with all your heart and all your soul. **When you are in distress and all these things have come upon you, in the latter days, you will return to the LORD your God and listen to His voice.** For the LORD your God is a compassionate God; He will not fail you nor destroy you nor forget the covenant with your fathers which He swore to them.

I have put in boldfaced type those major events that even a school-child would know as key elements in the history of Israel. A summary of these events would be as follows:

1. The Israelites and their descendants will remain long in the land.
2. The Israelites will act corruptly and slip into idolatry.
3. The Israelites will be kicked out of the land.
4. The LORD will scatter the Israelites among the nations.
5. The Israelites will be given over to idolatry during their wanderings.
6. While dispersed among the nations, the Israelites will seek and find the LORD when they search for Him with all their heart.
7. There will come a time of Tribulation, which is said to occur in the latter days, during which the Israelites will turn to the Lord in repentance and faith.
8. "For the LORD your God is a compassionate God; He will not fail you nor destroy you nor forget the covenant with your fathers which He swore to them" (Deut. 4:31).

If the first five events have happened to Israel—and no one would deny that they have—then it is clear from the text that the final events will also occur to the same people in the same way. This is most clear from the context. The Bible does not "change horses in midstream" so that suddenly Israel, who has received the curses, is dropped out of the picture and the church takes over and receives the blessings. Despite various systems of theology, the Bible nowhere teaches that God has forsaken Israel. Any reader of the text will have to admit that the same identity is referred to throughout the whole of the text under examination. If it is true that the same Israel is meant throughout the text, then the last three events have yet to be fulfilled for Israel in the same historical way in which the first five events are recognized by all to have taken place. Thus, a fulfillment of the final three events in the life of Israel will have to happen in the future. Israel was not rescued as a result of Tribulation in A.D. 70; instead, the nation was judged. Deuteronomy 4 pictures a return to the Lord after Tribulation, not judgment. This means that a futurist view of the Tribulation is supported in this early passage.

As significant as Deuteronomy 4 is in establishing the Tribulation and its purpose, an expanded narrative of Israel's future history is provided in chapters 28–32. "The last seven chapters of Deuteronomy (28–34)," says David Larsen, "are really the matrix out of which the great prophecies of the Old Testament regarding Israel emerge."[14] Dr. Larsen provides the following breakdown of Israel's future history:

26:3–13; 28:1–14	The conditions of blessing to follow obedience
31:16–21	The coming apostasy
28:15–60	The affliction that God will bring upon Israel, while still in the land, because of her apostasy
28:32–39, 48–57	Israel will be taken captive
Chapters 27, 32	The enemies of Israel will possess her land for a time
28:38–42; 29:23	The land itself will remain desolate
28:63–67; 32:26	Israel will be scattered among the nations
28:62	The time will come when Israel will be "few in number"
28:44–45	Though punished, Israel will not be destroyed, if she repents
28:40–41; 30:1–2	Israel will repent in her tribulation
30:3–10	Israel will be gathered from the nations to her divinely given land[15]

Exodus 23 and Leviticus 26 present similar material to that found above. Leviticus 26 evidences a striking similarity with that of Deuteronomy 28–30, except that Leviticus 26 presents the cursings (26:14–39) within the framework of five progressive stages to the covenantal curse. Each stage was to increase by a factor of seven (26:18, 21, 24, 28), resulting in the fifth stage, which would be devastation and deportation from the land. However, the chapter ends with hope that if the people repented of their sin, while in exile, they would be returned to the land and receive blessing (26:40–46). There are many significant parallels between Leviticus 26 and Deuteronomy 28–30.

Within Deuteronomy 28–30 we see a specific reference to the Tribulation when it says, "And the LORD your God will inflict all these curses [chap. 28] on your enemies and on those who hate you, who persecuted you" (30:7). Moses tells us that the Tribulation will include in its purposes a time of retribution on the Gentiles for their ill treatment of the Jews. This certainly did not take place at all either during the A.D. 70 destruction of Jerusalem or at any time in history yet past. Thus, we are beginning to find that the Bible does not regard the Tribulation as a time of punishment for the Jews, as preterists insist; instead, it is a time of preparation for the Jews leading to their conversion and deliverance.

It appears to be shaping up that while the A.D. 70 incident was indeed a prophesied event, it is not the same as the Tribulation. Dr. Harton concludes: "Inasmuch as Deuteronomy 28–30 is merely a restatement and amplification of this same promise in Deuteronomy 4, it may be concluded that Deuteronomy 28:15–68 will have an eschatological fulfillment."[16]

Deuteronomy 28 as Prophecy

After enumerating the relatively short list of blessings that God would bestow upon Israel in the land (Deut. 28:1–14), Moses commences to enumerate the much longer list of curses that God will inflict upon His people when they would inevitably disobey (vv. 15–68). The Lord will start inflicting the nation with mild curses at the inception of disobedience and gradually turn up the heat as insubordination persists. The most severe chastisement the Lord will inflict upon His wayward people will be expulsion from their land, being mediated through the agency of a foreign invader (vv. 49–68). The Lord's logic is something along the line that if Israel did not want to obediently serve Him in their own land, then they could go and serve other gods outside the land (vv. 47–48).

Interestingly, verses 49–68 record two specific instances of removal from the land. The first reference is clearly to the Babylonian captivity, which takes place in the sixth century B.C. (vv. 49–57). For example, verse 49 speaks of "a nation" that the Lord will bring against Israel in judgment. This is followed by a second statement of dispersion (v. 64), which says, "Moreover, the LORD will scatter you among all peoples, from one end of the earth to the other end of the earth." This was undoubtedly fulfilled by the Romans when they destroyed Jerusalem in A.D. 70. Luke 21:24, which speaks of the A.D. 70 Roman destruction of Jerusalem, says that the Jewish people "will be led captive into all the nations," a statement which reflects the language of Deuteronomy 28:64. Thus we see two different instances of the judgment of God's covenantal curse being worked out in history. But neither of them is the Great Tribulation.

We have seen thus far from our prophetic road map that Deuteronomy 28 has predicted two different instances when the ultimate covenant curse of expulsion from the land will be applied to national Israel.

However, we have also noted that Deuteronomy 28–30 indicates that the Tribulation will come after Israel has been regathered back into the land and Jerusalem; then God will bring to pass the Tribulation. Thus, since the second covenantal dispersion in A.D. 70 by the Romans led to Israel's scattering among the nations, that could not have been the Tribulation, which is to take place after a worldwide regathering. This makes the Tribulation a future event.

Prophetic Patterns

As we move progressively through the Bible from the Pentateuch to the Prophets, we find that the role of the prophets is similar to modern ambassadors who represent their government's positions and policy. The prophets provide divine commentary and rebuke to the nation on behalf of God, but always in terms of how the people measure up to their Mosaic covenantal responsibilities. For example, Isaiah the prophet is called up to the throne room of God for commissioning and consultations before he brings God's indictment against the nation for her disobedience (Isa. 6). Following the Lord's preordained pattern for Israel's history (as stated in Deuteronomy), the prophets speak about covenantal disobedience (which they document with many specific examples) and the resulting curse (ultimately involving expulsion from the land). But then they always include a future hope. This is often preceded with the Deuteronomic Tribulation, which gives rise to Israel's obedience and results in her ultimate blessing.

By the time of the exilic and postexilic prophets, all hope that the nation will accomplish her destiny through cooperative obedience has been abandoned. The hope for the nation, as well as for the entire Gentile world, is focused on the performance of a single individual—the *Messiah*. This prophetically prepares the nation for the first appearance of Messiah in the person of Jesus of Nazareth, whom the nation rejected, as she had the prophets who had come before Him. Thus, Jesus and the New Testament writers follow the Mosaic and prophetic pattern of documenting specific violations of Israel's covenant (see, for example, Matt. 21–23), and this provides the basis, not for the Tribulation, but for expulsion from the land and scattering among the nations. Thus, the ultimate rejection of God's Son Himself leads to the more severe application of the ultimate curse upon the nation than she previously experienced during her first expulsion in the sixth century B.C. under the Babylonians.

Just as Israel was regathered after the Babylonian captivity and returned to the land, so she will be returned from her A.D. 70 Diaspora from the nations. However, this time she will be regathered in preparation for a seven-year period that we know as the Tribulation, which will serve to prepare her for conversion and ultimate covenantal blessing. Such a scenario is supported by an examination of passages from the Old Testament prophets that expand upon—but do not contradict—the Mosaic prophecy of the Tribulation.

Prophetic Tribulation Terms

The Bible uses different terminology when referring to the Tribulation. Various descriptions are needed because of a multiplicity of aspects and purposes for the Tribulation. Dr. Randall Price has identified twenty-two terms and expressions used by Old Testament writers to describe the Tribulation, as noted in Figure 1.1.[17]

With this data as our guide, we will examine the major terms and passages relating to the Tribulation to gather a composite of what the Old Testament writers expected the Tribulation to be like. This profile will also provide a framework for examining the New Testament passages, which often are the basis for debate over when the Tribulation is to be fulfilled in history.

"Tribulation" or "Trouble"

The Prophets build upon the Mosaic introduction of the concept of "tribulation" in Deuteronomy 4:30. They use this term to refer to the future time of great distress at least four times in three passages. If we take these passages chronologically, the first one we will examine is Jeremiah 30:7, which deals with the well-known "Day of Jacob's Trouble." Notice the following observations from verses 1–11 about the "Day of Jacob's Trouble":

- It will be a time of restored fortunes for Israel and Judah (v. 3).
- It will be a time when Israel and Judah will be brought back into their land in order to possess it (v. 3).
- It will be a time of distress for Jacob (in other words, national Israel) from which he will be delivered (v. 7).
- It will be a unique time in history (v. 8).
- It will be a time when Israel's national slavery is ended (v. 8).
- It will lead to a time when Israel will serve the Lord and David, the nation's king (v. 9).
- It will lead to a time when Israel will be regathered from afar and dwell in the land in quiet and ease with no one making the nation afraid (v. 10).
- It will be a time when the nations to which Israel was scattered will be destroyed (v. 11).
- It will be a time when God will punish Jacob justly and destroy part of the nation (v. 11).

Old Testament Tribulation Terms and Expressions

Tribulation Term	Old Testament Reference
1. DAY OF THE LORD	Isaiah 2:12; 13:6, 9; Ezekiel 13:5; 30:3; Joel 1:15; 2:1, 11, 31; 3:14; Amos 5:18, 20; Obadiah 15; Zephaniah 1:7, 14; Zechariah 14:1
2. GREAT & TERRIBLE DAY OF THE LORD	Malachi 4:5
3. TROUBLE, TRIBULATION	Deuteronomy 4:30; Zephaniah 1:16
4. TIME/DAY OF TROUBLE	Daniel 12:1; Zephaniah 1:15
5. DAY OF JACOB'S TROUBLE	Jeremiah 30:7
6. BIRTH PANGS	Isaiah 21:3; 26:17–18; 66:7; Jeremiah 4:31; Micah 4:10 (cf. Jeremiah 30:6)
7. THE DAY OF CALAMITY	Deuteronomy 32:35; Obadiah 12–14
8. INDIGNATION	Isaiah 26:20; Daniel 11:36
9. THE [LORD'S] STRANGE WORK	Isaiah 28:21
10. OVERFLOWING SCOURGE	Isaiah 28:15, 18
11. DAY OF VENGEANCE	Isaiah 34:8a; 35:4a; 61:2b; 63:4a
12. DAY OF WRATH	Zephaniah 1:15
13. DAY OF THE LORD'S WRATH	Zephaniah 1:18
14. DAY OF DISTRESS	Zephaniah 1:15
15. DAY OF DESTRUCTION	Zephaniah 1:15
16. DAY OF DESOLATION	Zephaniah 1:15
17. DAY OF DARKNESS & GLOOM	Joel 2:2; Amos 5:18, 20; Zephaniah 1:15;
18. DAY OF CLOUDS & THICK DARKNESS	Joel 2:2; Zephaniah 1:15
19. DAY OF TRUMPET & ALARM	Zephaniah 1:16
20. DAY OF THE LORD'S ANGER	Zephaniah 2:2–3
21. [DAY OF] DESTRUCTION, RUIN, FROM THE ALMIGHTY	Joel 1:15
22. THE FIRE OF HIS JEALOUSY	Zephaniah 1:18

The composite in this passage does not fit any time of past judgment upon Israel, but it does fit the prophetic pattern of a future time when God's people will be returned from the nations to their land, put through the testings of the Tribulation, and rescued from that time of distress as the Lord judges the nations. This then leads to the Israelites' time of national obedience and blessing. This scenario characterizes the Tribulation, and thus it is yet future.

Daniel 12:1–2 provides us with another important tribulation passage. It reads as follows:

> *Now at that time Michael, the great prince who stands guard over the sons of your people, will arise. And there will be a time of distress such as never occurred since there was a nation until that time; and at that time your people, everyone who is found written in the book, will be rescued. And many of those who sleep in the dust of the ground will awake, these to everlasting life, but the others to disgrace and everlasting contempt.*

This Tribulation passage includes the following elements:

- "Now at that time" refers back to the previous section (11:36–45), which is descriptive of many of Antichrist's activities during the Tribulation (12:1).
- It will be a time when the archangel Michael "will arise," indicating that he will defend Israel against her enemies (12:1).
- It will be a time of distress such as has never occurred in Israel's national history up to that point (v. 1).
- It will be a time in which all elect Israelites will be rescued (v. 1).
- It will be a time followed by the resurrection of saved and unsaved Israelites (v. 2).

Once again we have the picture of national Israel during the time of greatest distress in which she is persecuted by her enemies. During this yet unfulfilled time period, God (through angelic intervention) will step in and rescue His elect nation. This fits the pattern of a future tribulation; but it does not correlate with the A.D. 70 judgment of Israel.

Zephaniah 1:14–18 is the final Old Testament passage under consideration. These verses heap together just about every term in the Bible that is used to describe and designate the Tribulation. More than half of the Old Testament tribulation terms noted in the above chart are found in Zephaniah 1:14–18. Interestingly, the emphasis in this passage is on the Lord's judgment of the nations when "all the earth will be devoured . . . all the inhabitants of the earth" (v. 18). This passage teaches us that during the Tribulation the Lord will judge the nations.

Day of the Lord

The "day of the Lord" is the most widely used term in the Old Testament to describe the time we call the Tribulation. Dr. Paul Benware summarizes the activities of the "day of the Lord" as a time when "the Lord will intervene in human history to judge the nations, discipline Israel, and establish His rule in the messianic kingdom."[18] Once again we see a recurring feature in the day of the Lord that we have observed in other Tribulation descriptions, namely, the Lord's defense of Israel against the nations. This is especially clear in Zechariah 14:1–8. "I will gather all the nations against Jerusalem to battle" (v. 2a). "Then the LORD will go forth and fight against those nations as when He fights on a day of battle" (v. 3). This hardly fits the A.D. 70 event or any historical possibility. It thus awaits future fulfillment.

Daniel's 70th Week

Daniel's "seventy weeks" (prophesied in Daniel 9:24–27) are the framework within which the Tribulation (or the seventieth week) occurs.[19] The seven-year period of Daniel's seventieth week provides the time span or length of the Tribulation. A graphic presentation of the seventy weeks (Figure 1.2) assists greatly in understanding this intricate prophecy.

Explanation of Daniel's 70 Weeks of Years

69 x 7 x 360 = 173,880 days
March 5, 444 B.C. + 173,880 days = March 30, A.D. 33

Verification

444 B.C. to A.D. 33 = 476 years
476 years x 365.2421989 days = 173,855 days
+ days between March 5 and March 30 = 25 days
Totals = 173,855 days + 25 days = 173,880 days

Rationale for 360-day Years

Half Week—Daniel 9:27
Time, times, half a time—Daniel 7:25, 12:7; Revelation 12:14
1,260 days—Revelation 12:6, 11:3
42 months—Revelation 11:2, 13:5
Thus: 42 months = 1,260 days = time, times, half time + half week
Therefore: month = 30 days; year = 360 days[20]

Daniel's Seventy Weeks
(Daniel 9:24–27)

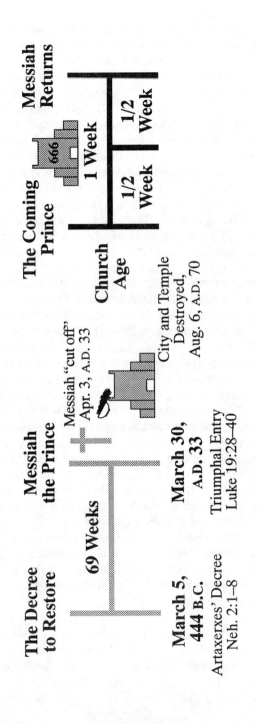

The Decree to Restore

69 Weeks

March 5, 444 B.C.

Artaxerxes' Decree
Neh. 2:1–8

Messiah the Prince

Messiah "cut off"
Apr. 3, A.D. 33

March 30, A.D. 33

Triumphal Entry
Luke 19:28–40

City and Temple
Destroyed,
Aug. 6, A.D. 70

Church Age

The Coming Prince

666

1/2 Week

1 Week

1/2 Week

Messiah Returns

The seventieth week of Daniel is the basis for our understanding that the future Tribulation will be seven years in length. This is confirmed in Revelation, where there are references to two three-and-one-half-year periods. The ministry of the two witnesses occurs in the first three-and-one-half years (11:3), while other Tribulation events are said to occur in the second half of the seven years (12:6; 13:5). Since the first sixty-nine weeks were fulfilled literally in history (explained above), it follows that the final week must be fulfilled in the same way. Any attempt to find a literal fulfillment of the final seven years requires a gap of time between the sixty-ninth and seventieth weeks. This provides the basis for the final week of Daniel's prophecy to be fulfilled literally in the future. But how is this possible?

The following is Dr. Randall Price's explanation and defense of a gap preceding the final week of Daniel's famous prophecy (emphasis in the original):

> The sixty-ninth week has already been set off as a distinct unit comprised of the seven and sixty-two weeks. This would imply in itself that the events of the seventieth week are to be treated separately. Further, the events in verse 26–"the cutting off of Messiah," and of the "people of the prince"— are stated to occur *after* the sixty-nine weeks. If this was intended to occur *in* the seventieth week, the text would have read here "during" or "in the midst of" (cf. Daniel's use of *hetzi,* "in the middle of," v. 27). This language implies that these events *precede* the seventieth week but do not *immediately* follow the sixty-ninth. Therefore, a temporal interval separates the two. It is also important to note that the opening word of verse 27 (*higbbir,* "confirm") is prefixed by the *waw* consecutive, a grammatical connective that indicates a close consequential relationship to a preceding verb. This use indicates that the events of verse 27 are *subsequent* to those of verse 26. Furthermore, the very language of these two verses, first speaking of "the prince [*nagid,* "leader"] who is to come" (v. 26), and then of that prince that later comes (the "he" of v. 27), implies that a separation of time exists between these events.[21]

Daniel's prophecy begins in verse 24 with six Hebrew infinitives that cite the goals to be fulfilled by the time the seventy weeks of years have ended. These goals are (1) "to finish the transgression;" (2) "to make an end of sin;" (3) "to make atonement for iniquity;" (4) "to bring in everlasting righteousness;" (5) "to seal up vision and prophecy;"

and (6) "to anoint the most holy [place]." The last three goals have yet to be fulfilled, especially the final one relating to the most holy place in the temple. If just one of these six goals is future, then it would strongly support the necessity of a yet future fulfillment of the seventieth week and the Tribulation. Dr. Price adds the following points:

> It is our contention that postponement does *not* affect the continuity of measured events, since the measured time allotted to Israel has been interrupted by a different measurement of time allotted to the Gentiles. If one does not understand the chronological reckoning in this sense, those who posit an A.D. 70 fulfillment must still contend with at least a forty-three-year interval of time (the crucifixion and destruction of Jerusalem) that is directly indicated as having occurred after the sixty-ninth week but prior to the seventieth week. Furthermore, those who hold to an A.D. 70 fulfillment have to explain the final clause of Daniel 9:27, namely, "that which is determined shall be poured out on the desolator," (i.e., the *appointed destruction* of the Desolator). This predicted judgment for the one who desecrates and attempts to destroy the temple and city, accords with an element in desecration motifs that have the Lord announcing the punishment of His instruments of judgment for their arrogance and self-actuated intent to destroy what is holy. Such an end was decreed for the Assyrian invaders (Isa. 10:23–26) and was repeated in more detail in Daniel 11:36 (cf. Rev. 13:5–8), a text that displays both the arrogance (Dan. 11 :36–38) and aggression (v. 39) of the future Desolator (the Antichrist). We could add to these chronological factors the critical observation that the six-fold restoration goal of Daniel 9:24 was not fulfilled immediately after the sixty-ninth week, but instead verse 26 indicated that both the city and the temple would be destroyed, followed by a determined period of desolations. This was all to be accomplished *before* the seventieth week in verse 27. It is not until the completion of the seventieth week that we find complete fulfillment of the goals.[22]

The Book of Zechariah

Zechariah was one of the final contributors to the Old Testament canon. It should prove especially helpful to anyone interested in the timing of the Tribulation. Zechariah's focus was not only on the nation of Israel; he also provides prophetic focus on Jerusalem. Chapters 12–14 involve prophetic details that I believe are descriptive of a future Tribulation, while preterists believe they were fulfilled in the

A.D. 70 destruction of Jerusalem. As we examine key passages, we once again see a pattern not found in the A.D. 70 event. Notice the following passages:

> *Behold, I am going to make Jerusalem a cup that causes reeling to all the peoples around; and when the siege is against Jerusalem, it will also be against Judah. And it will come about in that day that I will make Jerusalem a heavy stone for all the peoples; all who lift it will be severely injured. And all the nations of the earth will be gathered against it (12:2–3).*

> *Then the clans of Judah will say in their hearts, "a strong support for us are the inhabitants of Jerusalem through the LORD of hosts, their God" (12:5).*

> *In that day the LORD will defend the inhabitants of Jerusalem, and the one who is feeble among them in that day will be like David, and the house of David will be like God, like the angel of the LORD before them. And it will come about in that day that I will set about to destroy all the nations that come against Jerusalem. And I will pour out on the house of David and on the inhabitants of Jerusalem, the Spirit of grace and of supplication, so that they will look on Me whom they have pierced; and they will mourn for Him, as one mourns for an only son, and they will weep bitterly over Him, like the bitter weeping over a first-born (12:8–10).*

The passages above clearly depict a time when all the nations of the earth will have surrounded Jerusalem in a siege. When this event happens, the Lord does not use these Gentile armies as His agent of judgment, as in A.D. 70; instead, He will intervene to rescue Israel from this threat, which happens in the future Tribulation. That this language does not support a preterist interpretation would seem hard to circumvent when the text says, "In that day the LORD will defend the inhabitants of Jerusalem," and "in that day that I will set about to destroy all the nations that come against Jerusalem." Yet preterist interpreter David Chilton, apparently unable to deal with the details of the text, declares:

> Another passage parallel to this is Zechariah 12, which pictures Jerusalem as a cup of drunkenness to the nations (Zech. 12:2; cf. Rev. 14:8–9), a laver of fire that will consume the heathen (Zech. 12:6; Rev. 15:2). The irony of Revelation, as we have seen repeatedly, is that first-century Israel herself has taken the

place of the heathen nations in the prophecies: She is consumed in the fiery laver—the Lake of Fire—while the church, having passed through the holocaust, inherits salvation.[23]

This is an astounding demonstration, at least by this particular preterist, that he cannot produce a textually based interpretation of this passage that corresponds in any way with his A.D. 70 presumption. Thus, once again, without any basis in the text of Zechariah 12, he turns Jews into Gentiles and Gentiles into Jews, merely because he declares it to be so. Amazing! Such a deed makes it clear that the details of this passage cannot be made to fit an A.D. 70 fulfillment. This supports a yet future time when Israel is surrounded by hostile Gentile armies from all over the earth; yet this time the Lord intervenes to save the Jews, as the people of Israel are sovereignly converted to Jesus as their Messiah (as indicated by 12:10).

Preterists often say that Zechariah 12:10 was completely fulfilled at Christ's first coming because it is cited to that end in John 19:36–37: "For these things came to pass, that the Scripture might be fulfilled, 'not a bone of Him shall be broken.' And again another Scripture says, 'they shall look on Him whom they pierced.'" Clearly, the statement about Christ being pierced occurred at His first advent, for that took place at His crucifixion. John wanted to show that the piercing aspect of the prophecy was fulfilled by Jesus in His first-century crucifixion. John had this same intent when he quoted Exodus 12:46 in John 19:36: "not a bone of Him shall be broken." This does not mean that *all* the elements of the Zechariah 12:10 prophecy have been fulfilled. The late David Chilton erroneously believed that the original meaning of Zechariah 12:10 has been reinterpreted by the New Testament.

> Both Jesus and St. John thus reinterpreted this expression, borrowed from Zechariah 12:1–14, where it occurs in an original context of Israel's mourning in repentance. But Israel had gone beyond the point of no return; their mourning would not be that of repentance, but sheer agony and terror.[24]

Zechariah 13:1–2 supports the futurist interpretation that 12:10ff relates to a future conversion of Israel in conjunction with a time when Jerusalem will be surrounded by an international military force.

> *"In that day a fountain will be opened for the house of David and for the inhabitants of Jerusalem, for sin and for impurity. And it will come about in that day," declares the LORD of hosts,*

> *"that I will cut off the names of the idols from the land, and*
> *they will no longer be remembered; and I will also remove the*
> *prophets and the unclean spirit from the land."*

Further details relating to this fantastic time of future conversion are spelled out in the following passage in 13:7–9:

> *"Awake, O sword, against My Shepherd, And against the man,*
> *My Associate," declares the* LORD *of hosts. "Strike the Shep-*
> *herd that the sheep may be scattered; and I will turn My hand*
> *against the little ones. And it will come about in all the land,"*
> *declares the* LORD, *"that two parts in it will be cut off and*
> *perish; but the third will be left in it. And I will bring the third*
> *part through the fire, refine them as silver is refined, and test*
> *them as gold is tested. They will call on My name, and I will*
> *answer them; I will say, 'they are My people,' and they will*
> *say, 'the* LORD *is my God.'"*

Dr. Eugene Merrill's interpretation hits the mark as he recognizes the relationship between chapters 12 and 13 of the book of Zechariah:

> The cleansing fountain is opened specifically to the house of
> David and inhabitants of Jerusalem, for they are the two enti-
> ties singled out in 12:10, the ones upon whom YHWH will
> pour out the spirit of grace and supplication. They, however,
> are only representative of the whole redeemed people, as
> 12:12–14 puts beyond doubt. What is important to note here
> is that the cleansing fountain of 13:1 is presupposed by the
> divine initiative of grace in 12:10. It is only when the people
> of YHWH face up to Him as the one whom they have wounded
> and then repent sincerely of their wickedness that the foun-
> tain of cleansing is opened up to them. This is not in any way
> contrary to the Christian gospel message (Rom. 10:9–10; cf.
> Titus 3:5).[25]

The repentance described in Zechariah 12:10–13:9 did not happen in the first century. It remains prophetically unfulfilled as a future event related to what will be a time when Jerusalem is surrounded by a world-wide military force (I believe this will be the Battle of Armageddon at the end of the future Tribulation), and the Jewish people recognize that indeed Jesus was and is their promised Messiah. When they as a nation acknowledge the messiahship of Jesus, then they will call upon Him to deliver them from the impending threat. Christ will do this at

His Second Coming, as explained in chapter 14.

Zechariah 14:2–12 describes the Battle of Armageddon, which is interrupted by the second advent of Christ to Jerusalem to rescue His repentant and believing people.

> *For I will gather all the nations against Jerusalem to battle, and the city will be captured, the houses plundered, the women ravished, and half of the city exiled, but the rest of the people will not be cut off from the city. Then the LORD will go forth and fight against those nations, as when He fights on a day of battle. And in that day His feet will stand on the Mount of Olives, which is in front of Jerusalem on the east; and the Mount of Olives will be split in its middle from east to west by a very large valley, so that half of the mountain will move toward the north and the other half toward the south. And you will flee by the valley of My mountains, for the valley of the mountains will reach to Azel; yes, you will flee just as you fled before the earthquake in the days of Uzziah king of Judah. Then the LORD, my God, will come, and all the holy ones with Him! And it will come about in that day that there will be no light; the luminaries will dwindle. For it will be a unique day which is known to the LORD, neither day nor night, but it will come about that at evening time there will be light. And it will come about in that day that living waters will flow out of Jerusalem, half of them toward the eastern sea and the other half toward the western sea; it will be in summer as well as in winter. And the LORD will be king over all the earth; in that day the LORD will be the only one, and His name the only one. All the land will be changed into a plain from Geba to Rimmon south of Jerusalem; but Jerusalem will rise and remain on its site from Benjamin's Gate as far as the place of the First Gate to the Corner Gate, and from the Tower of Hananel to the king's wine presses. And people will live in it, and there will be no more curse, for Jerusalem will dwell in security. Now this will be the plague with which the LORD will strike all the peoples who have gone to war against Jerusalem; their flesh will rot while they stand on their feet, and their eyes will rot in their sockets, and their tongue will rot in their mouth.*

This passage describes a picture consistent with a futurist interpretation of these events: (1) The Tribulation ends with the second coming of Jesus to Jerusalem to rescue His repentant people Israel. (2) The coming of the Lord does not result in judgment upon Israel through the surrounding armies; rather, it leads to a divine judgment of the nations and rescue of Israel. This is the opposite of what happened in the first century. (3) After the Second Coming, the millennium begins in which Israel is blessed nationally. (4) Israel's reception of Jesus as her Messiah results in worldwide blessings to all the nations of the world.

Despite the above facts, preterist Dr. Kenneth Gentry insists, "The siege of Jerusalem described in Zechariah 14:1–2 has to do with the A.D. 70 devastation of Jerusalem. . . . Yet the Lord defends those who are truly His people, insuring their escape from the besieged city (vv. 3–4)."[26] While it is certainly true that the Lord defends His people in this passage, the point of Zechariah 14 is that the whole nation has become His people, not just a minority, as in A.D. 70. Zechariah 14:3 makes it clear that the Lord is not only defending His people, but that "the LORD will go forth and fight against those nations, as when He fights on a day of battle." When did the Lord fight against and defeat the Roman army in A.D. 70? Preterists teach rightly that the A.D. 70 event was a time when God used the Romans, as He had done previously with the Babylonians, to bring judgment upon national Israel. Dr. Gentry's interpretation of the text, no matter how brilliant it may seem, does not fit the broad features of the passage, let alone the details. Note further what Zechariah 14:12 and 13 prophesies:

> *Now this will be the plague with which the LORD will strike all the peoples who have gone to war against Jerusalem; their flesh will rot while they stand on their feet, and their eyes will rot in their sockets, and their tongue will rot in their mouth. . . . And Judah also will fight at Jerusalem; and the wealth of all the surrounding nations will be gathered, gold and silver and garments in great abundance.*

When did the Romans in A.D. 70 have their flesh rot while they stood on their feet, and their eyes rot in their sockets, and their tongue rot in their mouth? Does Josephus describe such an event? When, as a result of A.D. 70, did the wealth of all the surrounding nations stream into Jerusalem in great abundance? Of course, the answer is that it *did not.* This further shows that if we are to fit the A.D. 70 destruction of Jerusalem into biblical prophecy—and we must—then it fits as the second prophesied dispersion of the Jewish people for disobedience to the Mosaic covenant and their rejection of the messiahship of Jesus, as predicted in Deuteronomy 28:64–68. But the A.D. 70 event was not the Tribulation predicted early and often throughout the Old Testament. The Tribulation awaits a future time of fulfillment.

4

THE GREAT TRIBULATION IS FUTURE:

THE NEW TESTAMENT

Thomas Ice

The New Testament does not contradict the prophetic road map developed in the Old Testament. Instead, it develops and advances the notion that the Tribulation is a yet future event. The New Testament expands upon the two major events that were prophesied in the Old Testament, which are the Tribulation and the A.D. 70 judgment of God upon Israel for disobedience and rejection of the messiahship of Jesus. Preterists want to see the two prophecies as a single event, yet this is impossible because there is a major difference between them. That difference consists of the fact that it is impossible for God to be both judging and rescuing the nation at the same time. He clearly judged in the first century and will rescue His repentant people in the future. Let us examine the key New Testament passages and find out why the Tribulation is yet future.

The A.D. 70 Judgment

Preterists are right to note that the Roman siege and eventual destruction of Jerusalem and the temple in A.D. 70 was a major event in biblical history. However, it was neither the second coming of Christ nor a coming of Christ. It was an event that can be paralleled with the Babylonian destruction of Jerusalem in 586 B.C.

The ministry of Christ, leading up to His crucifixion, is similar to that of many Old Testament prophets. Jesus documents the offenses of national Israel that would lead to the A.D. 70 judgment and dispersion at the hand of the Romans. Matthew 21–23, in many senses, sounds like Isaiah and Jeremiah, as our Lord demonstrates legally Israel's

violation of specific stipulations found in the governing Mosaic
covenant. Thus, Israel's ultimate violation—the rejection of the
messiahship of Jesus—was met with the covenantal curse of Leviticus
26:27–39 and, specifically, Deuteronomy 28:64–68. Israel was under
the curse because of her failure to "recognize the time of [her]
visitation" (Luke 19:44) from Jesus the Messiah.

In a style similar to Jeremiah in Lamentations, Jesus weeps over the
impending judgment (A.D. 70) destined for Jerusalem (Matt. 23:37–39):

> *O Jerusalem, Jerusalem, who kills the prophets and stones*
> *those who are sent to her! How often I wanted to gather your*
> *children together, the way a hen gathers her chicks under her*
> *wings, and you were unwilling. Behold, your house is being*
> *left to you desolate! For I say to you, from now on you shall*
> *not see Me until you say, "Blessed is He who comes in the*
> *name of the Lord!"*

Also, in characteristically Old Testament prophetic style, Jesus does
not pronounce an impending judgment without at the same time holding
forth an ultimate hope for the people of Israel. The word "until" breaks
the pessimism of judgment and holds forth the future assurance that
one day Israel will bless the presence of Jesus. This is not stated as a
mere theoretical possibility; it is just as certain to take place as is the
nation's impending judgment that came to pass in A.D. 70. Thus, we
see the recurring theme of judgment that will be followed by
restoration—an ultimate restoration related to the end times.

Dr. J. Randall Price has argued that God expresses His cursing for
disobedience and blessing for obedience in relation to His people Israel within a pattern of "desecration/restoration," especially in relation to the temple, which is God's visible symbol of His dwelling in
favor with His people.[1] Thus, the A.D. 70 desecration is certainly an
important event in the flow of history, but this will be followed by an
eventual restoration of Israel to a future place of blessing. This explains
the important transitional role of the word "until" at the end of a major judgment passage.

Interestingly, the one passage within the Olivet discourse (Matt. 24–
25; Mark 13; Luke 21:5–36) that both preterists and futurists agree
refers to the A.D. 70 judgment is Luke 21:20–24:

> *But when you see Jerusalem surrounded by armies, then*
> *recognize that her desolation is at hand. Then let those who*
> *are in Judea flee to the mountains, and let those who are in*
> *the midst of the city depart, and let not those who are in the*

*country enter the city; because these are days of vengeance,
in order that all things which are written may be fulfilled. Woe
to those who are with child and to those who nurse babes in
those days; for there will be great distress upon the land, and
wrath to this people, and they will fall by the edge of the sword,
and will be led captive into all the nations; and Jerusalem
will be trampled under foot by the Gentiles until the times of
the Gentiles be fulfilled.*

This passage contains a second important "until" (v. 24), which provides the basis for a yet future event. That future event is the Tribulation described in 21:25–28.

*And there will be signs in sun and moon and stars, and upon
the earth dismay among nations, in perplexity at the roaring
of the sea and the waves, men fainting from fear and the expectation of the things which are coming upon the world; for
the powers of the heavens will be shaken. And then they will
see the Son of Man coming in a cloud with power and great
glory. But when these things begin to take place, straighten up
and lift up your heads, because your redemption is drawing
near.*

Further, the book of Hebrews is to be understood as containing
warnings to Israel upon the eve of God's judgment in the first century.
However, other New Testament passages in contention between
preterists and futurists are only understood properly as prophecy of a
yet future tribulation.

The Tribulation

Luke 21:20–28 provides the following outline of history: (1) the
destruction of Jerusalem in A.D. 70, which is called the "days of vengeance" (vv. 20–24a); (2) followed by the "times of the Gentiles"
(v. 24b); and then, (3) the Tribulation (vv. 25–26); followed by (4) the
second coming of Christ to rescue elect Israel (vv. 27–28). As in the
Old Testament, the second coming of Christ is associated with the salvation of Israel (called "your redemption" in v. 28). This did not happen in A.D. 70! Israel was under judgment, not redemption. Another
way of looking at the two aspects of the passage are the "desolation"
(v. 20) of Jerusalem in verses 20–24 as contrasted with her "redemption" (v. 28) prophesied in verses 25–28. The *desolation* of Israel occurred in A.D. 70, while the *redemption* of Israel will occur some time
in the future.

The Olivet Discourse

Since there is agreement between almost all preterists and futurists that Christ's prophecy in Luke 21:20–24 had a first-century fulfillment, I will start there and show that this passage (21:20–28) provides an outline of history that includes the current times of the Gentiles and a future Tribulation immediately followed by Christ's second coming. This outline fits nicely into the order already developed from the Old Testament, while at the same time it gives due prominence to the destruction of Jerusalem by the Romans in the first century.

All three Synoptic Gospels (Matthew, Mark, and Luke) record the Olivet discourse as given by Jesus. Matthew and Mark focus exclusively upon the future events of the Tribulation, while Luke's version includes past and future elements. In relation to Luke 21:20, Dr. Darrell Bock comments:

> The different emphases are most clearly indicated by what Luke lacks: he does not mention that the Tribulation in this period is the most intense ever to fall on humans; he does not mention that no human would have survived if the Lord had not cut short these days; he does not note that the time should not be in the winter; and he does not discuss the "abomination of desolation," only "its desolation." Conversely, Luke alone mentions "the time of the Gentiles." What do these differences mean? They indicate that Luke emphasizes a different element in Jesus' teaching at this point. He focuses on the nearer fulfillment in the judgment pattern described here, the fall of Jerusalem in A.D. 70, rather than the end (which he will introduce directly in 21:25). . . . So the instructions he offers here are like those that appear in the description of the end in 17:23, 31. He wants to make clear that when Jerusalem falls the first time, it is not yet the end. Nonetheless, the two falls are related and the presence of one pictures what the ultimate siege will be like.[2]

Indeed, many similarities can be noted between the various sieges set against Jerusalem. For instance, there are many similarities between the Babylonian siege and their destruction of Jerusalem in the sixth century B.C. and that of the Romans in the first century A.D. Conversely, there are sufficient dissimilarities to distinguish the two events. To note similarities between the Roman siege and a future siege does not prove that they are the same events any more than such similarities would mean that the Babylonian and Roman sieges were the same events. Dr. Bock recognizes the irreconcilable differences between the two events, despite clear similarities:

Jerusalem's fall pictures a horrific national judgment that is like the circumstances of the end-time as well as like judgments of old, a typological picture of what the consummation will be like—except that at the consummation, the nation of Israel will be rescued as the OT promised (13:35 also suggests hope for Israel).[3]

The template for Israel's history becomes clear in light of this passage. The favored status of the nation of Israel is temporally set aside through the first-century destruction of Jerusalem. This is the desecration phase of Dr. Price's "desecration/restoration" motif. The A.D. 70 desecration gives rise to the "times of the Gentiles" (Luke 21:24), which thus far has lasted almost two thousand years. The "times of the Gentiles" will conclude as they began, with a focus upon Jerusalem surrounded by armies (Zech. 12; 14:1–4; Matt. 24:4–31; Mark 13:5–27; Luke 21:25–28), but this time national Israel is converted and thus rescued. This is Dr. Price's restoration phase.

Thus, while Jerusalem was "desolated" (Luke 21:20) in A.D. 70, a quite different incident referred to as "the abomination of desolation" or "desolating sacrilege" is described in other passages as a yet future Tribulation event (Matt. 24:15; Mark 13:14; see Dan. 9:27; 11:31; 12:11; 2 Thess. 2:4; Rev. 13:15). While Luke 21:20 speaks about the first-century Roman invasion of Jerusalem, it supports the futurist interpretation of the other passages by providing a basis for contrast (not similarity, as proposed by preterists) with the other sections of the Olivet discourse yet to take place in history.

Hermeneutics

It should be observed at this point that neither preterists nor futurists resort to symbolic interpretation when explaining Luke 21:20–24. Preterist Dr. Kenneth L. Gentry Jr. says, "The context of Luke demands a literal Jerusalem (Luke 21:20) besieged by literal armies (Luke 21:20) in literal Judea (Luke 21:21)—which as a matter of indisputable historical record occurred in the events leading up to A.D. 70."[4] However, when expounding on 21:25–28, preterists resort to massive doses of *symbolic* interpretation in their attempt to give these verses a first-century fulfillment. The futurist does not need to make such adjustments and continues a *plain* reading of the text.

In these passages, the futurist is able to follow a consistently literal hermeneutic (namely, the historical-grammatical approach), while preterists have to interject symbolism at key points, without a textual basis, in order to avoid the futurist implications. ("Literal" means according to the text; in other words, interpretation based upon what the text actually says.) The consistent, literal hermeneutic of futurism recognizes figures of speech and symbols where introduced and supported by the text. Valid use of figures (such as God's Word pictured as a sword) and symbols (such as the "beast" of Revelation developed textually in Daniel 7 and supported by the various Revelation contexts) must have textual factors that can be cited to support the use of a figure of speech and a symbol.

Too often, preterists simply declare key textual elements to be symbols, without providing adequate contextual support. This is done time after time in key passages such as the Olivet discourse and Revelation. They apparently think that just citing a vaguely similar event from Josephus clinches the passage as a past fulfillment. A key factor in favor of futurism and literal interpretation is that even if one takes the symbolical approach to the text, the fact that Israel is rescued—not judged—in the Olivet discourse (except Luke 21:20–24) is unavoidable and thus a *fatal* blow to preterism. Further, this supports the plain reading of the entire Olivet discourse, which leads to the futurist understanding of the Tribulation.

Days of Vengeance

Further support that Luke 21:20–24 is a prophecy of judgment upon Israel two thousand years ago is seen in two key statements made in verse 22. Those first-century days are called "days of vengeance," for Jerusalem is under the divine judgment of covenantal sanctions recorded in Leviticus 26 and Deuteronomy 28. Luke notes that God's vengeance upon His elect nation is "in order that all things which are written may be fulfilled." Jesus is telling the nation that God will fulfill all the curses of the Mosaic covenant because of Israel's disobedience. He will not relent and merely bring to pass a partial fulfillment of His vengeance. Some of the passages that Jesus says will be fulfilled include the following: Leviticus 26:27–33; Deuteronomy 28:49–68; 32:19–27; 1 Kings 9:1–9; Jeremiah 6:1–8; 26:1–9; Daniel 9:26; Hosea 8:1–10:15; Micah 3:12; Zechariah 11:6. In an obvious prediction of Israel's rejection of Jesus as their Shepherd, the prophet announces an equally specific judgment against Israel that was fulfilled in A.D. 70.

> *"For I shall no longer have pity on the inhabitants of the land,"*
> *declares the LORD; "but behold, I shall cause the men to fall,*
> *each into another's power and into the power of his king; and*
> *they will strike the land, and I shall not deliver them from*
> *their power" (Zech. 11:6).*

Once again, Israel was not delivered in the first-century judgment, but in the future she will indeed be delivered from a similar setting (see Zech. 12:8; 14:3).

Great Distress

Another important contrast should be noted in Luke 21:23, where believers are instructed to flee from Jerusalem, "for there will be great distress upon the land, and wrath to this people." Dr. Bock notes the differences between the A.D. 70 judgment spoken of in this passage with similar language in Matthew and Mark that speak in a greater way about the future Tribulation.

> The parallels, which focus on the end-time, are longer. Matthew 24:19–21 equals Luke in almost the exact same terms (Luke lacks δέ [de, but] and uses ἀνάγκη [anankē] for suffering [as opposed to Matthew's θλίψις [thlipsis], distress, Tribulation]), and Mark 13:17 agrees verbally with Matt. 24:19. But Mark 13:18–19 = Matt. 24:20–21 goes on to speak about praying that the situation not develop in winter or on a Sabbath (the latter only in Matthew). Matthew speaks uniquely of "your flight" (ἡ φυγὴ ὑμῶν, [hē phygē hymōn]), while the subject of γενήται (genētai, happen) in Mark is unspecified. In contrast to Luke's general remark about distress, Matthew and Mark speak of unprecedented Tribulation (with Matthew calling it "Great Tribulation") and that no time is like it either before or after, thus showing their focus on the end-time. Attempts to apply this remark to A.D. 70 and make it rhetorical fail to come to grips with the unique judgment in view here, something that Jesus brings with his physical return.[5]

Interestingly the destruction of Jerusalem by the Romans is not called "Tribulation" but rather "distress" in Luke. On the other hand, those passages in Matthew and Mark that futurists argue refer to the future Tribulation are characterized as "Tribulation."

Times of the Gentiles

Three key events are noted in Luke 21:24. First, the Jews "will fall by the edge of the sword," which was clearly fulfilled by the Romans in the first century, but is contrasted with their deliverance in Tribulation passages. Josephus estimates that 1.1 million Jews were killed during this time. Second, these Jews "will be led captive into all the nations," which also was fulfilled in A.D. 70. Josephus says ninety-seven thousand captives were taken to Egypt and sold into slavery throughout the world, beginning what has been come to be known as "the Diaspora." Third, "Jerusalem will be trampled underfoot by the Gentiles until the time of the Gentiles be fulfilled." This prophecy began to be fulfilled in the first century and continues into our own day. This is descriptive of the Gentile domination of Jerusalem imposed by the Roman conquest that has been in place for almost two thousand years. However, it does speak about an end of the times of the Gentiles, which prepares the way for the context of Luke 21:25–28, which refers to a future tribulation period from which Israel will be delivered.

Dr. Bock makes the following observations about this passage:

> Because of his focus on the near future, Luke lacks reference to cutting short these days to spare the elect (Matt. 24:22 = Mark 13:20; see Isa. 54:7). . . . More intriguing is the note that Jerusalem remains trodden down until "the time of the Gentiles" are fulfilled . . . This phrase suggests three things. First, the city's fall is of limited duration, or why else mention a time limit? Second, there is a period of God's plan when Gentiles will dominate, which implies that the subsequent period is of a different nature (Ellis 1974: 245 says that the "times of the Gentiles" equals Gentile possession of Jerusalem that extends to the parousia; Zech. 8, 12–14). . . . But the question remains: Why describe this period this way unless there is an intended contrast between Israel and the Gentiles? . . . likely, the "times of the Gentiles" is a general way to describe the current period in God's plan, when Gentiles are prominent but that will culminate in judgment of those nations. . . . Third, it would thus seem that this view of Israelite judgment now but vindication later suggests what Paul also argues in Rom. 11:25–26: Israel has a future in God's plan. Israel will be grafted back in when the fullness of Gentiles leads it to respond (see also Rom. 11:11–12, 15, 30–32).[6]

A clear connection is established between Luke 21:24, which speaks about the current era of "the times of the Gentiles" being fulfilled and coming to an end, and Romans 11:25, which speaks about "the fullness of the Gentiles" having "come in." Both passages speak about Israel's redemption (Luke 21:28; Rom. 11:26–27). When we realize that the Old Testament pattern noted in the previous chapter says that Israel will pass through the Tribulation, repent toward the end when they recognize Jesus as the Messiah, experience conversion, and then the Second Coming will occur to rescue them from their enemies, it follows that "all Israel will be saved" (Rom. 11:26) in connection with the Tribulation. This is exactly the pattern of Luke 21:25–28. Preterist Kenneth L. Gentry Jr. believes the book of Romans teaches a future conversion of Israel, yet he does not associate it with the Tribulation (in contrast to Scripture, which repeatedly does). Dr. Gentry declares, "The future conversion of the Jews will conclude the fulfillment (Rom. 11:12–25)."[7] Yet only a futurist interpretation does justice to a harmonization of those passages that are clearly connected.

A Future Tribulation

The focus of Luke 21:25–28 indicates a distinct shift from the first-century description of verses 20–24. The differences include the local focus of Jerusalem in the first-century judgment versus the global perspective of the future Tribulation. The Tribulation will involve heavenly and global events that did not literally occur in A.D. 70. If preterists such as Dr. Gentry would interpret verses 25–28 in the same way they do verses 20–24, then they would see that the events of verses 25–28 are clearly global. And if these events are global, then they did not occur in the first century. And if these events did not occur in the first century, then they must take place in the future. In other words, these are *future* tribulation events that are prophesied by our Lord in this section of the passage.

Coming in a Cloud

In Acts 1, Luke records the final earthly event of our Lord, namely, Jesus' ascension to heaven. Two angels instructed Christ's disciples—who were "gazing intently into the sky" (v. 10)—that "this Jesus who has been taken up from you into heaven, will come in just the same way as you have watched Him go into heaven" (v. 11). This is a passage that even preterist Gentry believes refers to Christ's *future* Second Coming. "Here we have a clear and compelling reference to the Second Advent."[8]

One would think that such a clear and compelling statement about the Second Advent would lead to an understanding that Christ's triumphant departure in the Shechinah glory cloud (singular) to heaven in classic Old Testament fashion (reminiscent of Elijah) is reason enough to connect similar expressions to an equally victorious and global Second Coming. Instead, preterists want to make a symbol out of Christ's cloud coming in Luke 21:27 without a basis in the context. If this passage is a reference to a personal, literal coming to the earth, then it could not have happened in the first century and has to be a future event. If this is a future event, then it provides further support for a futurist understanding of the Tribulation, because the Second Coming at the end of the Tribulation is what is taught in this passage.

Dr. I. Howard Marshall says,

> Clouds may be a means of heavenly transport, but "cloud"
> (sing.) is an indication of the divine presence or rather of the
> glory which is associated with God and hides him from men
> (9:34 note); Luke's change here suggests that he is thinking of
> the Son of man accompanied by the glory of God (as the next
> part of the verse makes clear); there are links with 9:34f. and
> also with Acts 1:9 where Jesus ascends into a cloud, and it is
> prophesied that he will return in the same way (Acts 1:11).
> Perrin, 173f., notes that the change of word-order, as com-
> pared with Dn. 7:13, makes it clear that the cloud is associ-
> ated with the movement of the Son of man. . . . The original
> vision in Dn. refers to a coming to the earth (see Dn. 7:9, 22),
> and this is evidently what is meant here.[9]

Dr. Marshall gives further textual explanation for why this passage
is a description of the future return of Christ.

> On this view the cosmic phenomena described in the pre-
> ceding verses must be interpreted symbolically to refer to
> political disasters, and the gathering of the elect (Mk. 13:27)
> refers to the mission of the church. This interpretation de-
> serves careful attention, but it is exposed to various objec-
> tions. In particular it does not do justice to the language in
> Lk. where the cosmic signs cannot be interpreted as purely
> political events; there is no evidence that Dn. 7:13 was ap-
> plied to different stages of the vindication of the Son of man,
> and nothing in the context leads us to believe that an unusual
> sense is to be found here; in fact the clear temporal sequence
> (Mk. 13:24, 26) suggests that an event *after* the fall of Jerusa-
> lem is in mind. The solution is an attempt to deal with the
> problem that the parousia appears to follow immediately af-
> ter the fall of Jerusalem, an impression which is more pro-
> nounced in Mk. and Mt. than in Lk. where the 'times of the
> nations' intervene.[10]

This Generation

There is no more important passage for the preterist in his attempt
to refute futurism than those containing the phrase "this generation will
not pass away until all things take place" (Luke 21:32; see Matt. 24:34;
Mark 13:30). Gary DeMar writes, "Luke's account of the Olivet
Discourse confirms that the generation Jesus had in mind was the

generation to whom He was speaking."[11] Dr. Gentry contends that "the key to understanding the Great Tribulation in Matthew 24 is the *time statement* in verse 34. . . . This is *the* statement that must be reckoned with by the futurist or historicist viewpoints."[12]

I believe that the best interpretation of "this generation" in Luke 21:32 and in the two parallel passages is one I voiced about ten years ago.

> Instead, "this generation" is governed by its connection to verse 34. The qualifying factor is that this generation would "not pass away until all these things take place." Since the phrase "all these things" governs the timing of "this generation" (regardless of how it has been used in other contexts), one has to determine what "all these things" are and when they will be fulfilled. Then we will know whether "this generation" referred to those in Christ's day or to a future generation. Our position is that this generation is not the generation to whom Christ is speaking, but the generation to whom the signs will become evident.[13]

Dr. Bock concurs:

> What Jesus is saying is that the generation that sees the beginning of the end, also sees its end. When the signs come, they will proceed quickly; they will not drag on for many generations. It will happen within a generation. . . . The tradition reflected in Revelation shows that the consummation comes very quickly once it comes. . . . Nonetheless, in the discourse's prophetic context, the remark comes after making comments about the nearness of the end *to certain signs*. As such it is the issue of the signs that controls the passage's force, making this view likely. If this view is correct, Jesus says that when the signs of the beginning of the end come, then the end will come relatively quickly, within a generation.[14]

Despite the preterist chorus that "this generation" has to refer to the first century, an alternate *literal* interpretation relates it to the timing of the fulfillment of other events in context. While it is true that other uses of "this generation" refer to Christ's contemporaries, that is because they are *historical* texts. The use of "this generation" in the Olivet discourse in the fig tree passages are *prophetic* texts. In fact, when one compares the historical use of "this generation" at the beginning of the Olivet discourse in Matthew 23:36 (which is an undisputed reference to A.D. 70) with the prophetic use in 24:34, a contrast is obvious. Jesus is contrasting the deliverance for Israel in 24:34 with the judgment of 23:36. Once again the question arises, "When was Israel rescued in A.D. 70?" They were not. Neither were "all these things" (vv. 33–34) fulfilled in the first century. These will all be fulfilled in the Tribulation, which will take place in the future.

The Book of Revelation

Futurists and preterists believe that *the* major passage in all Scripture dealing with the Tribulation is found in Revelation. Predictably, futurists believe that chapters 4–19 are a prophecy about the future Tribulation. "The futurist approach to [Revelation]," according to futurist Dr. Robert Thomas, "views the book as focusing on the last period(s) of world history and outlining the various events and their relationships to one another."[15] Equally predictable is the preterist belief that it was virtually all fulfilled by A.D. 70. The late David Chilton, a preterist, declares: "The Book of Revelation is not about the Second Coming of Christ. . . . the word 'coming' as used in the Book of Revelation never refers to the Second Coming. . . . the main focus of Revelation is upon events which were soon to take place."[16] Whether the Tribulation is past or future in Revelation depends upon the overall thrust of the book.

Global or Local?

Once again, debate revolves around whether the language of Revelation is global or merely symbolic of the local judgment upon Israel and Jerusalem in A.D. 70. Since preterists advocate a symbolic interpretation of Revelation, they thus admit that a plain reading of the text does not yield their local perspective of the book and thus does not support a preterist interpretation. This is tacit admission that a plain reading supports a global and thus a future understanding of Revelation. Moderate preterists would contend that Jesus Christ did not return to earth in A.D. 70. Thus, those passages in Revelation that speak about Christ's coming are merely symbolic of His presence acting through the Roman army to judge Israel. However, if they refer to a return of Christ to earth, then their fulfillment is yet future. Even moderate preterists do not believe that Christ returned to earth in the first century.

Coming in the Clouds

It is hard to understand how Dr. Gentry believes that passages such as Acts 1:11 and 1 Thessalonians 4:16–17 teach a future second coming of Christ to the earth, yet he does not believe that passages in Revelation 1:7; 19:11–21; 22:12, 20 also teach the Second Coming. Christ did teach that in A.D. 70, through the Romans, He would judge Israel for covenantal unfaithfulness. However, Jesus did not use "coming" language to denote that event. Christ did say that He would "come" again to the earth.

It appears that an important event such as Christ's return to planet earth (which is admitted by Gentry in at least two instances to involve the expressions "coming" and "clouds") would be our Lord's intent when mentioned elsewhere, such as in Revelation. Certainly the burden of proof to take such expressions in another way, as preterists contend, would be on those who think that it is a *symbol* for something else. As with any literature, the proof would be textual, not just an argument that it could, maybe, or might mean something else, which just happens to fit into the futurists' particular eschatology. If one argues, as does Dr. Gentry, that Revelation 1:7 is a *symbolic* coming in A.D. 70, then why can't the same be argued in Acts 1:11 and 1 Thessalonians 4:16–17, as extreme preterists contend? It makes better sense to stay with the church's *traditional* interpretation that passages such as Revelation 1:7 are global and thus future in orientation.

BEHOLD, HE IS COMING WITH [meta] THE CLOUDS *[Dan. 7:13], and every eye will see Him, even those who pierced Him; and all the tribes of the earth will mourn over Him [an allusion to Zech. 12:10]. Even so. Amen. (Revelation 1:7)*

Preterists argue for their interpretation from the following points:

"He is coming with the clouds" is said to be the New Testament employment of the Old Testament motif of the Divine Warrior as a "cloud Rider" who engages in acts of divine wrath and judgment upon people. Gentry sees God as "poetically portrayed in certain judgment scenes as *coming in the clouds* to wreak historical vengeance upon His enemies."[17] Gentry cites the following passages as examples of the Lord's cloud judgments: 2 Samuel 22:8, 10; Psalm 18:7–15; 68:4, 33; 97:2–9; 104:3; Isaiah 13:9; 19:1; 26:21; 30:27; Joel 2:1, 2; Micah 1:3; Nahum 1:2ff.; Zephaniah 1:14–15.[18] Gentry uses Isaiah 19:1 as an example to illustrate his understanding: "The burden against Egypt. Behold, the LORD rides on a swift cloud, and will come into Egypt; the idols of Egypt will totter at His presence, and the heart of Egypt will melt in its midst." Gentry notes,

This occurred in the Old Testament era, when the Assyrian king Esarhaddon conquered Egypt in 671 B.C. Obviously it is not to be understood as a literal riding upon a cloud, any more so than Psalm 68:4: "Sing to God, sing praises to His name; Extol Him who rides on the clouds, By His name YAH, and rejoice before Him." The New Testament picks up this apocalyptic judgment imagery when it speaks of Christ's coming in clouds of judgment *during history*.[19] (emphasis mine)

I do not have a problem with Gentry's understanding of these passages as they are used in their Old Testament context. However, I do have a problem with how he is applying them to the Revelation 1:7 context. Some observations need to be made about the Old Testament passages so that we can see the significant differences between them and the Revelation 1:7 context.

First, I would agree that the "clouds are frequently employed as symbols of divine wrath and judgment."[20] In fact, this is why the second coming of Christ is spoken of in cloud language, for that is the Lord's way of showing up in history, and the Second Coming is no exception. Thus, to say that it is similar to the way the Lord shows up in the Old Testament is not a valid reason to declare that Revelation 1:7 does not refer to the Second Coming.

Second, in these Old Testament passages, the cloud Rider is normally pictured as one who *rides* the cloud. Never is He said precisely to be "coming with the clouds" or "with clouds" as described in Revelation 1:7. He is pictured as riding the clouds, and judgment is mediated through the clouds.

Third, the Lord is always pictured as riding the clouds in judgment *in defense of Israel,* against her enemies, but never is He pictured as riding against His own people Israel, as preterists insist with their A.D. 70 fulfillment. When Babylon, for instance, is used by God as His instrument of calamity against Israel, the cloud motif is never used. The clouds of judgment appear to have begun in the Exodus when the Lord delivered and lead Israel through the cloud by day and the pillar of fire by night. This would reinforce the idea that the Lord rides in judgment *in defense of Israel,* against her enemies, but never is He pictured as riding against His own people Israel. The Lord shows up throughout the Bible in the form of His Shechinah glory, and the Second Coming is no exception.[21]

Finally, there is no doubt that the divine-warrior motif is used throughout the Bible to picture God's judgment. It makes sense that such a characterization would be useful to picture the Second Coming and our Lord's global judgment. Longman and Reid note:

The overture to John's development of the divine-warrior motif is found in Revelation 1:6–7. The seer first speaks in doxology of the Exodus-like redemption worked on behalf of God's people, freeing them from their sins by blood and making them, like Israel, "a kingdom of priests" (see Ex. 19:6). The attention then shifts to the coming of the cloud rider in an echo of Daniel 7.[22]

Just because there is a divine-warrior motif in Revelation 1:7 and other passages that have our Lord coming on a cloud does not mean that it will not be a literal future coming in history. In fact, it will be. Revelation 1:7 is global (not local) and thus future.

"Quickly" in Revelation

Preterists believe they are driven to a first-century fulfillment of Revelation because, like the Olivet discourse, it says that it will be fulfilled soon. If such were not the case, then a plain reading of the text and a futurist interpretation would follow by default. What Bible verses do preterists appeal to in an effort to support their understanding of Revelation? "One of the most helpful interpretive clues in Revelation is . . . the *contemporary expectation of the author* regarding the fulfillment of the prophecies. John clearly expects the *soon* fulfillment of his prophecy,"[23] says Gentry (emphasis mine).

Preterist Gary DeMar has collected what he calls the "timing" passages in Revelation, which lead him to believe that the fulfillment of the Apocalypse had to occur during the first century. These are:

1. The events "must **shortly** *(en tachei)* take place" (1:1).
2. "For the time is *near*" *(engys)* (1:3).
3. "I am coming to you **quickly** *(tachy)*" (2:16).
4. "I am coming **quickly** *(tachy)*" (3:11).
5. "The third woe is coming **quickly** *(tachy)*" (11:14).
6. "The things which must **shortly** *(en tachei)* take place" (22:6).
7. "Behold, I am coming **quickly** *(tachy)*" (22:7).
8. "For the time is **near** *(engys)* " (22:10).
9. "Behold, I am coming **quickly** *(tachy)*" (22:12).
10. "Yes, I am coming **quickly** *(tachy)*" (22:20).[24]

It appears presumptuous at the outset of the interpretative process that these verses are labeled "timing" passages by DeMar. The timing of a passage is determined by taking into account all the factors in a given text. I hope to show that these terms are more properly interpreted as *qualitative indicators* describing how Christ will return. How will He return? It will be "quickly" or "suddenly."

Without a doubt, the exegetical survival of the preterist position re-volves around the meaning of these passages. When they arrive at pas-sages that do not appear to harmonize with their view, if taken plainly, they commonly revert to their "timing" Scripture texts and say, "What-ever this passage means, we have already established that it had to be fulfilled within the first century." In accordance with this belief, they search first-century "newspapers" for an event that comprises the clos-est fit to the passage and usually cite it as a fulfillment of the biblical text in discussion.

The Tachos *Word Group*

It is important to note from the outset that most words in the Greek New Testament usually have a range of usage and meaning. The mean-ings of words are discovered through studying how they are used in the various contexts that surround them. Therefore, if disagreement arises over how a word is used in a particular passage, the context of the passage must be the basis for determining exactly which nuance of meaning the Bible intends.

The Greek word *tachos* and its family of related words can be used to mean "soon" or "shortly," as preterists believe (relating to time), or it can be used to mean "quickly" or "suddenly," as many futurists con-tend (relating to the manner in which action occurs). The *tachos* fam-ily is attested in the Bible as referring to both possibilities. On the one hand, 1 Timothy 3:14 is a timing passage: "I am writing these things to you, hoping to come to you before long." On the other hand, Acts 22:18 is descriptive of the manner in which the action takes place: "and I saw Him saying to me, 'Make haste, and get out of Jerusalem quickly, because they will not accept your testimony about Me.'"

The "timing interpretation" of the preterists teaches that, based on the *tachos* word family used in Revelation (1:1; 2:16; 3:11; 11:14; 22:6, 7, 12, 20), Christ came in judgment upon Israel through the Roman army in the events surrounding the A.D. 70 destruction of Jerusalem. But how would the "manner interpretation" of the futurist understand the use of the *tachos* family in Revelation? Futurist John Walvoord explains:

> That which Daniel declared would occur "in the latter days" is here described as "shortly" (Gr., *en tachei*), that is, "quickly or suddenly coming to pass," indicating rapidity of execution after the beginning takes place. The idea is not that the event may occur soon, but that when it does, it will be sudden (see Luke 18:8; Acts 12:7; 22:18; 25:4; Rom. 16:20). A similar word, *tachys,* is translated "quickly" seven times in Revela-tion (2:5, 16; 3:11; 11:14; 22:7, 12, 20).[25]

Gentry is correct to note universal agreement among lexicons as to the general meaning of the *tachos* word family,[26] but these lexicographers generally do not support the preterist interpretation. Gentry's presentation of the lexical evidence is skewed, and thus his conclusions are faulty in his effort to support a preterist interpretation of the *tachos* word family. We now turn to an examination of how the *tachos* word family is used in Revelation.

Support for the Futurist Interpretation

1. *The lexical use.* The leading Greek lexicon in our day is Bauer, Arndt, and Gingrich (BAG),[27] which lists the following definitions for *tachos:* "speed, quickness, swiftness, haste" (814). The two times that this noun appears in Revelation (1:1; 22:6), it is coupled with the preposition *en*, causing this phrase to function grammatically as an adverb that indicates the "sudden" manner in which these events will occur.[28] They will take place "swiftly." The other word in the *tachos* family used in Revelation as an adverb is *tachy*, which occurs all six times with the verb *erchomai*, "to come" (2:16; 3:11; 11:14; 22:7, 12, 20). BAG gives as its meaning "quick, swift, speedy" (814) and specifically classifies all six uses in Revelation as meaning "without delay, quickly, at once" (815). Thus, contrary to the timing assumption of preterists such as DeMar and Gentry, who take every occurrence as a reference to timing, BAG (the other lexicons also agree) recommends a translation that is *descriptive* of the manner in which events will happen (Rev. 2:16; 3:11; 11:14; 22:7, 12, 20).

A descriptive use of *tachos* is also supported by the over sixty times it is cited as the prefix making up a compound word, according to the mother of all Greek lexicons, Liddell and Scott (1762). G. H. Lang gives the following example:

> *tachy* does not mean *soon* but *swiftly*. It indicates rapidity of action, as is well seen in its accurate use in the medical compound *tachycardia* (*tachy* and *kardia* = *the heart*), which does not mean that the heart will beat *soon*, but that it is beating *rapidly*. Of course, the swift action may take place at the very same time, as in Mt 28:7–8: "Go *quickly* and tell His disciples . . . and they departed *quickly* from the tomb": but the thought is not that they did not loiter, but that their movement was swift. Thus here also. If the Lord be regarded as speaking in the day when John lived, then He did not mean that He was returning *soon*, but swiftly and suddenly whenever the time should have arrived . . . it is the swiftness of His movement that the word emphasizes.[29]

2. *The grammatical use.* Just as BAG is the leading lexicon in our day, the most authoritative Greek grammar was produced by Blass, Debrunner, and Funk (Blass-Debrunner).[30] Blass-Debrunner, in the section on adverbs, lists four categories: (1) adverbs of manner; (2) adverbs of place; (3) adverbs of time; and (4) correlative adverbs (55–57). The *tachos* family is used as the major example under the classification of "adverbs of manner." No example from the *tachos* family is listed under "adverbs of time." In a related citation, Blass-Debrunner classifies *en tachei* as an example of "manner," Luke 18:8 (118). Greek scholar Nigel Turner also supports this adverbial sense as meaning "quickly."[31]

Not only is there a preponderance of lexical support for understanding the *tachos* family as including the notion of "quickly" or "suddenly," there also is further support that all the occurrences in Revelation are adverbs of manner. These terms are not descriptive of *when* the events will occur and our Lord will come, but rather, they are descriptive of the *manner* in which the events will take place (regardless of when they will occur). These adverbial phrases in Revelation can more accurately be translated "with swiftness, quickly, all at once, in a rapid pace [when it takes place]."[32]

3. *The Old Testament (LXX) use.* It is significant to note that the Septuagint uses *tachos* in passages that, even by the most conservative estimations, could not have occurred for hundreds or even thousands of years. For example, Isaiah 13:22 says, "Her (Israel's) fateful time also will *soon* come." This was written around 700 B.C. and foretold the destruction of Babylon, which occurred in 539 B.C. Similarly, Isaiah 5:26 speaks about the manner, not the time frame, by which the Assyrian invasion of Israel "will come with speed swiftly." Isaiah 51:5 says, "My righteousness is near, My salvation has gone forth, and My arms will judge the peoples; the coastlands will wait for Me, and for My arm they will wait expectantly." This passage probably will be fulfilled in the millennium; but no interpreter would place it sooner than Christ's first coming (at least seven hundred years after it was given). Isaiah 58:8 speaks about Israel's recovery as "speedily spring(ing) forth." If it is a "timing passage," then the earliest it could have happened is seven hundred years later, but most likely it has yet to occur. Many other citations in the Septuagint from the *tachos* family can be noted in support of the futurist interpretation of the usage in Revelation.

4. *The date of Revelation.* Gentry ends his presentation of the *tachos* word group by quoting a summary conclusion from Greek scholar and historian Kurt Aland, apparently thinking that Aland's statements support the preterist position.[33] Though Aland says that *tachy* "does

not mean 'soon,' in the sense of 'sometime,' but rather 'now,' 'immediately,'"[34] it does not support the preterist view for the following reasons.

First, Aland clearly understands Revelation's language as a reference to the yet future, bodily return of the Lord, not a stealth "coming" in judgment upon Jerusalem through the Romans, as argued by preterists. This is clear from reading his entire paragraph.

Second, Gentry's *selective* quotation did not contain the fact that in a preceding statement Aland says that Revelation was "written about the year 96."[35] If this is true, it renders the preterist interpretation impossible, for Revelation is a prophecy about a future event. Aland's understanding of *tachy* applies to the Second Coming. "It was the confident expectation of the first generations that the end of the world was not only near," says Aland, "but that it had really already come. It was the definite conviction not only of Paul, but of all Christians of that time, that they themselves would experience the return of the Lord."[36] Thus, Aland's interpretation of *tachy* better supports a futurist rather than the preterist understanding.

Third, at the end of the section from which Gentry quoted, Aland lectures his readers against the thought of the postponement of the Parousia (which is contrary to what modern preterism advocates).

> As soon as the thought of a postponement of the Parousia was uttered once—and indeed not only incidentally, but thoroughly presented in an entire writing—it developed its own life and power. At first, people looked at it as only a brief postponement, as the Shepherd of Hermas clearly expresses. But soon, as the end of the world did not occur, it was conceived of as a longer and longer period, until finally—this is today's situation—nothing but the thought of a postponement exists in people's consciousness. Hardly any longer is there the thought of the possibility of an imminent Parousia. Today we live with the presumption—I would almost say *from* the presumption—that this world is going to continue; it dominates our consciousness. Practically, we no longer speak about a postponement, but only seldom does the idea of the end of the world and the Lord's return for judgment even occur to us; rather, it is pushed aside as annoying and disturbing—in contrast to the times when faith was alive. It is very characteristic that in ages when the church flourishes, the expectation of the end revives—we think of Luther; we think of Pietism. If we judge our present time by its expectation of the future, our judgment can only be a very negative one.[37]

The majority of scholars today think it unlikely that Revelation was written before A.D. 70. Instead, they favor the A.D. 95–96 date. This being the case, an interpretation such as we have put forth would be required of the *táchos* family in Revelation, for it would have to refer to a future event.

    5. A "timing" interpretation would require an A.D. 70 fulfillment of the entire book of Revelation. In 22:6 we read, "And he said to me, 'These words are faithful and true'; and the Lord, the God of the spirits of the prophets, sent His angel to show to His bond-servants the things which must shortly *[tachos]* take place." This is passage #6 from DeMar's list of "time indicators" for Revelation, as noted above. However, Gentry cites Revelation 20:7–9 as a reference to the yet future Second Coming.[38] This creates a contradiction within Gentry's brand of preterism. Since 22:6 is a statement referring to the whole book of Revelation, it would be impossible to take *tachos* as a reference to A.D. 70 (as Gentry does) and at the same time hold that 20:7–9 teaches the Second Coming. Gentry must either adopt a view similar to futurism or shift to the extreme preterist view that understands the entire book of Revelation as past history, thus eliminating any future Second Coming and resurrection.

Literal Interpretation

    Preterist Gary DeMar mocks the futurist view because of our belief that it is the product of a consistent literal interpretation of the Bible and the correct approach to biblical interpretation. DeMar asks, "How consistent are dispensationalists in following the 'literal, plain, or normal' hermeneutical model when they deny the 'literal, plain, or normal' interpretation of 'near,' 'shortly,' and 'quickly'"?[39] In response, note that we do not deny or fail to use a consistent literal interpretation simply because we do not agree with DeMar's "timing" interpretation. By presenting his "timing" interpretation as the only possible literal approach, DeMar attacks and defeats a straw man constructed out of his own mischaracterization of the literal hermeneutic. He equates rejection of his "timing" interpretation as equivalent to a departure from a literal hermeneutic. He then boldly proclaims, "any student of the Bible who does not interpret these time texts to mean anything other than 'close at hand' is in jeopardy of denying the integrity of the Bible."[40] This is clearly not the case. He ignores other possible *literal* interpretative options. Our *manner* interpretation *is* a literal interpretation that we think *best* fits the passage for the reasons cited above.

    Another error made by DeMar in his interpretative process is his assumption that any time a form of *táchos* is used in the Bible, it has to be understood as a "time text." "The use of 'quickly' in other contexts will show that 'quickly' has but one meaning."[41] DeMar cites five examples that he believes proves his point.

- John 11:29: "She arose *quickly,* and was coming to him."
- John 11:31: "Mary rose up *quickly* and went out."
- John 13:27: "'What you do, do *quickly.*'"
- Revelation 3:11: "I am coming *quickly.*"
- Revelation 11:14: "The second woe is past; behold, the third woe is coming *quickly.*"[42]

DeMar then draws the following conclusion:

> If the time texts are understood in their "plain sense," then there are only two possible meanings: (1) John was mistaken and the Bible is filled with unreliable information, an unacceptable position; or (2) the events described therein came to pass soon after the prophecy was given.[43]

DeMar incorrectly labels these passages of Scripture as "time texts," for he has not properly interpreted them. I contend that they can be literally and plainly understood as emphasizing the *manner* in which or *how* an action takes place. "She arose quickly" simply means that Mary rose up quickly;" likewise, "do quickly" and "coming quickly" can easily be interpreted using a literal hermeneutic as calling attention to the *manner* in which something was done. It is true that these actions all came about "soon" after the prophecy was given, but that is understood from the context, not simply because of the use of "quickly."

Conclusion

It should be clear by now that the best understanding of how the *tachos* family is used in Revelation relates to the *manner* in which something will be done and *not to the timing* of the event. Thus, these eight adverbs carry the meaning that when Christ comes or certain events begin to happen, they will occur in a "quick manner," "all at once," "suddenly," or "at a rapid pace." "When the terror begins, the events will tumble," notes Mal Couch. "No one will have an opportunity to catch his breath or gain balance. The mighty, the leaders, and the common man will be swept away in the torrent of judgment."[44]

The late J. Barton Payne, who was not a futurist, has correctly noted the following:

In the last book of Scripture, Christ reiterates, "Behold, I come quickly" (Rev. 22:7, 12; see 3:11, 22:20), where the Greek adverb *tachy* means, not "soon," but "swiftly, all at once," that is before one can be aware and make preparations. . . . Does this mean then that it could be so soon as to happen right away, at any time? This is the thought that is associated with imminency, "ready to befall or overtake one."[45]

I believe the book of Revelation, through its use of the *tachos* family, teaches the doctrine of imminency (namely, that Christ could return for His church at any moment, but that He is not required to come soon). In fact, the New American Standard Bible translates a form of *táchos* in 2 Peter 1:14 with the English word "imminent." The New Testament believer is commanded many times to "eagerly wait for a Savior, the Lord Jesus Christ" (Phil. 3:20). The many different New Testament expressions of an expectant future return of our Lord are often encompassed by the theological term "imminence." John in Revelation uses the *tachos* family to teach imminence. But what about the two uses of "near" in Revelation?

"At Hand" in Revelation

Preterists contend that the twice-used phrase "the time is near" *(engys)* (Rev. 1:3; 22:10) demands a first-century fulfillment and justifies a non-futurist view of Revelation and the Tribulation. Gentry explains,

> How could such events so remotely stretched out into the future be "at hand"? But if the expected events were to occur within a period of from one to five years—as in the case with Revelation, if the book were written prior to A.D. 70—then all becomes clear.[46]

Just as "quickly" is used in Revelation to teach imminence, so also, "near" or "at hand" *(engys)* means imminency and thus does not support a first-century interpretation. Philip E. Hughes rightly says, "*the time is near,* that is to say, the time of fulfillment is imminent. This interval between the comings of Christ is the time of the last days, and the last of these last days is always impending."[47] William Newell calls it, "the nearness, the *next*-ness, the at-hand-ness, of its time is given by our Lord."[48]

The Meaning of Engys

Regardless of whether the preterist or futurist interpretation is correct, there is no disagreement about the basic meaning of *engys*. Gentry notes that it "is an adverb of time formed from two words: *en* ('in, at') and *guion* ('limb, hand'). Hence the meaning is literally 'at hand.'"[49] The disagreement between the two views concerns the event that is said to be at hand. Preterists say that it refers to the A.D. 70 judgment. In contrast, futurists believe that it refers to the "time of the end" that will culminate in Christ's bodily return.

It is true that *engys* can be and often is used to refer to something that takes place within a short span of time from when it is stated. Yet there are other instances when *engys* refers to something as "at hand," or "within reach"; but this does not mean that it must take place soon. An illustration from sports may help. A team may make it to the championship game. It may be said of that team that the championship is "at hand" or "within grasp." This does not mean that it is certain to come within a short period of time, just because it is at hand. Just ask the Buffalo Bills. The NFL championship has been "near" or "at hand" for a number of years for the Bills, but thus far it has yet to arrive.

The Kingdom of God Is "At Hand"

The same dynamics involved in the preterist versus futurist discussion are also seen in the meaning of the phrase "The kingdom . . . has drawn near" (a form of *engys*). The kingdom under discussion is the Davidic or messianic kingdom, not God's spiritual kingdom that has always been operative. Some think that "near" has the sense of "arrival." Others, including myself, see the sense as "close proximity."

I believe the Scriptures teach that Israel could have obtained her much-sought-after messianic kingdom by recognizing Jesus as the Messiah. We all know the sad reality—the Jews rejected Jesus. As a result, the kingdom is no longer near but postponed, awaiting Jewish belief, which will occur at the end of the Tribulation. However, during the intervening church age, which currently occupies history, there is the overhanging possibility that at any moment God will bring that last believer into His spiritual body, rapture the church, and resume Israel's final week (seven years) of history known as the Tribulation, which will induce the Jews' acceptance of Jesus as the Messiah.

Dallas Seminary professor Stanley Toussaint supports this interpretation in the following way:

> First, the hearers were to repent so that they could enter the kingdom when it arrived. This is clearly the emphasis of John's preaching in Matthew 3:7–12 (see Luke 3:7–17). . . . Those who expected to enter the future kingdom had to be prepared spiritually by repentance (see Ezek. 20:37–38). A second reason existed for the necessity of repentance: it was necessary

for Israel to repent for the kingdom to come. The fact that national repentance to allow the kingdom to come is also involved in these proclamations is clear from a number of passages. It is seen in the Lord's pronouncements of judgment on the cities of Chorazin, Bethsaida, and Capernaum (Matt. 11:20–24; Luke 10:13–15). The reason? They did not repent. In Matthew 12:41 Jesus said, "The men of Nineveh shall stand up with this generation at the judgment, and shall condemn it because they repented at the preaching of Jonah; and behold, something greater than Jonah is here" (see Luke 11:32). Because Israel did not repent, the kingdom could not come; instead the nation was doomed for judgment. Repentance is involved in and necessary for the coming of the kingdom (see Deut. 28:1–30:20; 2 Chron. 7:14; Ezek. 36:31; Hos. 5:14–15; 6:1–3; Zech. 12:10–14; Mal. 4:5–6). In addition, the concept of contingency in the proclamation of the proximity of the kingdom is clearly implied by other factors. . . . The amazing feature in all this is that the Lord predicted the kingdom of God will once again be near in the future during that great time of stress known as the Tribulation. In Luke 21:31 He prophesied, "Even so you, too, when you see these things happening, recognize that the kingdom of God is near." This is important, for it indicates that the kingdom is not now near. It was near; then it ceased to be near; in the future it will be near again. This strongly suggests that the kingdom was offered to Israel, but because the nation rejected its Messiah the kingdom was and is no longer near.[50]

I believe the language of the "at hand" passages in Revelation, in concert with "quickly," teach the notion of imminence. This makes good sense, especially in light of 22:10, which says, "Do not seal up the words of the prophecy of this book, for the time is near *(engys)*." To what is John referring? He has in mind a period of time from the book of Daniel. The phrase "time of the end" occurs five times in Daniel (8:17; 11:35, 40; 12:4, 9). The "time of the end" refers to Israel's final period of history, which Daniel was told to seal but John is told not to seal. Since 22:10 occurs at the end of the book and refers to the total message of Revelation, it is inconsistent to interpret part of the message as having already been fulfilled while another part is still future. It is better to see *engys* as a term that teaches the imminency of a period of time that could begin to happen without the warning of signs. F. C. Jennings explains:

In the one case the book is to be left open, "the time near;" in the other sealed up, for the time was still afar. . . . There is nothing to come between in the former—much in the latter. Nor do the words we are considering at all necessitate the immediate fulfillment of *all* the words. They do, however (what the Lord ever seeks), put us in the attitude of immediate and constant expectancy and watchfulness. Oh, look at time with God. "Long" will not be long then; any more than when we actually look back at it from eternity.[51]

The expectancy about which Jennings speaks is often labeled *imminence.*

Why Imminence?

A survey of the New Testament enables one to realize that there is an expectancy regarding the return of Christ and the consummation of His plan that is not found in the Old Testament. The passion of the Old Testament is for Israel to enter into her kingdom blessing with the Messiah. I think this is what Daniel was anticipating (Daniel 9) when he "observed in the books the number of years which was revealed as the word of the Lord to Jeremiah the prophet for the completion of the desolations of Jerusalem, namely, seventy years" (v. 2). The rest of the chapter conveys Daniel's desire to see the culmination of the plan of God in our Lord's kingdom reign. Daniel apparently thought that God would institute the messianic age upon Israel's return from their seventy–year captivity. However, God had other plans. As the rest of Daniel 9 reveals through an angel, God was stretching out Israel's history. It would not be seventy more years, but 70 times 7, or 490 years until the culmination of Israel's history in the kingdom.

When we come to the New Testament, we see the rejection of Jesus as Messiah by Israel and consequently the postponement of the kingdom. God is prolonging the time of Israel's kingdom. However, this time God promises that when the current age of grace comes to an end, the next period of time will include the restoration of the kingdom to Israel (Acts 1:6, 11; 3:19–21). Yet the length of our current church age is a mystery, part of the secret, unrevealed plan of God (Eph. 3:2–13). The length has been preordained by God, but He has not told us. Peter explains that the duration of this age is based upon our Lord's great patience (2 Peter 3:9), which has thus far been almost two thousand years long.

The whole outlook of this current age is built upon the imminency of our Lord's return, which will at last trigger the final week of years for which Daniel so longed. Therefore, the events of the book of

Revelation are said "to be at hand," that is, they are to be the next season
of events that will occur. God will not intervene with another new
program such as the church. We can be sure that the last phase of history
is the Tribulation leading up to the millennial kingdom. John Walvoord
is correct when he says:

> The expression "at hand" indicates nearness from the stand-
> point of prophetic revelation, not necessarily that the event
> will immediately occur. . . . The time period in which the tre-
> mendous consummation of the ages is to take place, accord-
> ing to John's instruction, is near. The indeterminate period
> assigned to the church is the last dispensation before end-time
> events and, in John's day as in ours, the end is always impend-
> ing because of the imminent return of Christ at the rapture
> with the ordered sequence of events to follow.[52]

Imminence in the Epistles

Revelation is not the only book to speak about future events as imminent and "at hand." Paul admonishes godly living in light of the fact
that the "night is almost gone, and the day is at hand" (Rom. 13:12).
Peter says, "The end of all things is at hand; therefore, be of sound
judgment and sober spirit for the purpose of prayer" (1 Peter 4:7). This
passage also makes the best sense when "at hand" is understood to
mean "overhanging," or "the next imminent event." Like Romans
13:12, this also means that the practical admonitions are still in effect,
for the end of all things has not yet come.

James joins the chorus of John, Paul, and Peter in his admonition
that "You too be patient; strengthen you hearts, for the coming of the
Lord is at hand" (James 5:8). Were believers supposed to be patient
only toward those who had wronged them until the destruction of
Jerusalem in A.D. 70? Of course not! This passage is speaking about a
still future return of our Lord. Because it is imminent, ongoing patience
is still required by believers in our day.

Conclusion

Preterists contend they are driven to their interpretation of a past
tribulation due to the meaning of "this generation" in the Olivet
discourse and "quickly" and "at hand" in Revelation. In their minds,
this justifies their nonliteral and symbolic handling of the text. This
turns the Tribulation from a global judgment of God centered on
Jerusalem (as a plain reading of the text requires) to a local event that
already took place in Israel alone. Additionally, preterists stand on end
the biblical statements about the Tribulation leading to the conversion

of Israel and the Lord's rescue of His elect at the Second Coming. Since we have relieved the interpretative compulsion they feel from "this generation," "quickly," and "at hand," there can no longer be a basis for avoiding a plain reading of the details of those passages. Once this approach is established, it is clear that the global scope of the Tribulation has not occurred and can be understood only as a future event.

A futurist understanding of the Tribulation is also the only view that makes sense of the Old Testament pattern of Bible prophecy. This pattern is reinforced in the New Testament by a literal—and thus futurist—interpretation. The future conversion of the Jews is brought about in history through various events that will transpire during the Tribulation, thus requiring both to be future events. The fact that the modern state of Israel was reconstituted in 1948 is historical verification that God is preparing the world for Tribulation events. This is the kind of development that futurists have taught for almost two thousand years would precede the beginning of the seven–year tribulation. The stage is set, and soon our Lord will bring to pass in history the events of a literal tribulation that will no doubt lay to rest forever the notion that the Tribulation is past. Dr. John Walvoord says,

> Of the many peculiar phenomena that characterize the present generation, few events can claim equal significance as far as biblical prophecy is concerned with that of the return of Israel to their land. It constitutes a preparation for the end of the age, the setting for the coming of the Lord for His church, and the fulfillment of Israel's prophetic destiny.[53]

Such development in the plan of God leads believers to rejoice in the *maranatha* hope. "He who testifies to these things says, 'Yes, I am coming quickly.' Amen. Come, Lord Jesus" (Rev. 22:20).

SECTION THREE

REBUTTALS

5

THE GREAT TRIBULATION IS PAST:

REBUTTAL

Thomas Ice

In this rebuttal section, I will provide direct interaction with Dr. Gentry's arguments found in this book. However, in addition, I also want to point out general weaknesses in the preterist approach to prophetic interpretation.

Preterism rises or falls upon whether the Tribulation is a past event. A first-century fulfillment of the Tribulation rises or falls, for preterists, on the meaning of their so-called "timing texts," which they believe provide the authority for extending this approach to include almost all the events of biblical prophecy. While the destruction of the temple and Jerusalem in A.D. 70 were certainly biblically prophesied events (see Deut. 28:64–68; Matt. 21–23), the preterist contention that the Olivet discourse, most of Revelation, and many other prophetic passages have been fulfilled falls considerably short of proving that this is what God meant in debated texts.

The "Time Texts"

This Generation

When challenged or threatened about the veracity of other interpretative details, preterists almost always fall back to what Gary DeMar calls the "time texts."[1] Their understanding of "this generation" (Matt. 24:34) in the Olivet discourse becomes, for them, the proof text that settles all arguments and justifies their fanciful interpretation of many other details found in Christ's discourse. Dr. Gentry is no exception when he says:

> We find the key to locating the Great Tribulation in history in
> Matthew 24:34: . . . This statement of Christ is indisputably
> clear—and absolutely demanding of a first-century fulfillment
> of the events in the preceding verses, including the Great Tribu-
> lation (v. 21) (pp. 26–27).

But does the phrase "this generation" in Matthew 24:34 demand a first-
century fulfillment? I do not believe it does. The passage in full says,
"'Truly I say to you, this generation will not pass away until all these
things take place.'"

First, I want to note that there is nothing in the Greek grammar of the
phrase ἡ γενεὰ αὕτη "this generation" that would disallow either Dr.
Gentry's or my interpretation. This is noted because some preterists say
that if Christ were referring to a future generation, He would have said
"that" instead of "this" generation. Not so! The timing of a passage is
determined by how words are used in a particular context. Thus, if one
is talking about something that will take place in the future, it is common to speak from the time perspective of the event. This is apparently
recognized by Dr. Gentry, for in earlier writings he declares,

> He employs the near demonstrative for the fulfillment of verses
> 2–34: These events will come upon *"this* generation." He uses
> the far demonstrative in 24:36 to point to the Second Advent:
> *"that* day."[2]

> Jesus clearly says that "all these things" will occur *before* "this
> generation" passes away. He employs the near demonstrative
> for the fulfillment of verses 2–34: these events will come upon
> *"this* generation." He uses the far demonstrative in 24:36 to
> point to the Second Advent: *"that* day" (emphasis original).[3]

Yet in this present work, Dr. Gentry does not restate his previous
inference. Perhaps he has come to correctly realize that his earlier statement is just an assertion that cannot be supported from the canons of
Greek grammar. The phrase "that day" in verse 36 refers grammatically to the previous section, namely, verses 32–35. Its referent is not
used as an ellipsis, as Dr. Gentry suggests, to an unmentioned second
advent of Christ. The sentence does refer to the Second Coming, but
that has already been introduced in the pervious section (vv. 26–35).
The parallel passage in Mark 13:32 supports the futurist view, for it is
clearly attached to the context of "the fig tree" illustration (vv. 28–32).
Matthew is using it to refer to the same event (the Second Coming),
not a first-century event.

Second, contextual surroundings determine the nuance of a specific word or phrase. It is true that every other use of "this generation" in Matthew (11:16; 12:41–42, 45; 23:36) refers to Christ's contemporaries, but that is determined by observation from each of their contexts, not from the phrase by itself. Thus, if the contextual factors in chapter 24 do not refer to A.D. 70 events, then the timing of the text would have to refer to the future. This is the futurist contention, namely, that the events described in chapter 24 did not occur in the first century. When were the Jews, who were under siege, rescued by the Lord in A.D. 70? They were not rescued; rather, they were judged, as noted in Luke 21:20–24. But Matthew 24 refers to a divine rescue of those who are under siege (24:29–31). This could not have been fulfilled during the first century due to the fact that the Jewish Christian community fled Jerusalem before the final siege. Matthew 24 refers to the deliverance of *all* Jews who are under siege. This did not happen under the first-century Roman siege.

The declaration just preceding Christ's "this generation" statement says, "even so you too, when you see all these things, recognize that He is near, *right* at the door" (Matt. 24:33, emphasis mine) The point of Christ's parable of the fig tree (vv. 32–35) is that all the events noted earlier in verses 4–31 are signs that tell those under siege that help is coming in the person of Christ at His return to rescue His people. In contradiction to this, preterists teach that "all these things" refer to the non-bodily, nonpersonal, coming of Christ through the Roman army in the first century. They are forced to say that the whole passage speaks about a coming of Christ via the events leading up to what Christ actually says will be His return. Yet, contrary to preterism, Christ says in the fig tree parable that preceding events instruct the reader to "recognize that He is near, *right* at the door." Had a first-century reader tried to apply a preterist understanding to chapter 24, it would have been too late for him to flee the city. They were told to flee the city when the siege first occurred, as noted in the first-century warning of Luke 21:20–24. Instead, the Jewish generation that sees "all these things" will be rescued, as noted in verses 27–28.

Dr. Randall Price has noted six major differences between the A.D. 70 temple and what would have to be another temple in another time.

The details of the progression of these latter events are given to us in the Gospels of Matthew and Mark. It is evident from Jesus' description of the times of the Gentiles in Matthew 24 and Mark 13 that things will go from bad to worse for Israel, culminating in a time of unparalleled Tribulation (Matt. 24:21; Mark 13:19). During this time Jesus speaks about a signal event connected with the Temple—its desecration by an abomination which was prophesied by the prophet Daniel (Matt. 24:15; Mark 13:14). What Temple is being spoken of here by Jesus? Was the Temple that was to be desecrated the same Temple as the one predicted to be destroyed? There are a number of contrasts within this text that indicate Jesus was talking about *two different* Temples:

(1) The Temple described in Matthew 24:15 is not said to be destroyed, only desecrated (see Rev. 11:2). By contrast, the Temple in Jesus' day (or Matthew 24:2) was to be completely leveled: "not one stone would be left standing on another" (Matt. 24:2; Mark 13:2; Luke 19:44).

(2) The Temple's desecration would be a signal for Jews to *escape* destruction (Matthew 24:16–18), "be saved" (Matthew 24:22), and experience the promised "redemption" (Luke 21:28). By contrast, the destruction of the Temple in Matthew 24:2 was a judgment "because you did not recognize the time of your visitation [Messiah's first advent]" (Luke 19:44b) and resulted in the Temple being level[ed] to the ground and your children [the Jews] within you" (Luke 19:44a).

(3) The generation of Jews that are alive at the time that the Temple is desecrated will expect Messiah's coming "immediately after" (Matthew 24:29), and are predicted to not pass away until they have experienced it (Matthew 24:34). By contrast, the generation of Jews who saw the Temple destroyed would pass away and two thousand years (to date) would pass without redemption.

(4) The text that Jesus cited concerning the Temple's desecration, Daniel 9:27, predicts that the one who desecrates this Temple will himself be destroyed. By contrast, those who destroyed the Temple in A.D. 70 (in fulfillment of Jesus' prediction)—the Roman emperor Vespasian and his son Titus—were not destroyed but returned to Rome in triumph carrying vessels from the destroyed Temple.

(5) The time "immediately after" (Matthew 24:29) the time of the Temple's desecration would see Israel's repentance (Matthew 24:30), followed by, as Matthew 23:29 implies, a restoration of the Temple. By contrast, the time following the destruction of the Temple only saw a "hardening" happen "to Israel," which is to last "until the fullness of the Gentiles has come in" (Romans 11:25), still two thousand years and counting.

(6) For the Temple that is desecrated, the scope is of a worldwide Tribulation "coming upon the world" (Luke 21:26;

compare Matthew 24:21–22; Mark 13:19–20), a global regathering of the Jewish people "from one end of the sky to the other" (Matthew 24:31; Mark 13:27), and a universal revelation of the Messiah at Israel's rescue (Matthew 24:30–31; Mark 13:26; Luke 21:26–27). This scope accords with the prophesied end-time battle for Jerusalem recorded in Zechariah 12–14, where "all nations of the earth will be gathered against it" (Zechariah 12:3). By contrast the A.D. 70 assault on Jerusalem predicted in Luke 21:20 is by the armies of one empire (Rome). Therefore, if there are two different attacks on Jerusalem, separated by more than 2,000 years, then two distinct Temples are considered in Matthew 24:1–2 and Matthew 24:15.[4]

The above points demonstrate that preterists fail in their attempt to cram still future prophecy into a past mold. Details of the Olivet discourse cannot be made to fit into a first-century fulfillment. Thus, "this generation" must refer to a future time when "all these things take place."

Dr. Gentry's Seven Arguments

Despite such difficulties, Dr. Gentry attempts to forge ahead with a first-century interpretation, as stated in a seven-point argument. He says, "I will offer a seven-point argument for interpreting the phrase 'this generation' at face value" (p. 28). The interpretative issue is not the "face value" meaning of the phrase "this generation" (for Dr. Gentry and I agree on the face value meaning of the phrase), but rather the time reference as determined by the surrounding context. There is no innate time reference latent within the phrase itself, as preterists often argue. Once again, the surrounding context determines the time reference of the phrase.

Dr. Gentry's First Argument

Dr. Gentry's first argument relates to matter that "the first-century temple is the focus of the disciples' question." This is clearly the case! But that does not mean that a later use of "this generation" must refer to Herod's temple. If such were the case, then the whole narrative in Matthew 24 should be taken to refer to the first century, as many preterists insist but Dr. Gentry does not. (Dr. Gentry understands Matthew 24:36–51 as a still future time resulting in a gap of at least two thousand years between the two events.) There are important breaks in the development of the narrative leading up to the Olivet discourse as follows:

(1.) Christ notes that the judgments of chapters 21–23 will fall upon "this generation" (23:36). Dr. Gentry and I agree that this was a prophecy about the first-century destruction of Herod's temple.

(2.) Christ then voices His concern for His wayward people in 23:37–39. Dr. Price explains:

> Even though Jesus announced to Jerusalem that "your house [the Temple] is being left to you desolate" (Matthew 23:38), He immediately adds, "For I say to you [Jerusalem], from now on you shall not see Me until you say, 'Blessed is He Who comes in the Name of the Lord'" (Matthew 23:39). Jesus' citation here is from Psalm 118, a psalm of thanksgiving sung when the people were in procession to the Temple. Note that Jesus put His words in the future tense by the use of the word "until." In other words, when the people of Jerusalem next see Jesus (and they will), it will be at the time they have turned to Him as Messiah (Zechariah 12:10). After that, the Temple will no longer be desolate—with the return of the Lord will come the return of His house.[5]

This proviso is a basis for Christ's later prediction in the Olivet discourse that Israel will one day be redeemed (24:29–31). But before that must come judgment.

(3.) Matthew 24:1–2 provides the next section leading up to the Olivet discourse. This section "begins with Jesus and His disciples viewing recent architectural additions to the Herodian Temple (verse 1). As they are leaving, Jesus uses the setting to announce the coming destruction of the Temple (verse 2)."[6] This event occurs as they are leaving the temple mount.

(4.) Some time later, the Olivet discourse begins with the disciples' question, "When will these things be, and what will be the sign of Your coming, and of the end of the age" (24:3)? Dr. Price says,

> The Gospel of Luke alone records Jesus' answer to the disciples' question as to when the destruction of the Temple ("these things") would occur. In Luke 21:20–24 He makes it clear that this disaster will not end the age nor bring the Messiah. Because it will be "the days of vengeance" (verse 22), it will begin the period of the Temple's desolation and the Messiah's absence—a time more specifically referred to in this passage as "the times of the Gentiles" (verse 24). Jesus again uses the word "until" here to assure them that *after* this time has run its determined course, Messiah will come and the age of Israel's national redemption will arrive (verses 27–28).[7]

We can see from the developments leading up to Christ's discourse that the first-century destruction of the temple was in view, but, at least in Christ's mind, so was Israel's future redemption (23:37–39). In fact, Christ will one day gather Israel "the way a hen gathers her chicks under her wings," when Israel is converted and becomes willing, which fits well with the Old Testament template for Israel's future. Christ says in 24:31 that "He will send forth His angels with A GREAT TRUMPET and THEY WILL GATHER TOGETHER His elect from the four winds, from one end of the sky to the other." The same Greek word, ἐπισυνάγω, is used in both passages. Of course, this did not happen in the first century. We see that our Lord set up the Olivet discourse with a focus upon the Herodian temple, but that He also held out a prophetic hope to Israel, which is something that the preterist interpretation does not.

The disciples, like preterists, erroneously thought that the destruction of the temple, the sign of Christ's coming, and the end of the age would be coterminous. "Yet if we make the reasonable assumption that in the disciples' mind their question as to the temple's destruction and the signs that will presage it are linked to the end of the age and Jesus' return (see 16:27–28; 23:39; Luke 19:11–27)," notes D. A. Carson, "there is little problem."[8] Dr. Stanley Toussaint adds,

> The disciples thought that the destruction of Jerusalem with its great temple would usher in the end of the age. The Lord separates the two ideas and warns the disciples against being deceived by the destruction of Jerusalem and other such ca-tastrophes. The razing of the temple and the presence of wars and rumors of wars do not necessarily signify the nearness of the end.[9]

The fact that the prophecy of the A.D. 70-temple destruction is in view is not a proof that "this generation" has to refer to the first cen-tury. By Dr. Gentry's own admission (p. 33), the same context includes a view to the Second Coming. Thus, the Olivet discourse could be about the future Second Coming and not the destruction of Herod's temple.

Dr. Gentry's Second Argument
Dr. Gentry's second argument says, "the first-century temple is, in fact, destroyed in Jesus' generation" (p. 29). This is not a disputed point between futurists and preterists. But it does not follow, contrary to what Dr. Gentry suggests, that since the first-century temple was destroyed it means "this generation" in Matthew 24:34 supports an A.D. 70 ful-fillment. In fact, in all three instances of the Olivet discourse (Matt. 24; Mark 13; Luke 21) the destruction of the temple is never mentioned,

though a discussion of its destruction precipitated Christ's sermon. Luke 21:20–24 is excepted, for both preterists and futurists believe it to have been fulfilled in A.D. 70.

Instead, the Olivet discourse closely parallels Zechariah 12–14, which refers to events in Jerusalem that take place during the future Tribulation period when Jerusalem is once again surrounded by armies. But this time "the LORD will go forth and fight against those nations, as when He fights on a day of battle" (14:3). Zechariah parallels the Olivet discourse, where the Lord rescues Israel from the armies of her enemies that have surrounded Jerusalem (see Matt. 24:29–31; Mark 13:24–27; Luke 21:27–28). Yet this aspect is absent from the preterist message.

Dr. Gentry's Third Argument

Dr. Gentry's third argument says, "the warning embedded in the prophecy indicates the primary focus of the events" (p. 31). What warning is Dr. Gentry referring to? "Then let those who are in Judea flee to the mountains" (Matt. 24:16). He comments, "This local coloring fits well with the temporally confined assertion that 'all these things' will happen in 'this generation' (vv. 33–34)" (p. 31). Once again, Dr. Gentry presents an "argument" that is not really an argument. This point does not support a first-century understanding of "this generation." The futurist viewpoint also has a Jerusalem-centered focus. Why, then, would this factor not equally argue for a future meaning of "this generation?" In reality, this point is a red herring and thus a nonfactor in determining the meaning of the debated phrase.

Dr. Gentry's Fourth Argument

Dr. Gentry's fourth argument says, "the same time designate indisputably applies to the scribes and Pharisees" (p. 31). Again, Dr. Gentry puts forth an "argument" that proves nothing. His statement of the argument assumes what he wants to prove. Supposedly by characterizing "this generation" as a "time designate," the phrase must then refer to the first century. Dr. Gentry next states that the disputed phrase refers to the scribes and Pharisees in Matthew 23—which it does— and then simply declares 24:34 to be a parallel phrase. But this is not proof; rather, it is mere assertion. As noted earlier, the context determines the time factor of "this generation," not merely the morphological fact that the same term is used in both passages. Since the precise context of chapter 23 is different than that of chapter 24, it does not follow that just because the phrases are the same, they must refer to the same thing.

Dr. Gentry's Fifth Argument

Dr. Gentry's fifth argument says, "the first mention of 'generation' in Matthew uses the Greek term in the sense of a life span" (p. 31). I am in total agreement with this point. Since Dr. Gentry does not attempt to further preterism in this argument, I have no further comment.

Dr. Gentry's Sixth Argument

Dr. Gentry's sixth argument says, "'generation' is used elsewhere in Matthew (and the other gospels) of those living in Christ's day" (p. 31). I am in agreement with Dr. Gentry on this point. Since the time relationship of "this generation" is dependent upon how it is used in 24:34, this is not a proof for its use there.

Dr. Gentry's Seventh Argument

Dr. Gentry's seventh argument says, "the phrase 'this generation' elsewhere in Matthew points to the contemporary generation of Christ's own day" (pp. 31–32). I am in agreement with Dr. Gentry on this point. It is true that the other passages cited by Dr. Gentry (Matt. 11:16; 12:4–45) refer to Christ's contemporaries, for the context of those passages support such a reading. However, I do not believe that such is the case in chapter 24 for reasons already stated. Thus, this point is no argument for Dr. Gentry's contention.

Other Arguments

I do not believe that Christ's Olivet discourse contains a single sentence, phrase, or term that *requires* a first-century fulfillment, except for Luke 21:20–24, as noted earlier. Since the timing of "this generation" is not innate in the phrase itself but is governed by its immediate context, which Dr. Gentry has demonstrated in arguments four, six, and seven, then I believe it refers to a future generation, for the events depicted have yet to take place. Dr. Gentry, along with other preterists, often commits the hermeneutical error of "illegitimate totality transfer." This error fits under the broad classification of taking a Scripture out of context. James Barr defines this hermeneutical blunder as follows:

> The error that arises, when the "meaning" of a word (understood as the total series of relations in which it is used in the literature) is read into a particular case as its sense and implication there, may be called "illegitimate totality transfer."[10]

Thus, just because a word has one meaning in all other passages, this does not imply that it will be used in the same way in another instance. Context is sovereign.

Dr. Gentry attempts an argument in which he claims that my futurist interpretation has an internal inconsistency.

> As I note above, though Dr. Ice denies Matthew 24 applies to the A.D. 70 events, he states that Luke 21 deals with A.D. 70. Interestingly, we find the same time designation in Luke 21 as we do in Matthew 24: "Truly I say to you, this generation will not pass away until all things take place" (Luke 21:32). Why should we not understand Matthew 24:34 in the same way? (p. 32).

Interestingly, Dr. Gentry holds that Luke 21:34–36 (note also parallel passages in Matt. 24:36–51 and Mark 13:32–37) refers to a yet future time. If I have a problem, then so would Dr. Gentry. But the answer to Dr. Gentry's question is provided in the flow of the context. Since Luke's account includes the answer to the disciples' question (Luke 21:20–24) about when there will come a time when "there will not be left one stone upon another which will not be torn down" (v. 6), multiple time references are necessary. This is evident in the wording of the question in verse 7.

The first part of the question—"when therefore will these things be?"—relates to the destruction of the temple in A.D. 70. This explains the first-century section in verses 20–24. Christ's answer to the disciples' second question—"what *will be* the sign when these things are about to take place?"—relates to "signs" preceding His Second Advent. This is a different event than that of their first question, and the event is still future to our day. The second question is answered in verses 25–28, which follows the long period of time described in the second half of verse 24—"Jerusalem will be trampled underfoot by the Gentiles until the times of the Gentiles be fulfilled." Thus, verse 32 ("this generation will not pass away until all things take place") will be fulfilled in the future, for the scope of "all these things" refers to verses 25–28, not verses 20–24. Dr. Arnold Fruchtenbaum explains:

> Then Jesus stated that the generation that sees this event, the abomination of desolation, will still be around when the Second Coming of Christ occurs three-and-a-half years later. . . . Verse 34 is intended to be a word of comfort in light of the world-wide attempt at Jewish destruction. It must be kept in mind that the abomination of desolation signals Satan's and the Antichrist's final attempt to destroy and exterminate the Jews. The fact that the Jewish generation will still be here when the Second Coming of Christ occurs shows that Satan's

attempt towards Jewish destruction will fail, and the Jewish saints of the second half of the tribulation can receive comfort from these words.[11]

Devil in the Details

A common response given by a politician to the media when they ask about specifics in an appropriations bill is that "the devil is in the details." Not only is the preterist "silver bullet" of "this generation" in error, but it also requires that the details of the Olivet discourse, the book of Revelation, and most other passages relating to the Tribulation to have a first-century fulfillment. It is not surprising that Dr. Gentry admits that his understanding of many of the details of Matthew 24 "appear contradictory to it" (p. 33). It is my contention that these details are in fact contradictory to the preterist position and thus require a future fulfillment.

In this book, Dr. Gentry has presented a first-century fulfillment exposition of verses 4–35. I will respond to selected portions of his exposition to show the error in the details of his preterist interpretation. I will not deal with items such as false Christs, wars, famine, and so on, for there were certainly events of that kind in the first century. However, they do not prove that the Tribulation is a past event. Other items from Dr. Gentry's commentary will be dealt with that show the impossibility of a first-century fulfillment.

Worldwide Witness

Matthew 24:14 says, "And this gospel of the kingdom shall be preached in the whole world for a witness to all the nations, and then the end shall come." Of course, Dr. Gentry says that this passage was fulfilled by A.D. 70, for other passages in the New Testament allegedly support such a view (pp. 44–45). Romans 1:8, 10:18, 16:19, and Colossians 1:6, 23 are cited by Dr. Gentry in support of the preterist view (pp. 44–45). But Matthew 24:14 does not support a preterist interpretation for the following reasons.

First, while it is true that "world" (οἰκουμένης) is used in the New Testament to refer to "the Roman Empire of the first century" (p. 44), its basic meaning is that of "the inhabited earth."[12] The word is a compound of the usual term for "world" (κόσμος) with the addition of a prefix from ὄικος, which means "house," thus the "inhabited" or "lived-in" part of the world. The inhabited world could refer to the Roman Empire, if supported by the context (for example, Luke 2:1), for Roman arrogance thought that nothing of significance existed outside of their realm. However, Acts 17:31 is surely speaking about the whole globe, for no individual will escape God's judgment. I think οἰκουμένης and κόσμος are used in basically the same ways, with their nuance (as always) being determined by the context.

Second, it is highly doubtful that the passages cited by Dr. Gentry from Romans and Colossians support a first-century fulfillment. Romans 10:18 is a quotation from Psalm 19:4, which was written about a thousand years before Paul and thus could hardly support a preterist view. Consider Romans 16:19, which says, "For the report of your obedience has reached to all." "All" in this context refers to those in the church. This is scarcely support for preterism. Romans 1:8 ("throughout the whole world") tells us that "News had spread to the entire empire of the presence of Christians in its capital city."[13] The two references in Colossians are used in a similar way, saying, in essence, that Christ's Great Commission (Matt. 28:19–20; Mark 16:15; Luke 24:47) was making progress, even in the first century. This is clear from the fact that Paul uses the Greek preposition "in" *(ἐν)* in all three passages (Rom. 1:8; Col. 1:6, 23) as a dative of sphere, telling us "the sphere or realm in which the word to which it is related takes place or exists."[14] This means that the three Pauline statements tell the reader that the gospel is spreading in or throughout the sphere of the whole world. James R. Gray explains:

> Paul's claim is to the universal appeal and scope of the gospel. That it is bearing fruit in the world—not that the gospel has been preached in all the world. . . . Paul is talking about the sphere of preaching, not that every creature was preached unto.[15]

These passages do not tell us that this process is complete and preparing the way for the A.D. 70 judgment, as preterists would lead us to believe. Instead, we learn that the evangelization of the world has only just begun in the first century and is making great progress.

Since "world" *(οἰκουμένης)* means "inhabited world," it depends upon what the inhabited world consists of at the time to which it refers. If it is a first-century focus, then it would likely mean the Roman empire. If it is a future reference, then the whole globe has become inhabited. Since the overall context supports a future time, then it should be understood as global—in other words, in every place where humanity inhabits the globe. In fact, Dr. Gentry does assign a global meaning to the phrase "all the nations" in Matthew 28:19.[16] Why should this not be the case for "all the nations" in 24:14 as well? "By implication the statement emphasizes the necessity of carrying out the great commission."[17] After all, both passages include an evangelistic commission. If Dr. Gentry's logic is followed, it would have required the total fulfillment of the Great Commission by A.D. 70. However, it is better to take both passages to include a future focus.

The final phrase in the passage is "and then the end shall come." This is a reference to end of the age about which the apostles ask the Lord (24:3). Three times Christ speaks about the end in His answer (vv. 6, 13–14). The context indicates that they all refer to the same time.

> Not the end of Jerusalem, . . . or of Judaism, or of the Jewish state; nor yet the end of the globe or habitable earth; but the end of 'the age,' 'the evil age,' the age that precedes the age or era of the Messiah's glorious presence and reign. In every other interpretation of the reference there is inextricable tanglement and inconsistency.[18]

Preterists are right to note the first-generation success of the spread of the gospel. However, such first-century attainments fall short of the greater global language of Matthew 24:14. This passage was no more fulfilled during the nativity of the church than was the Great Commission. The prophecy of 24:14 awaits a future fulfillment, specifically during the future Tribulation.

The Abomination of Desolation

Matthew 24:14 says, "Therefore when you see the abomination of desolation which was spoken of through Daniel the prophet, standing in the holy place (let the reader understand)." Predictably, Dr. Gentry believes that the famous "abomination of desolation" in 24:15 (see Mark 13:14) was fulfilled in the first-century destruction of Jerusalem (p. 45). Though there are similarities between the past destruction of Jerusalem and a future siege, there are enough differences to distinguish the two events.

One of Dr. Gentry's arguments for the preterist position rests on his confusion of Luke 21:20–24 with Matthew 24:15–22. I noted in chapter 2 that Luke 21:20–24 does refer to the A.D. 70 destruction of Jerusalem, but at the same time believe that all of Matthew 24 is still future. Before a determination can be made as to when the abomination of desolation is to occur in history, we need to examine what the Bible teaches concerning when this pivotal event is to occur.

The key passages that mention the phrase "abomination of desolation" are Daniel 9:27, 11:31, and 12:11. This is a technical phrase, which means that it has a precise and consistent meaning in all passages. The phrase refers to an act of abomination that renders something unclean (in this case the temple). Daniel 11:31 refers to an act that was fulfilled in history before the first coming of Christ. Dr. John Walvoord explains:

In Daniel 11:31, a prophecy was written by Daniel in the sixth century B. C. about a future Syrian ruler by the name of Antiochus Epiphanes who reigned over Syria 175–164 B. C., about 400 years after Daniel. History, of course, has recorded the reign of this man. In verse 31, Daniel prophesied about his activity: "they shall pollute the sanctuary of strength, and shall take away the daily sacrifice, and they shall place the abomination that maketh desolate." This would be very difficult to understand if it were not for the fact that it has already been fulfilled. Anyone can go back to the history of Antiochus Epiphanes and discover what he did, as recorded in the apocryphal books of 1 and 2 Maccabees. He was a great persecutor of the children of Israel and did his best to stamp out the Jewish religion and wanted to place in its stead a worship of Greek pagan gods. . . . One of the things he did was to stop animal sacrifices in the temple. He offered a sow, an unclean animal, on the altar in a deliberate attempt to desecrate and render it unholy for Jewish worship (see 1 Macc. 1:48). First Maccabees 1:54 specifically records that the abomination of desolation was set up, fulfilling Daniel 11:31. In the holy of holies, Antiochus set up a statue of a Greek god. . . . In keeping with the prophecy the daily sacrifices were stopped, the sanctuary was polluted, desolated, and made an abomination.[19]

This passage sets the pattern and provides the details concerning the abomination of desolation. Daniel 9:27 says that this abomination is to take place in the middle of a seven-year period. We read that "in the middle of the week he will put a stop to sacrifice and grain offering; and on the wing of abominations will come one who makes desolate." "In other words, the future prince will do at that time exactly what Antiochus did in the second century B.C."[20] But Daniel goes on to say that the one who commits this act will be destroyed three-and-a-half years later. Daniel 12:11 provides "the precise chronology."[21] The text says, "And from the time that the regular sacrifice is abolished, and the abomination of desolation is *set up,* there will be 1,290 days."

In addition to the three passages in Daniel, the two references by our Lord in Matthew and Luke, as well as 2 Thessalonians 2:4 and Revelation 13:14–15, also have this event in view. Therefore, the abomination of desolation, which the reader is to understand, includes the following elements:

1. It occurs in the Jewish temple in Jerusalem (Dan. 11:31; 2 Thess. 2:4).

2. It involves a person setting up a statue in place of the regular sacrifice in the holy of holies (Dan. 11:31; 12:11; Rev. 13:14–14).
3. This results in the cessation of the regular sacrifice (Dan. 9:27; 11:31; 12:11).
4. There will be a time of about three-and-one-half years between this event and another event and the end of the time period (Dan. 9:27; 12:11).
5. It involves an individual setting up a statue or image of himself so that he may be worshiped in place of God (Dan. 11:31; 2 Thess. 2:4; Rev. 13:14–15).
6. The image is made to come to life (Rev. 13:14).
7. A worship system of this false god is thus inaugurated (2 Thess. 2:4; Rev. 13:14–15).
8. At the end of this time period the individual who commits the act will himself be cut off (Dan. 9:27).

Despite this information about the abomination of desolation, Dr. Gentry identifies it as simply the Roman invasion and destruction of Jerusalem and the temple in A.D. 70 (pp. 47–48). Rather than going to Daniel for an understanding of what our Lord wanted the reader to understand, Dr. Gentry goes to Luke 21:20–22, with a little help from Josephus, to conclude that "Christ is warning about Jerusalem's devastation by military assault, not just the temple's desecration by profane acts" (p. 47). Let's see whether this interpretation measures up to the biblical explanation concerning the abomination of desolation.

As noted above, the Luke 21:20–24 passage does refer to the A. D. 70 destruction of Jerusalem. Therefore, when verse 20 says, "when you see Jerusalem surrounded by armies, then recognize that her desolation is at hand," it is describing in clear language the destruction of the holy city. This is vindicated by the language of the rest of the passage, especially verse 24, "and they will fall by the edge of the sword, and will be led captive into all the nations; and Jerusalem will be trampled underfoot." In context, the desolation is the destruction of Jerusalem, not the technical term relating to the temple (as Dr. Gentry suggests).

In contrast, the Matthew 24:15 passage has a context of its own that differs from the account in Luke. Matthew says, "when you see the abomination of desolation which was spoken of through Daniel the prophet [not Luke], *standing in the holy place.*" A comparison of the description in Matthew and Daniel with the passage in Luke yields significant differences, which proves that they are two separate events.

In the A.D. 70 destruction of Jerusalem there was:

1. No image set up in the holy place.
2. No requirement to worship the image.
3. No three-and-one-half year period of time between that event and the coming of Christ. This is especially true since the destruction of Jerusalem occurred at the end of the siege by Rome. It was over in a matter of days. D. A. Carson notes, "by the time the Romans had actually desecrated the temple in A.D. 70, it was too late for anyone in the city to flee."[22]
4. No image came to life and summoned people to worship it.

Josephus tells us that Titus did not want the temple burned, but that he wanted it spared. However, the Roman solders were so upset with the Jews that they disobeyed his orders and burned the temple anyway. All Titus was able to do was to go in and tour the holy place shortly before it was burned.[23] This does not agree with the biblical picture of the image to be set up on the altar in the middle of Daniel's seventieth week, resulting in cessation of the regular sacrifice and a rival worship system set up in its place for three-and-one-half years. Dr. Stanley Toussaint says,

> Because Christ specifically related the prophecy of the abomination of desolation to Daniel's prophecy, it seems best to see some correspondence between the abomination of desolation committed by Antiochus Epiphanes and that predicted by Christ. If this is so, it would entail not only defilement on the altar by sacrifices offered with impure hearts, but also an actual worship of another god using the temple as a means for such a dastardly act. Those preterists who agree with this take it to be the worship of the Roman standards in the temple precincts. However, if this interpretation is taken, Matthew 24:16–20 is difficult if not impossible to explain. By then it would be too late for the followers of the Lord Jesus to escape; the Romans had already taken the city by this time. If the abomination of desolation spoken by Daniel 9:27 and 12:11 is foreshadowed by Antiochus Epiphanes (11:31), it would be best to say it is a desecration carried out by a person who sacrilegiously uses the temple to promote the worship of a god other than Yahweh. This is what is anticipated in 2 Thessalonians 2.[24]

Another major dissimilarity between Dr. Gentry's preterism and Matthew 24 is that according to Matthew "neither the city nor the temple are destroyed, and thus the two situations stand in sharp contrast."[25] The Luke 21:20–24 reference does record the "days of vengeance" that befell Jerusalem. Let us look at some other details related to the fact that the future fulfillment of Matthew 24 is one in which Christ delivers the Jews rather than allowing them to be overtaken by their enemies, as in A.D. 70.

First, as Luke shifts from the A.D. 70 destruction of Jerusalem in 21:20–24, to the second coming of Christ in 21:25–28, he says in verse 28 to "straighten up and lift up your heads, because your redemption is drawing near." This is the language of deliverance from the threat of the nations, not a warning about the Jews' destruction. This language of deliverance is reflected in Zechariah 12–14, as noted in chapter 1. These three chapters of Zechariah include three important factors: (1) Jerusalem will be surrounded by the nations, who will seek to destroy the holy city (12:2–9; 14:2–7); (2) The Lord will fight for Israel and Jerusalem and defeat the nations, who have come up to lay siege against the city (14:1–8); (3) At this same time, the Lord will also save Israel from her sins and she will be converted to the Messiah—the Lord Jesus (12:9–14).

Factor one fits well into the language of Matthew 24. The nations have surrounded Jerusalem. It does *not* fit the A.D. 70 destruction of Jerusalem, for that was accomplished by one nation, namely, Rome. Zechariah 14:2 says, "I will gather *all the nations* against Jerusalem to battle."

Factor two also fits Matthew 24, but not the preterist view. Zechariah 14:3 says, "Then the Lord will go forth and fight against those nations, as when He fights on a day of battle." Matthew 24:22 speaks about God's intervention into the affairs of that time when it says, "unless those days had been cut short no life would have been saved; but for the sake of the elect those days shall be cut short." Luke 21:28 says to look up for the redemption that is near. This interventionist language parallels the Zechariah account, but not the A.D. 70 destruction of Jerusalem.

Factor three refers to the conversion of Israel. This certainly did not happen in A.D. 70, for the whole purpose of the destruction of Jerusalem at that time was due to the nation's rejection of the Messiah. As already cited above, the picture in the Gospels is one of conversion: the Jews are to "look up" to the advent of the Lord for their redemption. This occurs later when the elect are gathered from the four winds of the earth (Matt. 24:31). All the inhabitants of the Jewish nation are the ones under siege. It cannot be a reference to just the first-century Hebrew Christians, as Dr. Gentry supposes (pp. 48–50), for in the A.D. 70 event, the remnant had already fled the city by this point in the siege. Furthermore, Zechariah 14:5 describes the Lord as coming with all His holy ones. Verse 6 speaks of how "in that day there will be no light; the luminaries will dwindle." This is language similar to Matthew 24:29–31, which pictures the Lord coming in the clouds and darkening the light and luminaries to rescue His people and Jerusalem. There is no judgment here of the Jews; rather, there is a judgment of the armies that have laid siege to the holy city.

Further, Daniel 9:27 says that the one leading the siege of Jerusalem will himself be cut off; "even until a complete destruction, one that is decreed, is poured out on the one who makes desolate." This did not happen in A.D. 70. The Roman general Titus went back victoriously to Rome and lived a number of years after that noteworthy event. But Daniel 9:27 refers to one being cut off in the course of the siege.

There are great parallels between Matthew 24 and Zechariah 12–14. I believe that our Lord's discourse in Matthew 24 and the siege of Zechariah 12–14 refer to the same future event. Both prophesy a time when Jerusalem is surrounded by armies and the Lord moves to rescue His people and judge the invaders. Since Dr. Gentry wrongly attempts to equate Luke 21:20–24 with Matthew 24 (and thus, I believe, Zech. 12–14), I think it is helpful to note the differences between the two scenarios. Dr. Randall Price has provided the following helpful chart (Figure 6.1).

Despite a few similarities (such as both passages are set in Jerusalem, there is a Gentile siege, and so on), it is the differences that are determinative. Once again, we see that the events of Matthew 24 and the Tribulation have yet to occur.

The Great Tribulation

Matthew 24:21–22 says, "for then there will be a Great Tribulation, such as has not occurred since the beginning of the world until now, nor ever shall. And unless those days had been cut short, no life would have been saved; but for the sake of the elect those days shall be cut short." Predictably, Dr. Gentry (following the normal preterist approach) teaches that the Tribulation and the Great Tribulation are past, having occurred in the first century A.D. While admitting that this passage of Scripture "seems to preclude an A.D. 70 Great Tribulation" (p. 51), Dr. Gentry, however, insists that these verses have already be fulfilled. The core of Dr. Gentry's argument on this (and a number of other points) is that it had to have a first-century fulfillment. Thus, I believe, preterists have to find some explanation. Dr. Gentry asks, "Is the destruction of first-century Jerusalem a disaster 'such as has not occurred since the beginning of the world until now, nor ever shall'"? (p. 51). He concludes concerning this passage that "we should not interpret Christ's language literally after all. It is dramatic hyperbole, well justified by the gravity of the situation" (p. 53).

Contrasts Between Luke 21:20–24 and Zechariah 12–14

Luke 21:20–24	Zechariah 12–14
Past fulfillment—"led captive to all nations" (v. 24)	Eschatological fulfillment—"in that day" (12:3–4, 6, 8, 11; 13:1–12; 14:1, 4, 6–9)
Day of the desolation of Jerusalem (v. 20)	Day of deliverance of Jerusalem (12:7–8)
Day of vengeance against Jerusalem (v. 22)	Day of victory for Jerusalem (12:4–6)
Day of wrath against Jewish nation (v. 23)	Day of wrath against Gentile nations (12:9; 14:3, 12)
Jerusalem trampled by Gentiles (v. 24)	Jerusalem transformed by God (14:4–10)
Time of Gentile dominion over Jerusalem (v. 24)	Time of Gentile submission in Jerusalem (14:16–19)
Great distress upon the land (v. 23)	Great deliverance for the land (13:2)
Nations bring the sword to Jerusalem (v. 24)	Nations bring their wealth to Jerusalem (14:14)
Jerusalem destroyed (A.D. 70) "in order that all things which are written [concerning the Jewish people] may be fulfilled" (in the future; v. 22)	Jerusalem rescued *and redeemed* so that *all things* written (concerning the Jewish people) may be fulfilled (13:1–9); see Rom. 11:25–27
Jerusalem's desolation is given a time limit: "until the times of the Gentiles be fulfilled" (v. 24). This implies that a time of restoration for Jerusalem will then follow.	The attack on Jerusalem is the occasion for the final defeat of Israel's enemies, thus ending the "times of the Gentiles" (14:2–3, 11)
The Messiah comes in power and glory to be seen by the Jewish people only *after* "these things," namely, the events of vv. 25–28, which are yet future to the events of vv. 20–24.	The Messiah comes in power and glory *during* the events of the battle (14:4–5)[26]

Before I further address this issue, I want to deal with a statement
that Dr. Gentry makes in this section. He says, "The Lord is not referring to His Second Advent, or else we should wonder why His disciples should pray about fleeing from Judea (Matt. 24:16). What good
would running to the hills be at the return of Christ?" (p. 53). It is hard
to know where someone would come up with a point such as this. I
have never heard of a futurist who believes that this will occur "at the
return of Christ." Clearly, we believe that this will occur "in the middle
of the week" (Dan. 9:27), which is three-and-a-half years before the
Second Coming. Such a scenario does make sense in light of the biblical text. However, Dr. Gentry's "straw man" argument does not make
sense.

In support of his "prophetic hyperbole" argument, Dr. Gentry cites
Exodus 11:6, Ezekiel 5:9; 7:5–6, and Daniel 9:12 as examples of other
passages using similar language (pp. 52–53). Further, Dr. Gentry argues that the flood of Noah was a worse judgment than the one described in Matthew 24, for it "destroys the entire world except one
family" (p. 52). I believe there are a number of errors in the thinking
of Dr. Gentry (and other preterists) at this point. For instance, they gen-
eralize many of the specifics of a given text, which limits the scope of
these absolute descriptions. The passages that preterists cite are all limited in scope, not simply the greatest disaster of any time or place.
Several years ago I wrote to Hebrew Christian scholar Dr.
Fruchtenbaum and presented these same arguments made by Dr.
Gentry's fellow preterist Gary DeMar. Here is Dr. Fruchtenbaum's
response:

> As for Exodus 11:6, the focus here is specifically on one coun-
> try, which is the nation of Egypt. Furthermore, the verse is not
> saying that what happened with the ten plagues was the worst
> judgment that Egypt will ever experience and, therefore, the
> correlation between 14 million and 55 million is irrelevant.
> The text is saying that there was not such a great cry in all the
> land of Egypt in the past, nor will there be such a great cry in
> the land of Egypt in the future. The emphasis is not on the
> judgment itself but on the Egyptian response to the judgment.
> The first-born son of every Egyptian family died, but the re-
> mainder of the family was spared, and so every family was
> affected. In the tribulation, there is no need to assume that
> every family will be affected and, furthermore, rather than
> merely one or two members of the family, whole families might
> be destroyed; and if whole families are destroyed, there will
> be no one to mourn for that particular family. Another point is

that the Bible says that one quarter of the world's population will be destroyed. Because it mentions the world population in general, it does not mean that exactly twenty-five percent of the Egyptian population will be destroyed. In other words, whether we speak about twenty-five percent or seventy-five percent of the earth's population being destroyed, most of it is among the nations outside of the Middle East and, therefore, it will not effect Egypt to the same degree that it will affect, let's say, North America or Europe. Therefore, there might be a lot less death in Egypt than there would be elsewhere, and it still might be less than those who died in the tenth plague. In other words, Exodus 11:6 simply does not present such a great problem. Finally, concerning Ezekiel 5:9–10 . . . there are two implications. The first implication is that what happened in A.D. 70 was far more severe than what happened in 586 B.C. That point is true. But the point about Ezekiel 5:9 is that God, in this case, is going to perform a judgment of the type that He has not done before and will not do again; and the type of judgment is that one third will die by plague and famine, one third will die by the sword, and one third will be scattered to the four winds. It did not happen that way in A.D. 70, and it will not happen that way in the tribulation. What Ezekiel is describing is something that happened uniquely in the Babylonian destruction of Jerusalem when the inhabitants were equally divided into thirds, with two thirds dying in two different ways, and one third surviving, though under divine judgment and being scattered. No such three-fold division equally happened in A.D. 70. Even the tribulation (where it does mention in Zechariah 13:8–9 that two thirds will die and one third will survive) it does not say that the two thirds will die by sword and by famine in an equally divided two halves. Furthermore, the remaining surviving third is not under divine judgment and scattered, but rather they are saved and regathered. So, Ezekiel's words can be taken as literally true; what he said did happen to Jerusalem and was unique to the Babylonian destruction. The second implication is his statement under point 4: "The flood was obviously a greater tribulation." This is true as far as general tribulations are concerned. However, here we are dealing specifically with the Jewish people and Jerusalem. The focus of the flood was not on the Jewish people, for Jewish history had not begun as yet. Nor was the focus on Jerusalem, for that city had not existed yet. The Noahic flood destroyed the world in general and was the worst flood that ever was or will be. But Ezekiel's prophecy focuses specifically on the Jewish people and Jerusalem, which had not been nor will be destroyed by a flood. And while God will once again destroy the mass of humanity, according to Isaiah 24, it will not be by means of water but by means of fire. So, none of these "problems" that Gary DeMar is presenting are in any sense a great problem. They are all solvable, especially if we remain within the original context of the verses in question, and if we move carefully through the actual words and consider the things to which they are referring.[27]

Thus, these issues are not a problem, especially if one pays attention to the context that governs the words of these passages. But another objection can be raised to the preterist handling of these verses, as noted by Dr. Toussaint.

✦ However, the tribulation referred to in Matthew 24:21 is explained further in verse 22. "And unless those days had been cut short no life would have been saved; but for the sake of the elect those days shall be cut short." This verse must be considered along with verse 21. What is meant by "life" in the clause "no life would have been saved"? DeMar explains this as referring "to life in the land of Israel." The noun translated "life" is *sarx.* It should be noted, however, that the Greek construction is *pasa sarx,* or all flesh, a technical term that refers to all humanity. The following are all the occurrences of "all flesh" in the Greek New Testament text—Matthew 24:22; Mark 13:20; Luke 3:6; John 17:2; Acts 2:17; Romans 3:20; 1 Corinthians 1:29; 15:39; Galatians 2:16; 1 Peter 1:24. In every case, except 1 Corinthians 15:39, the expression describes all humans. In the passage, Paul is discussing the nature of the resurrection body: "All flesh is not the same flesh, but there is one flesh of men, and another of beasts." Here he is using it in an even broader sense, all human and animal life.

BAG takes *pasa sarx* to mean *every person, everyone.* With the negative they take it to mean *no person, nobody,* and list Matthew 24:22 and Mark 13:20 as instances of this meaning. The expression *pasa sarx* comes from the Septuagint, which in turn looks at the Hebraism *kol basar,* "all flesh." Gesenius says this Hebrew construction means "all living creatures . . . especially *all men,* the whole human race." Therefore, to interpret "all flesh" in Matthew 24:22 and Mark 13:20 as referring to Jews living in Judea in A.D. 70 is too limiting. "All flesh" describes all humanity. In other words, the tribulation described in Matthew 24:21 is of such huge proportions that human life stands in jeopardy on planet earth. This could not be said in A.D. 70, as horrible as the decimation of life was in Judea at that time. Matthew 24:21–22 must look beyond the past destruction of Jerusalem.[28]

It is quite clear that once again, if the plain meaning of the text is allowed to stand, then a first-century A.D. interpretation is precluded. Preterists must revert to sophistry in order to say why the text does not mean what it says so that they can suggest a meaning in support of their view. Interestingly, they tend to only take this approach with given passages that do not appear to support their thesis, but take other verses plainly that appear to support their views, even when figures of speech are embedded in the text. No, the Great Tribulation has not yet happened, but the world is now being prepared for this future time (2 Thess. 2:6–7).

Coming as Lightning

Matthew 24:27 says, "For just as the lightning comes from the east, and flashed even to the west, so shall the coming of the Son of Man be." Since Christ did not bodily return to earth in A.D. 70, Dr. Gentry and his fellow preterists are bound by their system to say that this verse "is a providential *judgment coming,* a Christ-directed judgment, rather than a miraculous visible bodily coming" (p. 53). Dr. Gentry continues, "it is not *Christ Himself* who is *corporally present.* Rather He directs the Roman armies by His providence" (p. 54). The logic of such an approach would demand that Christ comes many times every day through the vehicle of His providence. Yet, such an approach strips the hope of our Lord's actual return of significance. Instead of looking for a future event, preterist logic suggests that we should be seeking the many *mystical* comings of Christ.

There are a number of issues to be dealt with concerning this passage. For instance, Dr. Gentry compares Christ's coming in Matthew 24:27 with a statement to Israel's Sanhedrin in 26:63–64 "that they will 'see' His coming. Obviously, they are not still alive today! Jesus must be referring to an event in their first-century life spans" (p. 53). The preterist misuse of 26:63–64 is better explained as an event that will literally take place. The Sanhedrin will see Christ's glorious return, even if it is a few thousand years after their time, just as all people of all ages will see this event, regardless of whether they are alive. Paul says the same sort of thing in Philippians 2:9–11, namely, that all will bow the knee to Christ, regardless of whether they are alive at His moment of glorification. Paul says "that at the name of Jesus every knee should bow, of those who are in heaven, and on earth, and under the earth, and that every tongue should confess that Jesus Christ is Lord, to the glory of God the Father" (vv. 10–11). Further, it is likely that hardly any of the Sanhedrin would have lived another forty years to see a coming of Christ in the sense advocated by the preterists. Instead, Christ was saying that though He was in a position of humiliation before them, He would not always be that way. One day He will return as the same Jewish Messiah in power and great glory. The Sanhedrin (and all who are living on earth) will one day see this great event.

In all Dr. Gentry's effort to explain why "the coming of the Son of Man" in Matthew 24:27 is not a literal advent of Christ, Dr. Gentry fails to tell his readers that the Greek word παρουσία is used in this verse. Three of the four times that παρουσία is used in chapter 24, Dr. Gentry admits that it refers to the yet future Second Coming (p. 53). BAG says that παρουσία means "presence," "coming," "advent," and "of Christ, and nearly always of his messianic advent in glory to judge the world at the end of this age."[29] BAG cites all four uses of παρουσία in chapter 24 as a reference to Christ's second advent. In fact, BAG does not even recognize Dr. Gentry's stated meaning as a possible category. The *Theological Dictionary of the New Testament* (TDNT), in concert with BAG, tells us that the core idea of the word means "to be present," "denotes esp. active presence," "appearing."[30] TDNT describes παρουσία as a technical term "for the 'coming' of Christ in messianic glory."[31] Thus, παρουσία carries the idea of a "presence coming," contrary to the preterist notion of a "nonpresence coming," or an invisible coming. Our Lord's use of παρουσία demands His physical, bodily presence when He returns to earth at the Second Advent.

Dr. Toussaint provides further reasoning for the futurist understanding of παρουσία in this passage:

> "What will be the sign of your coming?" (Matt. 24:3). What does "coming" *(parousia)* mean? That term is filled with significance. This noun occurs four times in the Olivet Discourse (the only times Matthew uses *parousia* and the only occurrence in the Gospels). The first occurrence is in the question asked by the disciples. Very interestingly, the remaining three are in identical clauses, "thus, shall be the coming of the Son of Man" . . . (Matt. 24:27, 37, 39). . . . The problem with this interpretation is the meaning of *parousia* before verse 36 and after. If the coming of the Son of Man in Matthew 24:37, 39 is the Second Advent, one would expect *the identical clause* in

24:27 to refer to the same event. The word would also have the same meaning in 24:3. It must be the Second Advent in each case.

Furthermore, the word *parousia,* as found in the New Testament, is always used of an actual presence. It may be employed of the presence of persons, as in 1 Corinthians 16:17; 2 Corinthians 7:6–7; 10:10; Philippians 1:26; 2:12, and 2 Thessalonians 2:9. In each of these above cases the person is *bodily* present. In all the other cases, *parousia* is used of the Lord's presence at His Second Coming; see 1 Corinthians 15:23; 1 Thessalonians 2:19; 3:13; 4:15; 5:23; 2 Thessalonians 2:1, 8; James 5:7, 9; 2 Peter 1:16; 3:4, 12; 1 John 2:28. The only occurrences in the Gospel of *parousia* are in Matthew 24. It would seem that they, too, refer to a yet future coming of Christ.[32]

Dr. Gentry attempts to say that the "lightning" description in Matthew 24:27 "reflects the Roman armies marching toward Jerusalem from an easterly direction" (p. 54). It is hard to imagine that the time-consuming march of the Roman armies is the true interpretation of this passage. Once again, I follow Dr. Toussaint's explanation of the text.

What then is Matthew 24:27 saying? It is simply saying that people should not be misled by false teachers or counterfeit messiahs who make their deceptive claims in some wilderness or inner sanctum (24:26). They may even fortify their pretensions by fantastic miracles (24:24). The reason the Lord's followers should not be drawn aside is because the coming of the Lord Jesus will be so spectacular that no one will miss seeing it. It will be like a bolt of lightning that streaks from one horizon to the other. This is why the Lord used the correlatives *hosper. . . . houtos;* He is simply using an analogy or comparison. His Second Advent will be as obvious as a brilliant sky-spanning bolt of lightning. So will be the unmistakable and actual presence of the Lord Jesus Christ in His Second Coming to earth.[33]

Cosmic Disturbances

Matthew 24:29 says, "But immediately after the tribulation of those days THE SUN WILL BE DARKENED, AND THE MOON WILL NOT GIVE ITS LIGHT, AND THE STARS WILL FALL from the sky, and the powers of the heavens will be shaken." "Here we encounter remarkable cosmic disturbances that seem too catastrophic for applying to A.D. 70," says Dr. Gentry.

He believes that "this portrays historical divine judgment under the dramatic imagery of a universal catastrophe" (p. 55). How does he arrive at such a conclusion? "To understand it properly we must interpret it covenantally, which is to say biblically, rather than according to a presupposed simple literalism" (p. 55). Dr. Gentry believes that this verse "draws upon the imagery from Old Testament judgment passages that sound as if they are world-ending events" (p. 56). I wish that Dr. Gentry would draw upon the Old Testament prophetic pattern that I mentioned in chapter 1. Dr. Gentry admits that this passage sounds as if it did not occur in the first century A.D. This is why, by his own admission, he must introduce his particular theology as a factor for interpreting the text. (If *covenant* were a true synonym for *biblical,* why must he tell us?) Meanwhile, those following the normal canons of *sound* hermeneutics—the historical, grammatical, contextual approach—cannot find Dr. Gentry's view taught in the passage. Thus, since preterists erroneously believe that these events had to occur in the first century, they are forced to advocate views unsupported by the words, phrases, and context of the passage.

When I study the Old Testament figures that preterists insist refer to the passing of a great political power, I wonder how they know what the original figures mean? I do not see a textual basis either in the Old Testament or in Matthew 24. There are no biblical passages that establish the preterist use of these figures. In 1857, the Rev. D. D. Buck made the following hermeneutical points about interpreting Matthew 24:29:

> (1) The use of metaphoric language implies a knowledge or idea about what would be understood if such language were applied literally. No one ever uses figures without having in view the literal things from which the figures are derived. . . . If we say that Christianity is the sun of the world, it implies that we have a previous understanding of the nature and fact of the sun. (2) Now, whence did this ancient figurative use of the darkening of the luminaries arise? How did it happen that it was so common for the prophets to speak about ordinary, limited judgments, in language which all admit would, if used literally, apply to the general judgment? How became it so common to speak metaphorically about the darkening of the sun, moon, and stars, and the passing away of the heavens? Figures are the shadow of the literal. Where is the substance that originates the shadow? Metaphors are borrowed from literal speech. Where is the literal speech, and the revelation of the literal idea, of the blotting out of the bright heavens, and

the downfall of the world? (3) This question is to be settled by those who seize upon every reference to these great events, and pronounce them figurative. Will they please tell us where there is a spot in all the Bible where the literalist may plant his feet, and stand up in defense of orthodoxy, and give a philosophical explanation of the commonness of such language as appears to refer to the day of judgment?[34]

Matthew 24:29 is not a new revelation by our Lord. Old Testament passages such as Isaiah 13:9–10 and Joel 2:31; 3:15 also reference this "black out," which will occur "immediately after the Tribulation," in preparation for Christ's Second Coming in Matthew 24:30. These Old Testament passages refer to the same future events about which Christ spoke in verse 29. We see reinforced from the contexts of these Old Testament passages, especially Joel 2 and 3, that Christ Himself will rescue Israel from her Tribulation. Notice the following passages from Joel:

> *The sun will be turned into darkness, and the moon into blood, before the great and awesome day of the LORD comes (2:31).*

> *For behold, in those days and at that time, when I restore the fortunes of Judah and Jerusalem, I will gather all the nations, and bring them down to the valley of Jehoshaphat. Then I will enter into judgment with them there on behalf of My people and My inheritance, Israel, whom they have scattered among the nations; and they have divided up My land (3:1–2).*

It is clear that our Lord has quoted part of His declaration about the sun and moon in Matthew 24:29 ("But immediately after the tribulation of those days THE SUN WILL BE DARKENED, AND THE MOON WILL NOT GIVE ITS LIGHT") from Joel 2:31. Both passages are referring to the same time and events, namely, the future tribulation. Thus, it is interesting to take note of Joel 3:1–2, which provides a "time text" saying that the "black out" (2:31) will occur "in those days and at that time" (3:1). In conjunction with this is described a time when the Lord will "restore the fortunes of Judah and Jerusalem" (3:1). The reference is not judgment, but deliverance, as in Matthew 24. This event is said to be a time when the Lord "will gather all the nations" (Joel 3:1) in the valley of Jehoshaphat just north of Jerusalem. Further, it will be a time in which Israel will have been regathered from among the nations (v. 2). This will be the time in which the sun and moon will be darkened.

I showed in chapter 2 that Luke 21:24 ("and they will fall by the edge of the sword, and will be led captive into all the nations; and Jerusalem will be trampled under foot by the Gentiles until the times of the Gentiles be fulfilled") provides an outline of the history of Jerusalem from the time of the destruction of the city until Israel's redemption at the Second Coming (see vv. 25–29). The time in which the sun and moon will be darkened will follow the end of "the times of the Gentiles," according to verse 25. The fact that the blackout of Matthew 24:29 is to come at the end of the times of the Gentiles ("immediately after the tribulation of those days") makes it clear that it could not have happened in the first century, for, according to Luke 21:24, the Roman destruction of the holy city would commence that time which has gone on now for almost two thousand years. This event must be future and occur in conjunction with a time in which the Lord will deliver His people, not judge them (as in A.D. 70).

If the preterist interpretation of Matthew 24:29 is left to stand, it creates tremendous contradictions between the text and the historical records of the Roman siege. The Rev. Richard Shimeall explains the preterist problem as follows:

> Historically, therefore, the state of the case amounts to this:
>
> 1. The high priest of the Jewish nation and many of his associates had been murdered, and the whole body of the priesthood overthrown; and, if there were any religious services, they were conducted by such wretches as the robbers saw fit to appoint.
>
> 2. Their temple was changed into a citadel and stronghold of an army of the vilest and most abominable robbers and murderers that ever disgraced the human race.
>
> 3. Their "holy houses" (synagogues) throughout the land had been pillaged and destroyed by the ruthless and bloody Sicarii.
>
> 4. Their judiciary and temple officers had either fled for their lives to the Romans, or had been murdered by the robber-gangs of the city, while their nobles and men of wealth perished by myriads. And finally,
>
> 5. Whether within the capital or throughout the borders of Judea, east, west, north, and south, the *ecclesiastical* and *civil* institutions of the nation were exterminated, and the country conquered and laid waste by the Romans, or ravaged by organized banditti.
>
> And thus, reader, it continued to the end. These, we repeat, are the *historical facts* of the case. And yet, our commentators have trusted the interpretation of some of the most important

parts of the Bible to the theory, the principal argument to sustain which lies in the assumption that the Jewish ecclesiastical and civil governments were destroyed *"after"* the destruction of Jerusalem!

What shall the writer say more? He claims to have settled the question by *undeniable* historic facts. If anything, let it be in the form of the following appeal to logic:

1. If by the heavenly luminaries be meant the ecclesiastical and civil states and rulers of the Jews, and the darkening of them refers to their destruction; and if this was effected by the Roman legions, it follows that it must have occurred either *before* or *during* the Tribulation that resulted in their ruin.

2. But, inasmuch as the *object* of the war was to reduce the nation to obedience, or to bring it to ruin, it could not have *preceded* it.

3. It must therefore have occurred *during* the war. Recollect we are now speaking of the darkening of the sun, moon, and stars, as denoting the so-called *Jewish Tribulation* at the hands of the Romans. We repeat, then, it must have occurred during the war. Now, it is undeniable that that war did not cease until its object was effected. It is also undeniable, that the nation was in ruins *before* the war was ended. And it is a fact, also, that the predicted Tribulation continued undiminished, if indeed it did not increase in severity, *to the last.*

It is, therefore, we submit, settled—historically and logically settled—that it was during, and *not* after, that time of trouble, that the so-called Jewish luminaries were darkened. And, what is decisive of this point, are those notable words of Christ, *"Immediately after* Tribulation of those days, the sun shall be darkened,"* etc.; which shows conclusively that our Lord was not speaking of *that event* in the 29th verse of this chapter.[35]

Preterists admit that if Matthew 24 requires a literal blackout, then it did not happen in the A.D. 70 event. Is a literal occurrence of such an event so far-fetched as preterists insist? Stars literally do fall from heaven. They are called "falling stars," "shooting stars," "comets," or "meteors." The Greek word for *star* can be used in this way.[36] "Stars" that fall to the earth often disintegrate and burn up as they enter the earth's atmosphere. Robert Gundry has said, "The falling of the stars refers to a shower of meteorites, and the shaking of the heavenly powers of God's displacing 'the spiritual forces of wickedness in the heavenly places' (Eph 6:12)."[37] In a similar passage, this is what causes the people of the earth to hide in caves (Rev. 6:12–17). Perhaps this is similar to the Lord's raining down of fire and brimstone upon Sodom and Gomorrah (Gen. 19:23–26)?

It makes sense that the heavens and earth are physically affected by humanity's sin at the end of history, just as it was when humanity fell at the beginning of history. With the literal view, Genesis and Revelation recount the beginning and ending of history. Revelation notes the magnitude of the shaking of the heavens and the earth in judgment. Noah's flood had physical effects, and so too will the judgment of the Tribulation prior to Christ's return.

I believe Dr. Gentry takes a number of similar, yet smaller in scale, incidents of biblical history to be literal. These other events put his preterism at risk. The question must be raised: Did the sun literally not shine over the land of Egypt and at the same time shine in the land of Goshen during the ninth plague (Exod. 10:21–29)? Of course. Similarly, during the crucifixion of our Lord, did darkness really fall over the whole land of Israel about the sixth hour until the ninth hour (Luke 23:44–45)? Sure it did. It was a pattern of the final darkness that will accompany the final judgment at the end of the world. "When He died, the sun refused to shine (Lk. 23:45). When He comes again it will not shine (Mt. 24:29)."[38] Why shouldn't grandiose, supernatural phenomenon accompany the glorious return of our Lord? Only a naturalist mentality would say that a literal occurrence of Matthew 24:29 is impossible. After all, God said in Genesis 1:14 that one of His purposes for the sun, moon, and stars is to serve as "signs" in the heavens. It would be absurd to think that these references to the sun, moon, and stars are to be taken merely as symbols with no physical referent. Why shouldn't the One who created the heaven and earth have the heavens reflect His global judgment upon a sinful world? There may be objections in the minds of people to such heavenly displays, but no such problem exists in Scripture.

The Sign of the Son of Man

Matthew 24:30 says, "and then the sign of the Son of Man will appear in the sky, and then all the tribes of the earth will mourn, and they will see the SON OF MAN COMING ON THE CLOUDS OF THE SKY with power and great glory." Once again Dr. Gentry's preterist interpretation of this passage is an exercise in why the text does not mean what it appears to say. He teaches that

> "The sign" of verse 30 is "when the Romans lay waste the temple (vv. 6 and 15 anticipate this) and pick apart Jerusalem (v. 28). That is, when the government of Israel utterly collapses

(v. 29), then it will be evident that the one who prophesies her destruction is "in heaven." The "sign" is not a visible token in the sky. Rather, the sign is that the "Son of Man" rejected by the first-century Jews is *in heaven*. The destruction of Israel vindicates Christ (p. 58).

It is hard to believe that such an interpretation is what Christ intended when He prophesied this event. Since Dr. Gentry wants the passage to teach that the sign appeared in heaven (namely, the throne room of God), rather than as a sign in heaven to be seen by humanity, he insists upon a certain word order for the verse. The word order of the Greek is as follows: "And then shall appear the sign of the Son of Man in the heaven." It is true that this allows for the possibility of Dr. Gentry's understanding that there was a sign within heaven itself. However, the Greek also allows for the possibility that the intent of the passage is that sign of the Son of Man will appear in the heaven or sky. To take it as a humanly visible sign in the sky, as I would, Dr. Gentry says, "requires a restructuring of the text" (p. 58). It does not *require* a restructuring, though many who take a futurist view do put forward translations that do not retain the original word order. The difference amounts to whether "in heaven" refers to the preterist invisible sign that takes place in the throne room of God or to the futurist sign in the sky that is seen by humanity. Grammarian Nigel Turner says, "Mt 24:30 is ambiguous; either *the sign which is the S.M.* (appos.), or *the sign which the S.M. will give* (possess.)."[39]

I believe that the context argues in favor of the futurist interpretation that the sign is visible to the human eye in heaven, which is the sky. First, the Greek word οὐρανὸς can mean either "throne room," as preterists believe, or the visible heaven or sky that can be seen by the human eye, as futurists believe. The majority of New Testament occurrences fall into this latter use.[40] BAG classifies it as the latter and says *"then the sign of the Son of Man (who is) in heaven will appear;* acc. to the context, the sign consists in this, that he appears visibly in heavenly glory Mt. 24:30."[41]

Second, the surrounding verses focus upon heavenly meteorological disturbances (see vv. 27, 29, 30b, 31) that are visible to humanity. The appearance of a sign in the sky would certainly fit the contextual theme of a heavenly focus.

Third, "It must, in the nature of the case, be *luminous*. This is indicated by the original word for *appear*. But it must be luminous from this single consideration: it will appear, or shine, at a time of *total darkness*," declares the Rev. Buck. "The sun will be previously turned to darkness, and the moon and the stars will have withdrawn their shining. All the great sources of light being thus totally obscured, whatever shall *appear* must be luminous in its nature."[42]

Fourth, the time relationships of the passage support a visible, and thus, a future understanding. Matthew 24:30 begins "and then" referring back to the meteorological events of verse 29, which will occur "immediately after the Tribulation of those days." Thus, verse 30 tells us that "the sign . . . will appear;" "and then" there will be human mourning in response to the sign; followed by Christ's glorious return. Amazingly, Dr. Gentry says that the sign of verse 30 means that the Jews "must flee the area if they are to preserve their lives" (p. 60). How can this happen if the sign is the Roman conquest of Jerusalem? It will be too late. Such folly does not fit an A.D. 70 sequence of events, as noted by the Rev. Shimeall:

> Yes, reader. This is the theory of our Lord's *Second Coming,* . . . Briefly, then, as it respects the *first* branch of this theory, its inconsistency, we submit, will become apparent, from the following arguments and facts:
>
> (1.) If the coming of the Lord at the time here specified was merely "the coming of the Roman army to destroy Jerusalem and the unbelieving Jews," then it will follow, of necessity, that it occurred at the same time, since, in fact, it is affirmed to be the same event.
>
> (2.) Again, the destruction of the Jewish church and state, and city, and people, resulted from the coming of the Romans, and must, of course, have been after that coming, because results must be subsequent to the causes that produce them. Accordingly, as our blessed Lord delivered the whole of this remarkable prophecy with special regard to the chronological order of the events,
>
> (3.) He describes the appearance of the "sign" of His coming, of the mourning of all the tribes of the earth, and of His actual coming in the clouds of heaven, as being "after the tribulation of those days," and subsequent, in the order of time, to the darkening of the sun, moon, and stars.
>
> Reader, which shall we believe—the comments and opinions of men, or the teachings of Christ?[43]

Fifth, I believe that "the sign" will likely be a display of the Shechinah glory that has been manifested throughout history.[44] After all, it was the sign of Christ's first coming—the Shechinah glory—that flashed upon a darkened sky announcing His birth to the shepherds. It was the Shechinah glory star that led the wise men from the east. So it is that His sign—the sign of the Son of Man—will once again be His trademark, the Shechinah glory cloud. Dr. Fruchtenbaum explains:

> At this point Matthew states that the sign of the Second Coming will appear (v. 30a); and since this sign is coupled with God's glory, it is obviously the Shechinah glory light that will signal the Second Coming of Christ. So the answer to the second question, "What will be the sign of the Second Coming?" is the Shechinah glory. So *immediately after the tribulation of those days* there will be a total blackout with no light penetrating at all, followed by a sudden, glorious, tremendous light that will penetrate through the blackout. This Shechinah light will be the sign of the Second Coming of Christ. The light will be followed by the return of Christ Himself (v. 30b).[45]

Dr. Gentry argues that "they will see" Christ's "coming on the clouds" and that this is (once again) neither visible sight (the eyes of faith) nor a physical coming (pp. 60–61). He goes so far as to evidence "exegetical vertigo" when he says that Christ's "coming on the clouds" "actually refers to Jesus' ascension" (p. 61). At this point, preterists confuse coming with going. This is despite the fact that Dr. Gentry, unlike some preterists, understands Acts 1:11 as a Second Coming passage.[46]

> And after He had said these things, He was lifted up while they were looking on, and a cloud received Him out of their sight. And as they were gazing intently into the sky while He was departing, behold, two men in white clothing stood beside them; and they also said, "Men of Galilee, why do you stand looking into the sky? This Jesus, who has been taken up from you into heaven, will come in just the same way as you have watched Him go into heaven" (1:9–11).

The language in Acts 1:9 is clear that Christ is ascending upward to heaven. It is equally clear that verse 11 refers to His return as a coming down from heaven on a cloud. Further, the Greek word for "coming" in both Matthew 24:30 and Acts 1:11 is ἔρχομαι. Thus, once Christ has ascended into heaven, His next act of coming could not be up, but only down, namely, down from heaven to earth. This is clearly the picture our Lord paints, not only in the specific passage (Matt. 24:30), but throughout the overall context (vv. 27–31). Dr. Stanley Toussaint adds the following:

It will be conceded by all that the first part of Matthew 24:30 looks back to Zechariah 12:10. However, it is important to notice that in Zechariah the mourning of 12:10 is explained by the verses that follow. It is a repentant lamentation by Israel because it results in the purification of the nation (Zech. 13:1). The context of Zechariah 12:10 is most significant. Rather than prophesying the destruction of Jerusalem, it is predicting the opposite. "And it will come about in that day that I will set about to destroy all the nations that come against Jerusalem" (Zech. 12:9). This is the tenor of Zechariah 12:1–8. It looks ahead to God's future deliverance of Israel when Jerusalem will again be surrounded by enemies. "In that day" is prophetic of a time of deliverance of Israel, not judgment. (Note the constant repetition of "in that day" [12:3, 4, 6, 8 (2x), 9, 11; 13:1, 2, 4]). It is clear that the context of Zechariah is a mourning that results in cleansing and deliverance for Israel. Whatever the sign of the Son of Man is, it results in the national repentance of Israel. This parallels perfectly what Paul says in Romans 11:25–27. This explanation of Matthew 24:30a sets the stage for the understanding of the last half of the verse. It is true that in the vision of Daniel 7:13, as it is translated in the NASB, the Son of Man came up to the Ancient of Days to receive the dominion to rule. However, the Hebrew verb has no idea of direction; it simply means to arrive or to reach. This specific verb is only used in Daniel, where it may refer to something reaching up as Nebuchadnezzar's greatness did in 4:22, or it may describe something going down as in 6:24 where the detractors of Daniel were thrown into the lion's den. It has no intrinsic sense of direction. Nor does the following preposition indicate direction in itself. The construction simply means the Son of Man approached the Ancient of Days. But even if it describes the Son of Man coming up to the Ancient of Days, it only looks at the bestowment of authority. The question is: Where is the authority expressed? Keil says it well when he writes:

> In this very chapter before use there is no expression or any intimation whatever that the judgment is held in heaven. No place is named. It is only said that judgment was held over the power of the fourth beast, which came to a head in the horn speaking blasphemies, and that the beast was slain and his body burned. If he who appears as the son of man with the clouds of heaven comes before

the Ancient of Days executing the judgment on the earth,
it is manifest that he could only come from heaven to earth.
If the reverse is to be understood, then it ought to have
been so expressed, since the coming with clouds of heaven
in opposition to the rising up of the beast out of the sea
very distinctly indicates a coming down from heaven. The
clouds are the veil or the "chariot" on which God comes
from heaven to execute judgment against His enemies;
see Ps. xvii;10f., xcvii 2–4, civ. 3, Isa. xix 1, Nah. i. 3.
This passage forms the foundation for the declaration of
Christ regarding His future coming, which is described
after Dan. vii. 13 as a coming of the Son of man with, in,
on the clouds of heaven; Matt. xxiv. 20, xxvi. 64; Mark
xiii. 26; Rev. 1.7, xiv. 14.[47]

In summary, Matthew 24:30 describes a visible appearance of the
sign of the Son of Man, the repentance of Israel and the triumphant
return of Christ to reign on planet earth.[48]

An Angelic Gathering

Matthew 24:31 says, "And He will send forth His angels with A GREAT
TRUMPET and THEY WILL GATHER TOGETHER His elect from the four winds,
from one end of the sky to the other." In keeping with his localized
and nonsupernatural interpretation, Dr. Gentry teaches that "Matthew
24:31 continues the poetic imagery" (p. 61). He explains the verse as
"the gathering of the saints into local assemblies or churches (Heb.
10:25; James 2:2) and the universal assembling of the saints into the
body of Christ, the church universal (compare Matt. 22:7–13)" (p. 64).
Mention of "a great trumpet" refers to "the destruction of the temple
trumpets in the *ultimate* Jubilee Year" (p. 61). Finally, angels do "not
seem to refer to the supernatural heavenly beings here, but to those
who now proclaim the message of full salvation" (p. 63).

This section in Dr. Gentry's argument (pp. 61–65) provides us with
another blatant example of the hermeneutical error termed by Dr. Barr
as "illegitimate totality transfer."[49] While totally ignoring contextual
uses, Dr. Gentry seeks to establish his own context for trumpets, gathering, and angels. For example, he fails to note that the verb ἐπισυνάγω
("they will gather together") is used earlier in this passage. Other than
an insignificant use in verse 28, ἐπισυνάγω is used twice in Matthew
23:37, where Jesus weeps over Jerusalem as He pronounces the A.D.
70 judgment and declares, "How I wanted to gather [ἐπισυνάγω] your
children together, the way a hen gathers [ἐπισυνάγω] her chicks under her wings, and you were unwilling." Chapter 24 is about a future

time when Jerusalem is again in peril, but this time the Jews are willing to believe. Thus, our Lord will gather (ἐπισυνάγω) His elect (saved Jews at the end of the Tribulation) from around the world and bring them to Jerusalem, rather than scatter them as He did in A.D. 70 (Luke 21:24).

Preterists such as Dr. Gentry often talk about interrupting a passage in accordance with the Old Testament, yet he misses an opportunity with the phrase quoted from the Old Testament: "they will gather together." Just such a regathering was predicted in the Old Testament.

> *So it shall be when all of these things have come upon you, the blessing and the curse which I have set before you, and you call them to mind in all nations where the LORD your God has banished you, and you return to the LORD your God and obey Him with all your heart and soul according to all that I command you today, you and your sons, then the LORD your God will restore you from captivity, and have compassion on you, and will gather you again from all the peoples where the LORD your God has scattered you. If your outcasts are at the ends of the earth, from there the LORD your God will gather you, and from there He will bring you back (Deut. 30:1–4).*

> *And He will lift up a standard for the nations, and will assemble the banished ones of Israel, and will gather the dispersed of Judah from the four corners of the earth (Isa. 11:12).*

The only item missing from the Old Testament that our Lord expands upon in His discourse is that He will use the agency of angels to accomplish this task (rather than El Al airline!). Deuteronomy 30:1–4 reveals an important covenantal promise made by the Lord to His people Israel. Matthew 24:31 reveals that our Lord, the same One who made the promise in Deuteronomy, will fulfill His promises in history, even if it requires a miraculous solution.

Surely Dr. Gentry does not have a bias against our Lord's use of the supernatural and the angelic in this way in order to support the naturalistic explanations of preterism. We know that Elijah was translated to heaven without dying. Second Kings 2 records this interesting event, with an emphasis upon the mode of Elijah's transportation to heaven. Verse 1 says that he was taken "by a whirlwind to heaven." In verse 11 the whirlwind is further described as "a chariot of fire and horses of fire." No doubt this was an appearance of the Shechinah glory of God, for Hebrews 1:7 says, "and of the angels He says, 'Who makes His angels winds, and His ministers a flame of fire.'" Since Elijah was taken to heaven by angels (mere human messengers could not accomplish such a task), why not have a group operation? This is exactly what we find in conjunction with an important event such as Christ's Second Advent.

The Deuteronomy passage also provides an answer for why our Lord used the term "elect" in Matthew 24:31 to characterize His people. It is because at this pivotal point in history, the Jews will fulfill the requirements of Deuteronomy 30:2. In other words, they will turn "to the LORD your God and obey Him with all your heart and soul according to all that I command you today." This was also our Lord's own requirement for the Second Coming mentioned in Matthew 23:39. The passage makes great sense with such a futuristic interpretation, and it is also in harmony with clear Old Testament teaching about Israel and that wonderful day when the Jewish people will be converted to the Messiah and receive in history their long-awaited blessing. Dr. Arnold Fruchtenbaum says,

> In the New Testament, the final regathering revealed by the Old Testament prophets is summarized in Matthew 24:31 and Mark 13:27. In this passage, Jesus stated that the angels will be involved in the final regathering and they will bring the Jews back into the land. As to locality, the emphasis is on the world-wide regathering. The two passages are a simple summary of all that the prophets had to say about the second facet of Israel's final restoration. The Matthew passage is based on Isaiah 27:12–13 and the Mark passage is based on Deuteronomy 30:4. Its purpose was to make clear that the worldwide regathering predicted by the prophets will be fulfilled only after the Second Coming.[50]

Concluding Observations Concerning Preterism

The heart and soul of preterism is built around the belief that the Great Tribulation has already occurred in the past through events surrounding the Roman battle in A.D. 70. No doubt this was a pivotal event and of great importance to a proper understanding of the Bible. When one contemplates the warnings recorded in the Epistle to the Hebrews, one should do so against the backdrop of the impending destruction of Jerusalem. No matter how great this first-century event was, it does not do justice to the biblical description of a coming seven-year tribulation that will engage the whole world (not just the Roman empire). Though the focus of preterism is its understanding of the Tribulation, its deviant doctrine also distorts the focus of many other biblical periods. I will note some of the other problems created by the preterist interpretation.

First-Century Christians

If the preterist interpretation of the Olivet discourse, the book of Revelation, and many other eschatological passages were the actual biblical teaching, then why did those who stood to benefit the most from this teaching (namely, first-century Christians) not even appear to know about such a view? Preterists commonly tell us how important it was that prophecy relate directly to those who were the first-century recipients. Yet all admit that there is no actual evidence that any first-century believers benefited from what they were supposedly living through. When he discusses the matter, Dr. Gentry is unable to produce any first-century or early second-century preterists from church history.[51] In fact, Dr. Gentry admits that systematic preterism can only be traced back to 1614.[52]

New Heavens and New Earth

Not only does Dr. Gentry believe that the Great Tribulation is a past event, he (along with most preterists) actually believes that current history is to be identified as the new heavens and new earth of Revelation 21–22 and 2 Peter 3:10–13.[53] Talk about lowering expectations! Dr. Gentry provides four major reasons why "the new creation begins in the first century."[54] It stretches credulity to think about the implications of the details of such a conclusion. If we are currently living in the new heaven and new earth, the following must be concluded from Revelation 21–22:

- The one thousand years and the new heaven and earth must be equated (compare 20:1–9 with 21–22).
- Satan has been removed from any more influence in history (20:10).
- There is no longer any sea (21:1).
- There is no longer any death, crying, or pain (21:4).
- All things have been made new (21:1).
- There is no longer any need for the sun or the moon (21:23).
- There is no longer any night (21:25).
- There is no longer any unclean, nor those practicing abomination and lying (21:27).
- There is no longer any curse (22:3).
- Believers are now able to see the Father's face (22:4).
- There is no longer any sun (22:5).

If Revelation 21–22 is a description of the state in which we are now living, then most of the New Testament is rendered obsolete and impractical, for it relates to believers and how they should live between

Christ's two comings. The logic of the preterist position would lead to this conclusion, even though preterists do not think this way in practice. They don't, but they should!

Implications of the Forty-Year Interval

Since prophecy and subjects relating to prophecy dominate virtually every page of the New Testament, then according to the logic of preterism, most of the New Testament does not relate to the church today. Instead, it was for believers who lived during the forty-year period between the death of Christ and the destruction of Jerusalem in A.D. 70.

Many preterists believe that passages such as Titus 2:13 refer to the coming of Christ in A.D. 70. This would mean that it was a hope only for those Christians living between the time that the epistle was written and the destruction of Jerusalem, namely, A.D. 65–70. Paul says that Christ's appearance the first time impacts the lives of believers in the "present age." Verse 12 says, "instructing us to deny ungodliness and worldly desires and to live sensibly, righteously and godly in the present age." The grammar of verse 13 relates the activities of verse 12 to activity of "looking for the blessed hope and the appearing of the glory of our great God and Savior, Christ Jesus."

If 2:13 is a reference to A.D. 70, then the "present age" mentioned in verse 12 would have ended when verse 13 was fulfilled. Therefore, the total admonition of verse 12 was temporary and applicable only to Christians up until A.D. 70. This would mean that the instruction "to deny ungodliness and worldly desires and to live sensibly, righteously and godly in the present age" would not directly apply to the current age, but only to the past age that ended in A.D. 70 when "the appearing of the glory of our great God and Savior, Christ Jesus" was manifested in the destruction of Jerusalem. This (sadly) would have to be the practical implications of the preterist view, as applied to this passage and to most of the New Testament.

Practical application of the Christian life is impacted in two major areas, depending on whether Titus 2:13 is a past prophecy or a future event. First, if this is a past event, the *motivation* of the blessed hope as it relates to living a godly life in "the present age " (2:12) would not apply to believers today. Second, the *ethical* admonitions of 2:12 would not apply to believers today, for the basis for compliance would have been fulfilled in A.D. 70.

The preterist view relating to the current work of Satan and the demons should reflect their theology on the subject. According to the preterist view, Satan is currently bound (Rev. 20:2–3) and crushed (Rom. 16:20). The enemy was not just defeated *de jure* (legally) at the cross, but has been crushed *de facto* (in fact). Therefore, there is no spiritual road block prohibiting Christians from reigning and ruling now.

On the other hand, if the binding and crushing of Satan and his company is still future, then the commands in the epistles make sense in this present age. Such commands include the following: "resist the devil and he will flee from you" (James 4:7b); "Be of sober spirit, be on the alert. Your adversary, the devil, prowls about like a roaring lion, seeking someone to devour. But resist him, firm in your faith, knowing that the same experiences of suffering are being accomplished by your brethren who are in the world" (1 Peter 5:8–9); "Be angry, and yet do not sin; do not let the sun go down on your anger, and do not give the devil an opportunity" (Eph. 4:26–27); "For our struggle is not against flesh and blood, but against the rulers, against the powers, against the world forces of this darkness, against the spiritual forces of wickedness in the heavenly place" (6:12).

These instructions are the tactics that must be applied by believers in this present age, for we are not yet in the new heaven and new earth. If Satan is bound and crushed (as the preterist interpretation insists), then advocates of this view are unfaithful to their understanding of Scripture when (as they often do) they apply the above passages to the Christian life today. A crushed and bound enemy does not prowl, or wage war, and so on. This becomes crystal clear when one realizes that Satan resumes his war with God only after the devil has been "released from his prison" (Rev. 20:7b).

Similar thinking could—even should—be applied from the implications of preterism to many passages and subjects in the Christian life. Just think, there is no more suffering! And if there is no more suffering, then there is no need for endurance. There is also no need for the sanctification process, which involves suffering, endurance, faith, and hope. There's no hope, for Christ supposedly returned in A.D. 70 and ushered in a new day. There is no apostasy of the church, as well as no pain, suffering, or death. Therefore, since we are obviously not living under such conditions, it means that preterism must be incorrect.

Preterism Can Lead to Heterodoxy

Dr. Gentry is a moderate preterist. Yet, as noted earlier, there is a growing number of preterists who believe that all prophecy has already been fulfilled. For instance, extreme preterists believe that all prophecy was fulfilled in A.D. 70 and that there will never be a future Second Coming. Allegedly Jesus' return occurred in that year.

Such a position not only denies the hope of the Second Advent, but it also means that there will be no future resurrection of the saints. Such views are heretical. Dr. Gentry affirms, "hyper-preterism is heterodox. It is outside of the creedal orthodoxy of Christianity. No creed allows any Second Advent in A.D. 70. No creed allows any other type of resurrection than a bodily one."[55]

Yet it seems that many preterists are becoming hyper-preterists. Dr. Gentry's moderate preterism may satisfy him and others that they have a systematic answer to dispensational futurism, but it opens the door for too many to move into the heretical position of hyper-preterism. Within Dr. Gentry's own reconstructionist circle we have already seen the late David Chilton take this route. More are following in his footsteps. Once one partakes of the preterist approach, it seems hard to stop its growth and resist its appeal to preterize all Bible prophecy.

Back to the Future

When Bible prophecy is taken literally, it leads to a proper understanding of God's plan for history and the individual believer. Such an understanding provides a great hope, indeed a "blessed hope" that Christ's prophetic program for the church and Israel will yet provide some of the greatest moments of history. A futurist eschatology provides a fitting climax for history that began in a garden and concludes in a city—the new Jerusalem. Christ's church will be raptured before the Tribulation so that our Lord can complete His plan for His ancient people Israel. In fact, with the modern restoration of national Israel, Jesus is, even in our own day, preparing the stage for the Tribulation. The Tribulation is a time in which God will rescue, not judge the Jews so that "all Israel will be saved." No, the Tribulation is not past; rather, it is future. If it is in the past, then we have no future. *Maranatha!*

6

THE GREAT TRIBULATION IS FUTURE:

REBUTTAL

Kenneth L. Gentry Jr.

In this response section, Dr. Ice and I each have less space available than in our positive presentations above. Consequently, my rejoinder will be somewhat clipped and rapid. I will divide my response into three categories: (1) general observations; (2) Luke 21 issues; and (3) Revelation issues. Though my response is relatively short, I think the reader will sense Dr. Ice's tendency to obfuscation, misrepresentation, and self-contradiction.

General Observations

Missed Opportunity

As I begin my response, I remind you of the title of our book: *The Great Tribulation: Past or Future?* If you consult your Bible concordance, you will discover that the phrase "the great Tribulation" occurs *only* in Matthew 24:21; Revelation 2:22 and 7:14. Yet despite our debate focus, *Dr. Ice omits an exposition of the very passage containing explicit reference to "the great Tribulation."* Only rarely does he allude to Matthew 24; nowhere does he analyze it. Obviously, the entire book of Revelation (wherein we find "the great tribulation," Rev. 2:22; 7:14) might overwhelm us due to our current limitations.[1] But surely Matthew's record of the Lord's discourse is not too cumbersome—and it is precisely to the point.[2]

Interestingly, Ice himself argues that Matthew 24 is devoted solely to the (allegedly) future Great Tribulation, which is our topic of debate.

165

Why does he not analyze the passage? Why does he go to other passages that, as he admits (p. 99), do not even use the phrase "the great Tribulation" (e.g., Luke 21)? I suspect this is due to the difficulties facing dispensationalism in the text. For instance, dispensationalist David L. Turner writes of the Olivet discourse (especially Matt. 24) in the *Grace Theological Journal:* "The manner in which dispensationalism has traditionally handled this section is thus weak on several fronts. . . . Contemporary dispensationalists should rethink this area of NT exegesis."[3] "It must be concluded that the futurist view, held by traditional dispensationalists, is unconvincing. It does not satisfactorily handle the contextual emphasis on the fall of Jerusalem."[4]

Careless Exegesis

Space constraints forbid a thorough analysis of Ice's numerous exegetical anomalies. I will in this section, however, highlight a couple of samples from sections which provide the foundation for his Tribulational theology. Rephrasing the psalmist, we might ask: "If the foundations are destroyed, what can the interpreter do?"

First, under the heading "The Mosaic Covenant," Ice provides a section he calls "A Prophetic Road Map" (p. 75). There he alerts us to the great importance of Deuteronomy 4:30 to his argument: "This is important because it is within this framework that the Tribulation is first mentioned in the Bible as an event in Israel's history that will occur in 'the latter days' and will lead to their repentance and conversion to Jesus as their Messiah (Deut. 4:30)" (p. 74). In the same paragraph he notes: "this is a significant observation for dealing with *when* the Tribulation will occur in history because Deuteronomy provides a prophetic road map of Israel's history" (emphasis mine, p. 74). Elsewhere he comments: "As significant as Deuteronomy 4 is in establishing the Tribulation. . . ." (p. 78).

The biblical text in question reads: "When you are in distress and all these things have come upon you, in the latter days, you will return to the LORD your God and listen to His voice." Ice vigorously asserts that Deuteronomy 4:30 is "important" and "significant" because here "the Tribulation is first mentioned." Unfortunately for Ice, most evangelical commentators hold that this passage does *not* speak of the eschatological last days. Rather "the latter days" statement serves as a *general* warning regarding *Israel's future after Moses's death;* not the eschatologically pregnant end-time events. Consider the following commentators' observations:

P. C. Craigie: "'In the days ahead' (or 'in the latter days') comes to have an eschatological significance at a later date, though in this context the reference is simply to the future."[5] "The primary reference is still to the immediate future, and the book of Judges provides some insight into the type of disunity that appeared in the period following the initial part of the conquest. But as history unfolded, the danger contained in this warning was illustrated more dramatically in the fall of the two kingdoms and the subsequent dispersal of many of the Israelites from their promised land."[6]

Others agree. J. A. Thompson: "The phrase *in the latter days* need not be interpreted eschatologically, but merely in the sense of 'in the future.'" J. Ridderbos: "It appears to refer merely to 'a later time,' or 'the future.'" A. D. H. Mayes: "The phrase often has the general sense of 'days to come.' . . . The eschatological ideas present in Isaiah 2:2; Micah 4:1 are not expressed." Keil and Delitzsch: It refers to "all the dispersions which would come upon the rebellious nation in future times." W. L. Alexander: "it simply indicates futurity."[7]

There even seems to be some confusion over this passage among classic and revised dispensationalists, as recent comments by one of Ice's teachers and mentors, John F. Walvoord, suggests.[8] What Ice deems "important" and "significant" as a first occurrence of "the Tribulation" in prophecy is really a more general covenantal warning to Israel about her conduct in the approaching future within the Old Testament. This error fits the pattern of concern I have with Ice's whole presentation. In my comments above I note he *avoids* a passage that even he admits is directly relevant to our debate (Matt. 24); here he *misapplies* a passage, making it a specific eschatological prophecy rather than a general covenantal warning.

Second, in his "prophetic road map" Ice continues applying Moses' general covenantal threats as if they were specific eschatological prophecies: "Within Deuteronomy 28–30 we see a *specific reference* to *the Tribulation*" (emphasis mine, p. 78). For instance, Ice writes:

> Interestingly Deuteronomy 28:49–68 records two specific instances of removal from the Land. The first reference is clearly to the Babylonian captivity that took place in the sixth century B.C. (Deut. 28:49–57) when 28:49 speaks of "a nation" that the Lord would bring against Israel in judgment. This is then followed by a second statement of dispersion (Deut. 28:64) which says, "Moreover, the Lord will scatter you among all peoples, from one end of the earth to the other end of the earth; . . ." This was undoubtedly fulfilled by the destruction of Jerusalem in A.D. 70 by the Romans. (p. 79)

Evangelicals widely concede that this is a covenant sanctions passage serving as an ethical warning to Israel.[9] That is, the covenant stipulations would apply upon *any* occasion in which Israel rebels against God; they do not outline a "prophetic road map." They begin with "if" (Deut. 28:1–2. 9; 13. 15, 58), not "thus saith the LORD."

Nevertheless, Ice finds in Deuteronomy 28 "two specific instances of removal from the land." "The first reference" he associates with the Babylonian captivity (ending in 536 B.C.); "a second statement" he applies to the Jewish War with Rome (ending in A.D. 70). Once again he manufactures his specific eschatology from a general covenant sanction/ethical warning passage. Even Ice's fellow dispensationalists recognize circumstances *other than* the Babylonian and Roman holocausts where these curses apply. The curses of Deuteronomy 28 (and Lev. 26) are not properly predictive prophecy at all. Rather, they are ethical warnings of the consequences of covenantal breach. They have prophetic *character,* but not prophetic *purpose.* In fact, Dallas Theological Seminary's *The Bible Knowledge Commentary* observes regarding one of the particular curses in Deuteronomy 28:53–57: "This curse was literally fulfilled when the Arameans besieged Samaria (2 Kings 6:24–29) and when the Babylonians besieged Jerusalem (Lam. 2:20; 4:10)."[10] *The Bible Knowledge Commentary* also applies verses 58–68 to the Assyrian invasion. Deuteronomy 28 does not prophesy *two* future events. Dispensational scholars apply them to no less than *three* episodes—as do others.[11]

The Bible Knowledge Commentary also clearly relates the Deuteronomy 28 curses to Amos's prophecies regarding the fall of the northern kingdom to the Assyrians. The commentary refers the reader to a chart on "Covenant Chastenings," where we find that Amos 4 applies the Deuteronomy 28 curses to the siege of "the Northern capital" of Israel during the Assyrian invasion in 722 B.C. The Assyrian siege and conquest is a separate and distinct historical invasion ante-dating by over one hundred years the Babylonian captivity of Judah.[12]

In fact, Israel suffers *three* major expulsions from the land: by the Assyrians when the northern kingdom falls at the siege of Samaria (722 B.C.), by the Babylonians when the southern kingdom of Judah collapses with the capture of Jerusalem (586 B.C.), and by the Romans when first-century Israel falls to Titus (A.D. 70). Ice's "prophetic road map" scenario outlines only *two* applications of Deuteronomy 28: the Babylonian and the Roman exiles. What about the Assyrian deportation, which is so important in Israel's prophecy and history? This illustrates the fallacy of Ice's scenario: his alleged "road map" leaves out an important stop along the way.

What is more, the Deuteronomy passage expressly mentions exile in *three* sections, not two (Deut. 28:36–37; 28:49; 28:64). Ice is quite mistaken when he asserts: "We have seen thus far, from our prophetic road map, that Deuteronomy 28 has predicted two different instances when the ultimate covenant curse of expulsion from the land will be applied to national Israel" (p. 79).

Naïve Hermeneutic

Ice's exegetical problems flow directly from his naïve hermeneutic. He claims to follow a "consistently literal hermeneutic" (p. 97), a "consistent literal interpretation of the Bible and the correct approach to biblical interpretation" (p. 112), a "plain reading of all of the Olivet discourse" (p. 98), "a plain reading of the text" (pp. 104, 118). Indeed, Ice's approach to Scripture is such that he confidently declares that "even a schoolchild" (p. 77) can easily recall the events of Israel's history as suggested by his system.[13]

But dispensationalist theologians are now forsaking so-called literalism. For instance, John S. Feinberg, a noted contemporary dispensationalist, complains of one of Ice's mentors: "Ryrie is too simplistic" in his literalism.[14] Craig A. Blaising warns that: "consistently literal exegesis is inadequate to describe the essential distinctive of dispensationalism. Development is taking place on how to characterize a proper hermeneutic for dispensationalists."[15]

Darrell L. Bock (whom Ice abundantly and enthusiastically quotes on Luke 21) notes: "hermeneutical methodology has been rethought and is no longer perceived as an exclusively dispensational hermeneutic."[16] This rethinking is due to the "conceptual naïveté" of Ryrie's hermeneutic which involves a "methodological deficiency in the very hermeneutic that it proposed." This is gravely serious in that "this hermeneutical deficiency was structured into the very meaning of dispensational thought and practice in its advocacy of clear, plain, normal, or literal interpretation."[17]

Hermeneutics

For Ice the question of hermeneutics is absolutely crucial. He thinks the preterist's occasional employment of symbolism not only obscures God's message but reflects negatively on the Lord's abilities to communicate: "God's reputation in the area of clearness of speech and His veracity are at stake" (p. 70).

By way of quick rejoinder I would note:

(1) The apostle Peter confesses a problem in understanding Paul, one of God's premiere speakers: "As also in all his letters, speaking in them of these things, in which are some things hard to understand" (2 Peter 3:16). Is "God's reputation in the area of clearness of speech" at stake because of Paul's "hard to understand" writings?

(2) Ice himself *admits* that biblical writers employ symbolism from

time to time: Despite his alleged "consistently literal" hermeneutic, he allows "a valid use of figures . . . and symbols" (p. 98). Regarding my statement that the Old Testament often represents divine judgments in history symbolically as cloud-comings, Ice confesses: "I do not have a problem with Gentry's understanding of these passages as they are used in their Old Testament context" (p. 106). In fact, he observes: Jesus' teachings in "Matthew 21–23, in many senses, sound like Isaiah and Jeremiah" (p. 93). He refuses to admit, however, that in Matthew 24 (and Luke 21) Jesus *also* sounds like an Old Testament prophet. And this refusal is despite the intimate connection of Matthew 24 with the three preceding chapters (see my analysis in chap. 1 above), and its clear allusions to Old Testament prophets in verse 29 (cp. Isa. 13:10; 24:23; Ezek. 32:7; Joel 2:10; 3:15), verse 30 (cp. Dan. 7:13), and verse 31 (cp. Isa. 27:13; Zech. 9:14). Such an admission would be problematic for Ice, though. For then we could interpret Matthew 24 (and Luke 21) symbolically at places, *like the Old Testament prophets*. Indeed we should, for as Lane remarks: "The OT plays an essential part in the structure and imagery of the prophetic discourse."[18] Interestingly, Darrell Bock, upon whom Ice depends for his exposition of the Olivet discourse (pp. 96–104), notes of the Luke 21 material: "These descriptions recall OT pictures of judgment and captivity for unfaithfulness, as Jesus speaks like an OT prophet."[19]

Ironically, after a lengthy use of Bock's exposition of Luke 21, Ice titles his next section: "Hermeneutics." But Bock is one of the "progressive dispensationalists" who so alarmingly (to Ice) disposes of literalism! Thus, Ice employs the argument of his hermeneutic nemesis, despite his attacking Bock on this very matter in his (Ice's) chapter in *Issues in Dispensationalism*.[20]

(3) Ice's own system of theology admits obscurities in Scripture. He argues that in the Old Testament God hides the *entire* church age as an unrevealed "parenthesis" in God's original plan. This makes it appear (wrongly, in his view) that Israel's age continues uninterrupted into the future. And as I will show below, Ice allows huge hidden gaps in biblical time frames—such as with the four hundred and ninety weeks of Daniel, wherein hides a gap of two thousand years (pp. 84–87, 117). Why do these matters not reflect negatively upon God's "reputation in clearness of speech"?

(4) Ice is inconsistent with his own literalism principle. He applies the (allegedly) "significant" and "important" Deuteronomy 4:25–31 passage to Israel's dispersion beginning in the first century. He notes that "the first five events [in the list] have happened to Israel" so that "it is clear from the text that the final events will also occur to the same people in the same way" (p. 77). Here he even condescendingly asserts

of this "road map" approach to Israel's history that "even a schoolchild would know [these] as key elements in the history of Israel" (p. 77).

In summarizing his "road map" approach to prophecy, however, he notes as his fifth point: "Israel would be given over to idolatry during their wanderings" (p. 77). Deuteronomy 4:28 warns of Israel's experience during her (current, according to Ice) exile: "And there you will serve gods, the work of man's hands, wood and stone, which neither see nor hear nor eat nor smell." Deuteronomy 28:64 (which Ice clearly applies to Israel after A.D. 70, p. 79) reads: "Moreover, the LORD will scatter you among all peoples, from one end of the earth to the other end of the earth; and there you shall serve other gods, wood and stone, which you or your fathers have not known." And yet Ice knows full well that after A.D. 70 Israel did not nor does she today *literally* worship idols made by "man's hands, wood and stone." The late Merrill F. Unger, a dispensational biblical scholar who taught at Dallas Theological Seminary and whom Ice highly regards, states: "The Babylonian captivity cured the Jews of idolatry. Up to that time, despite everything, they continually fell into idolatry. From that day forward, however, whatever sins the Jews have been guilty of, they have not been idolatry."[21] What becomes of Ice's "consistent literalism" in these "significant" and "important" Tribulation passages that (allegedly) prophesy a literal return to idolatry in Israel after A.D. 70?

Poisoning the Well

Sadly, Ice charges (erroneously) that "preterists have to introduce symbolism at key points, without a textual basis" (p. 97). A few sentences later he continues: "Too often preterists simply declare key textual elements to be symbols, without providing adequate contextual support. This is done time after time in key passages like the Olivet discourse and Revelation, apparently thinking that just because they can cite a vaguely similar event from Josephus, that it clinches the passage as a past fulfillment" (p. 98). This bold charge is quite mistaken, for:

(1) Ice himself knows that this charge is not true. Later he admits: "Preterists believe they are driven to a first-century fulfillment of Revelation because, like the Olivet discourse, it says it will be fulfilled soon" (p. 107). "Preterists contend that they are driven to their interpretation of a past Tribulation due to the meaning of 'this generation' in the Olivet discourse and 'quickly' and 'at hand' in Revelation. In their minds, this justifies their nonliteral and symbolic handling of the text" (p. 118). This is a far cry from an argument for symbolic interpretation "without a textual basis" because preterists "can cite a vaguely similar event from Josephus." Time-frame indicators in Scripture lead to our interpretation.

(2) The whole discourse in question (Matt. 24) appears in a specific context. It follows Jesus' intensifying denunciation of Israel in Matthew 21–23. In Matthew 23 Christ charges that God will judge first-century Israel ("this generation," v. 36), whereupon he weeps over Jerusalem (v. 37), declares the temple "desolate" (v. 38), then ceremoniously departs from it (24:1). His surprised disciples then show him the majesty of the temple (24:2a). In response, Jesus prophesies the temple's stone-by-stone destruction (24:2b), which leads to their question: "When shall these things be?" (24:3). Jesus warns them to flee Jerusalem (24:16) when desolation in that very temple begins (24:15), which will be in "this generation" (24:34) to which he speaks. *Every datable item in the context points to a first-century fulfillment.*[22]

Revelation Questions

Perhaps nowhere is Ice's interpretive naïveté more evident than in the book of Revelation: "Since preterists advocate a symbolic interpretation of Revelation, they thus admit that a plain reading of the text does not yield their local perspective of the book and thus does not support a preterist interpretation. This is a tacit admission that a plain reading supports a global and thus a future understanding of Revelation" (p. 104). I gladly confess that I advocate a "symbolic interpretation of Revelation." And for good reason—please note:

(1) Ice himself allows a symbolic approach to key figures in Revelation. He admits a "valid use of figures (such as God's Word pictured as a sword) and symbols (such as the Beast of Revelation developed textually in Daniel 7 and supported by the various Revelation contexts)" (p. 98).

(2) All interpreters recognize abundant symbols within. Do we not see creatures filled with eyes (Rev. 4:6)? Locusts with faces of men, teeth of lions, crowns of gold, and tails like scorpions (9:6)? Lion-headed, scorpion-tailed horses belching fire and smoke (9:17)? Fire-breathing prophets (11:5)? A seven-headed, red dragon with ten horns and seven crowns who pulls stars down from heaven (12:3–4)? A woman with eagle's wings standing on the moon (12:14)? A serpent vomiting a river of water (12:15)? The seven-headed beast compounded of four carnivores (13:2)? Frogs coming out of the mouth of a dragon (16:13)? A prostitute riding the seven-headed beast while she is drunk on blood (17:6)? Christ returning with a sword in his mouth and on a horse from heaven (19:15)? A city the size of a fifteen-hundred-mile-high cube floating down out of heaven (21:10, 16)? On and on we could list such oddities. If these are compatible with a "plain" and "consistently literal" approach, then language has lost all meaning.

(3) John informs us in his introduction that Revelation was "sent

and communicated" (Gk., *esemanen*) (Rev. 1:1). According to the great Baptist Greek scholar, A. T. Robertson, the Greek word here is *esemanen* "from *sema,* sign or token, for which see John 12:33; Acts 11:28." He continues: "*semaino* (only here in the Apocalypse) suits admirably the symbolic character of the book."[23] Even Ice's mentor, Revelation commentator John F. Walvoord, confesses: "Apocalyptic literature is in a place all by itself because all agree that this is not, strictly speaking, literal in its revelation. Outstanding examples, of course, are the Books of Daniel, Ezekiel, and Revelation."[24] In fact, he says of Revelation 1:1 that it means "revelation *through symbols,* as in this book"[25] (emphasis mine).

(4) John even provides us with clues for interpreting a number of his symbols. In Revelation 1:20 John informs us that stars are angels and lampstands are churches. In 5:6 eyes are spirits. In 5:8 bowls of incense represent prayers. In 12:9 a dragon represents Satan. In 17:9–10 heads represent mountains. In 17:12 horns represent kings. In 17:15 waters represent peoples.

(5) Literalism leads to absurdity in Revelation. For example, Robert Thomas, a friend of Dr. Ice, holds that the locusts of Revelation 9 and the frogs of Revelation 16 are demons literally taking these peculiar physical forms; that the two prophets of Revelation 11 literally spew fire from their mouths; that every mountain in the world will be abolished during the seventh bowl judgments; that Babylon will smolder for more than one thousand years; that Christ will return from heaven on a literal horse; and that the new Jerusalem is literally a fifteen-hundred-mile-high cube.[26]

Argumentative Confusion

My friend Dr. Ice claims the "road map" of prophecy is so "plain" and "simple" that it is readily accessible to the average "schoolchild." Unfortunately, his own presentation is often hamstrung with argumentative confusion and self-contradiction.

Schematic Pandemonium

One major area of confusion appears in Dr. Ice's proposed order of events in Israel's "prophetic road map," especially as they lead to the Tribulation. And this confusion arises despite Ice's claim that even a "schoolchild" should know these (p. 77).

First, Ice presents a confused scenario regarding Israel's regathering to the land. In some places he states that Israel's regathering is already accomplished. In other places he writes as if it is not: He observes that "just as Israel was regathered after the Babylonian captivity and returned to the land, so she *will be* returned from her A.D. 70 Diaspora from the nations" (p. 80, emphasis mine). Of the prophecy of "Jacob's trouble" he writes: "It *will* be a time of when Israel and Judah *will* be brought back into their land in order to possess it" (p. 13, emphasis mine). He continues explaining this passage, noting that "the composite in this passage does not [fit] any past time of judgment upon Israel, but does fit the prophetic pattern of a future time when she will be returned from the nations to her land" (pp. 81–82).

Note carefully that Ice presents a prophetic picture of a *future* regathering to the land. Yet he knows Israel is *already* back in the land: "The fact that the modern state of Israel was reconstituted in 1948 is historical verification that God is preparing the world for Tribulation events" (p. 119). Indeed, for him the current "nation of Israel" is "prophetically significant" (p. 69). In fact, Ice approvingly cites Walvoord: "Of the many peculiar phenomena which characterize the present generation, few events can claim equal significance as far as biblical prophecy is concerned with that of the return of Israel to their land" (p. 119).

Consequently, Ice's "prophetic road map" informs us of a *future* return of Israel to the land from the A.D. 70 dispersion, even though he admits Israel has *already* returned to the land in our recent past. Any future immigration to Israel by more Jews will only augment the nation's population. Furthermore, any proposed future dispersion to allow for a future return would counter Ice's Deuteronomy 28 scenario wherein he finds *two* dispersions: the Babylonian Exile in the Old Testament and the Roman exile in the New Testament.

Second, Ice presents two different prophetic scenarios for Israel's future. In one place he presents the following order: Tribulation-repentance-regathering. In other places his pattern is: regathering-Tribulation-repentance. Note the following.

Interestingly, Ice provides this contradictory prophetic scenario immediately after stating that any "schoolchild" could list "key elements in the history of Israel" (p. 77). He enumerates the key elements in Israel's history, stating that "the first five events have happened to Israel." He then observes that it is "clear from the text that the final events will also occur to the same people in the same way" (p. 77). In this listing we observe two remarkable problems: (1) The list of the "key elements in the history of Israel" do not mention a return to the land. Surely Israel's regathering would be a "key" element in her history! (2) According to Ice, Israel's "tribulation" occurs *after* repentance *during* her exile, contrary to what he suggests as the pattern elsewhere.

Ice's sixth and seventh points claim that:

> 6. While dispersed among the nations, Israel would seek and find the LORD when they search for Him with all their heart.

7. There would come a time of tribulation, said to occur in the latter days, during which time they would turn to the LORD. (p. 77).

"The latter days" suggests for Ice the *eschatological* tribulation. So here, according to his enumeration, the Tribulation (#7) occurs *after* Israel's repentance (wherein she will "seek and find the Lord") but "*while* dispersed among the nations" (from A.D. 70 onwards; #6).

Only one paragraph later, Ice cites David Larsen's work on the Deuteronomy 28–34 prophecy. Note especially the following two consecutive entries in Ice's list (p. 78):

28:40–41; 30:1–2	Israel will repent in her tribulation
30:3–10	Israel will be gathered from the nations and brought back to her divinely given land

But what do we find elsewhere in Dr. Ice's presentation? An inverted scheme:

Deuteronomy 4 pictures a return to the Lord after Tribulation, not judgment. This means that a futurist view of the Tribulation is supported from this early passage.

We have also noted that Deuteronomy 28–30 indicates that the Tribulation will come after Israel has been regathered back into the land and Jerusalem, then God will bring to pass the Tribulation." (p. 79)

Just as Israel was regathered after the Babylonian captivity and returned to the land, so she will be returned from her A.D. 70 Diaspora from the nations. However, this time she will be regathered in preparation for a seven-year period we know as the Tribulation, which will serve to prepare her for conversion and ultimate covenantal blessing." (p. 80)

Third, Ice outlines the plight of Israel following upon the A.D. 70 holocaust as follows:

28:15–60	The affliction that God would bring upon Israel, while still in the land, because of her apostasy
28:32–39, 48–57	Israel will be taken captive
27; 32	The enemies of Israel will possess her land for a time

| 28:38–42; 29:23 | The land itself will remain desolate |
| 28:63–67; 32:26 | Israel will be scattered among the nations (p. 78) |

Notice that, according to Ice's scenario, Deuteronomy warns that "the land itself will remain desolate." Indeed, one of the passages to which he refers is Deuteronomy 29:23: "All its land is brimstone and salt, a burning waste, unsown and unproductive, and no grass grows in it, like the overthrow of Sodom and Gomorrah, Admah and Zeboiim, which the LORD overthrew in His anger and in His wrath." Yet who would say Israel's land "remain[s] desolate" today—especially to the degree of Deuteronomy 29:23? What happens to Ice's "consistent literalism" in all of this?

Purpose Blurring

Ice contradicts himself regarding the *judgment* nature of the Great Tribulation. In one place he denies it is a judgment on Israel, asserting rather that it is a judgment on the Gentiles:

> Within Deuteronomy 28–30 we see a specific reference to the Tribulation when it says, "And the LORD your God will inflict all these curses [Deut. 28] on your enemies and on those who hate you, who persecuted you" (Deut. 30:7). Moses tells us that the time of tribulation will include in its purposes a time of retribution to the Gentiles for their ill treatment of the Jews. (pp. 78–79)

Indeed, he castigates preterists for suggesting it is Israel's judgment: "the Bible does not regard the Tribulation as a time of punishment for the Jews, as preterists insist, instead it is a time of preparation for the Jew leading to his conversion and deliverance" (p. 79).

But in other places Ice admits the Great Tribulation is a judgment on the Jews:

(1) Of Jeremiah's prophecy regarding "Jacob's distress" (Jer. 30:7), Ice himself states: "It will be a time when God will *punish* [!] *Jacob justly and destroy part of her* (30:11)" (p. 81). The "part" of her God destroys is fully *two-thirds* of her population: Ice cites Zechariah 13:8 as a Great Tribulation text, wherein we read: "two parts in it will be cut off and perish; but the third will be left in it" (p. 90).[27] If this "punishment" is not judgment, what is? As Abraham Lincoln mused long ago: "If I call a tail a leg, how many legs does a dog have? Only four, because calling a tail a leg does not make it a leg."

(2) Ice comments on the future Great Tribulation: "We have the

picture of national Israel during the time of greatest distress from her enemies in all her history" (p. 83). If a time "of greatest distress" is not "judgment," what is?[28] If her Babylonian exile and Roman conquest are judgments (as all agree), how can those *judgments* be *less* intense than the *non*-judgment "great tribulation" which brings her time of "greatest distress"? This does not make sense. With apologies to Shakespeare: "What is in a name? that which we call a 'tribulation' by any other name would judge as vigorously."

(3) Ice's chart lists "twenty-two terms and expressions used by Old Testament writers to describe the Tribulation" (p. 81). Here he begins to "examine the major terms and passages relating to the Tribulation to gather a composite of what the Old Testament expected the Tribulation to be like" (p. 81). Interestingly, we find three of these terms (which define the character of "the Tribulation") applying directly to Israel: Deuteronomy 4:30; Jeremiah 30:7; and Zephaniah 1:15 (see Ice's discussion of these passages, pp. 81–83).

Consider just Zephaniah 1:15. According to Dr. Ice this verse employs one of his "tribulation terms" (p. 82). Surprisingly, Ice later (p. 99) argues vigorously that Luke calls Israel's woes in A.D. 70 a time of "great distress" (Gk., *anankē*, Luke 21:23) rather than a "great tribulation" (Gk., *thlipsis*). In fact, this difference of terms supposedly *proves* for Ice that Luke 21:23 refers to A.D. 70 and does not parallel Matthew 24:21 which prophesies the future Great Tribulation: "Interestingly the destruction of Jerusalem by the Romans is not called 'tribulation' but rather 'distress' in Luke. On the other hand, those passages in Matthew and Mark which futurists argue refer to the future tribulation are characterized as 'tribulation'" (p. 99). I would have the reader note, however, that Luke's term *anankē* appears in Zephaniah 1:15a in the Septuagint[29]: "A day of wrath is that day, A day of trouble and distress *[anagke]*." How can Ice argue that "the Tribulation" is not upon Israel if one of his tribulation terms speaks expressly of Israel? I believe Ice's presentation is confused.

Furthermore, note that Ice insists Zephaniah 1:14–18 refers to the *future tribulation:* "These verses heap together just about every term in the Bible that is used to describe and designate the Tribulation" (p. 83). Actually, Zephaniah is referring to the Babylonian captivity in the Old Testament as a judgment upon Israel. Please note: (a) The prophet specifically warns that the events are "near" (Zeph. 1:14). (b) The context relates the judgment to (Old Testament) Jerusalem: "And it will come about at that time that I will search Jerusalem with lamps" (Zeph. 1:12).[30] (c) Dispensational commentators recognize its immediate reference to the Babylonian assault. Walvoord deals with this passage under the heading: "The Impending Judgment of the Day of the Lord on Judah and

Jerusalem." He writes: "*Zephaniah 1:4–18*. Zephaniah declared the word of the Lord against Judah and Jerusalem." And: "This coming time of judgment, though extending to all the earth (1:2–3), was primarily on Judah and Jerusalem (1:4–2:3)."[31] Dallas Seminary's *The Bible Knowledge Commentary* observes: "This section (Zeph. 1:4–2:3) clearly indicates that Judah's wicked people would be destroyed at the Babylonian invasion in 586 B.C."[32] The translation Dr. Ice and I are using for our debate is the New American Standard Bible. Its heading over Zephaniah 1:1–18 reads: "Day of Judgment on Judah."

(4) Ezekiel 20:33–38 speaks of God *judging* Israel: "I shall bring you into the wilderness of the peoples, and there I shall enter into judgment with you face to face." Two of Ice's mentors apply this passage to the Tribulation. Walvoord: "This important prophecy was never fulfilled in the history of Israel and is connected to the judgments at the Second Coming."[33] Pentecost: "Since these things have never been fulfilled, and since an eternal and unconditional covenant demands a fulfillment, we must include such a program in our outline of future events."[34] This tribulational passage mentions *Israel's* judgment: "I shall enter into *judgment* with you face to face."

(5) According to Ice, Deuteronomy 4:30 is "the Mosaic introduction of 'tribulation.'" After enumerating the events Moses lists therein, Ice comments: "If the first five events have happened to Israel, and no one would deny that they have, then it is clear from the text that the final events will also occur to the same people in the same way. This is most clear from the context" (p. 77). But Deuteronomy 4 does *not* mention judgment on the *nations,* but only upon the *Jews*. Read it for yourself: "When *you* are in distress and all these things have come upon *you*, in the latter days, you will return to the LORD your God and listen to His voice" (emphasis mine). Once again, Ice's tribulation theology seems hopelessly confused.

Temporal Contortions

Dr. Ice frequently calls for a "plain reading" of the biblical text, defending his interpretations with statements such as: "The futurist does not need to make such adjustments and continues a plain reading of the text" (p. 97) Unfortunately, almost invariably he misreads plain and self-evident time indicators in Scripture. Regarding biblical prophecy, we could say that Dr. Ice cannot tell time.

Preterism receives its starting point in the various time statements of Scripture, not from any predisposition regarding eschatology.[35] The relevant time qualifiers are clear, numerous, varied, and strategically placed, leaving a remarkably consistent testimony to even the casual reader of God's Word. A few samples include the following: Matthew

24:34; Mark 9:1; Romans 16:20; 1 Peter 4:7; James 5:8; Revelation 1:1, 3; 3:10; 22:6, 10.

Yet Dr. Ice argues in effect that: "this generation" (Matt. 24:34) really means "that generation"; "shortly take place" (Rev. 1:1) really means "takes place rapidly—though thousands of years later"; "the time is near" (Rev. 1:3) really means "the time is theoretically imminent though delayed for two thousand years." In fact, he attempts various hermeneutical sleights-of-hand to remove the significance of these time texts from their original first-century audiences, after which he confidently asserts: "we have relieved the interpretative compulsion they feel from 'this generation,' 'quickly,' and 'at hand'" (p. 119).

At this point I will quickly respond to Dr. Ice's understanding of Daniel 9. Afterward I will grant a little more space to his reinterpretation of the prophetic time texts. Space limitations, of course, prevent a thorough analysis.

Ice's Seventy Weeks

The dispensational view of Daniel's seventy weeks is popular among laymen, but is fraught with enormous difficulties. Unfortunately, Ice's presentation transforms the difficulties into absurdities.

Keep in mind that Daniel 9 is important to Ice's Tribulation views: "Daniel's 'seventy weeks,' prophesied in Daniel 9:24–27 are the framework within which the Tribulation or the seventieth week occurs. The seven-year period of Daniel's seventieth week provides the time span or length of the Tribulation" (p. 84). Of Daniel 9 in its context, Ice comments: "Daniel apparently thought that God would institute the Messianic age upon Israel's return from their seventy–year captivity. However, God had other plans. As the rest of Daniel 9 reveals through an angel, God was stretching out Israel's history. It would not be seventy more years, but seventy times seven, or four hundred and ninety years until the culmination of Israel's history in the Kingdom" (p. 117). Just a few sentences later, Ice contrasts the time frame of the church with that of Israel, when he observes: "The length [of the church age] has been preordained by God, but He has not told us" (p. 117).

According to Ice, then, God reveals the seventy-weeks prophecy specifically to correct Daniel's anticipating a soon establishment of the Messianic age. The prophecy informs Daniel that "God was stretching out Israel's history," so that the Messianic age would "not be seventy more years, but seventy times seven, or four hundred and ninety years." I agree that God designs the prophecy to measure time for Daniel, for it opens with these words: "Seventy weeks [or four hundred and ninety years] have been decreed for your people" (Dan. 9:24a).[36] But Ice then *totally destroys* the measuring function, once

again showing that his system cannot tell time. I will provide just a
brief analysis of a few problems with his treatment of Daniel 9.[37]

First, under the heading "Verification," Ice justifies his count of the
days involved in the first sixty-nine weeks, which he thinks (wrongly,
I believe) culminates on March 30, A.D. 33. I will leave aside certain
huge problems confronting Ice's precise computations, such as the
controversy over the date of Christ's birth (probably around 4 B.C.) and
the date he begins his ministry (apparently when he was "about thirty,"
Luke 3:23). Even one of Ice's favorite theologians, L. S. Chafer, admits: "Recent scholarship has placed the death of Christ as late as A.D.
33, *although most interpreters date it A.D. 30 or earlier.*"[38]

Even granting these large assumptions, we may still discern enormous debilitating problems for Ice. Notice his rather strained math-
ematical intricacies: To make his calculations fit, he adopts a
definition of a year which provides the year length of 365.2421989
days (rather than 365 days)— as if Daniel had this figure in mind!
The decimal is necessary to Ice's precise calculation. The formula
computes down to a fraction of a day, exactly .2421989 of a day, that
is, 5 hours and 48 minutes and 45.98496 seconds! Then, employing
this technically precise time measure, he comes up with 173,855 days.
(Actually, he should come up with 173855.2866764 days, but we will
let that slide, too.)

What surprises me in all of this is that after all of his high-tech com-
putation, Ice arbitrarily throws in an enormous *open-ended* gap in
Daniel's precise measurement: "Any attempt to find a literal fulfillment of the final seven years requires a gap of time between the sixty-
ninth and seventieth weeks. This provides the basis for the final week
of Daniel's prophecy to be fulfilled literally *in the future*" (emphasis
mine, p. 86). This brings Ice's own judgment down upon himself, for
this not only generates a problem with "God's reputation in the area
of clearness of speech" (p. 70)—who would have surmised this open-
ended gap when reading Daniel? But it also contradicts Daniel's assertion that a specific time is established for Israel (Dan. 9:24a)—as
Ice well knows (see his comments from p. 117 cited above). What is
more, the unforeseen gap in Daniel's time frame *presently* measures
almost two thousand years—or *four times Daniel's entire time frame!*

Dr. Ice is fundamentally mistaken when he asserts that every evangelical view must incorporate a gap (p. 86). I do not employ a gap,
even though I *do* see the time frame as literal.[39] Nor does J. Barton
Payne, a premillennialist.[40] Furthermore, this sort of *deus ex machina*
gap destroys other observations by Ice, such as: "God will not intervene with another new program such as the Church. We can be sure
that the phase of history is the Tribulation leading up to the millennial

kingdom" (p. 118). How does Ice know God will not intervene with another new program? Was not the church age itself wholly unforeseen, in Ice's system? Prophetic calculation is impossible with such a methodology.

"This Generation"

When Dr. Ice considers the time text in the Olivet discourse, he once again distorts the obvious. Luke 21:32 reads: "Truly I say to you, this generation will not pass away until all things take place." Ice writes: "our position is that this generation is not the generation to whom Christ is speaking, but the generation to whom the signs will become evident" (p. 103). He then cites Darrell Bock as supporting evidence: "Dr. Bock concurs."

At this juncture the reader should recall my observations in chapter 1 above. My exposition of "this generation" provides a linguistically sound, morally relevant, and historically dramatic fit; it does not require a reinterpretation of "this generation" between Matthew 23:36 and Matthew 23:34. I believe the presentation there withstands Ice's counterintuitive approach. In addition, I would offer the following rejoinders:

First, Ice admits that the phrase *can* be interpreted according to my analysis: "it is true that other uses of 'this generation' refer to Christ's contemporaries" in other contexts (p. 103).

Second, the obvious implications of this phrase, which give rise to the "highly artificial" (Carson) and "weak" (Turner)[41] alternatives of dispensationalism, cause great interpretive problems for them. In 1957 dispensational scholar J. Dwight Pentecost argued: "The word generation is to be taken in its basic usage of 'race, kindred, family, stock, breed.'"[42] He has since renounced this view and adopted one like Ice's: "This generation" means that "the generation that sees the beginning of these signs will 'not pass away until all these things have happened' (v. 34)."[43] Dispensationalists are dancing around the obvious interpretation. Read Matthew 24:34 for yourself and see.

Third, when Ice writes that "Dr. Bock concurs," then quotes Bock, he omits the following admissions by Bock (p. 103): "This view is a strong possibility and is the best of the options. . . . The main objection to this view is that *genea* usually refers to the present generation, rather than to a deferred generation, a correct point. . . . If this view is correct. . . . It is hard to be dogmatic about the meaning of this difficult text."[44] Bock is not as sure as Ice: it is a "strong possibility," "if," "it is hard to be dogmatic." You would never know this, however, from Ice's selective citation from Bock.

Fourth, the logical question to ask of Ice's counterintuitive interpretation is: Why did not Jesus simply say *"that* generation"? This would be perfectly clear, if Ice's view were correct.

Fifth, on page 103 Ice tries to distinguish Jesus' use of "this generation" in Matthew 23:36 from the same phrase in 24:34 on the basis that 24:36 is "historical" while 24:34 is "prophetical" (Matt. 24:34). But note: (1) *Both* are prophetic. In Matthew 23 Jesus prophesies *future* persecution for his own disciples (23:34) and the catastrophic calamity to befall the Pharisees in A.D. 70 (23:35). Declaring future events in advance is, by definition, "prophetic." (2) As I show in Chapter One, Matthew 24 flows directly from Matthew 23: As Jesus declares Israel's first-century temple "desolate" (23:38), dramatically leaving it (24:1a), the disciples point out the beauty of the temple (24:1b), to which Jesus responds about its destruction (24:2), causing the surprised inquiry of the disciples "when" shall these things be (24:3). The two chapters are interlocked— and so must be the similar time-frame language.

"Shortly Take Place"

Another area in which Dr. Ice exhibits his penchant for reinterpreting the obvious time texts is in Revelation. John opens Revelation with these words: "The Revelation of Jesus Christ, which God gave Him to show to His bond-servants, the things which must *shortly* take place" (Rev. 1:1a, emphasis mine). Because of this text and others similar to it (e.g., 1:3; 22:6, 10), I believe the first century witnesses the fulfilling of the great majority of the events of Revelation, especially in conjunction with the destruction of the temple and Jerusalem.[45] Ice and other dispensationalists, of course, vigorously disagree. But at this juncture I am demonstrating Ice's problems with prophetic time texts. Due to space limitations I cannot provide an exposition of Revelation.[46]

Ice cites my observations on the shortness of Revelation's time frame, then launches into another massive reinterpretive effort. He suggests that the term translated "shortly" in Revelation 1:1 means: "'quickly' or 'suddenly' as many futurists contend (relating to the manner in which action occurs)" (p. 108). Thus, "shortly" (Gk., *tachos*) does not speak of the temporal *proximity* of the events, but of their *rapidity* of succession whenever they begin erupting on the scene. I will briefly rebut his major arguments.

First, immediately after introducing the preterist focus on the nearness of Revelation's prophecies (Rev.1:1), Ice writes: "It appears presumptuous at the outset of the interpretative process that these verses are labeled 'timing' passages" (p. 107). This is an incredible assertion. "Presumptuous"? When speaking of the word *tachos* in Revelation 1:1, Ice himself admits that *tachos:* "can be used to mean 'soon' or 'shortly' as preterists believe (relating to time)" (p. 108). Of the similar term in

Revelation 1:3 ("near," Gk., *engys,* see below), Ice notes that "it is true that *engys* can and often is used to refer to something that takes place within a short span of time from when it is stated" (p. 115). If such are "often" legitimate meanings of the terms, how can the soon/near interpretation be "presumptuous at the outset"? As usual, he overstates his concerns.

Second, after Ice agrees that we may translate the term as I prefer, he says: "If disagreement arises over *how* a word is used in a particular passage, the context of the passage must be the basis for determining exactly which nuance of meaning the Bible intends" (p. 108). Unfortunately, he does not inform his reader that *all* standard versions of the Bible translate these terms in a preterist-like way, rather than his way. Check them out for yourself.[47] *None* of the versions agree with Ice; absolutely no disagreement exists among the professional linguists on the Bible translation committees. Had John wanted to speak of the soonness/nearness of the prophecies, how else could he have stated it? He clearly states they are "shortly to come to pass" and "the time is near."

Third, amazingly Ice uses Acts 22:18 as his first sample of the term's meaning "quickly" rather than "soon": "And I saw Him saying to me, 'Make haste, and get out of Jerusalem quickly, because they will not accept your testimony about Me'" (p. 108). After discussing whether this phrase means "soon" or "quickly" in Luke 18:8, Marshall uses Acts 22:18 as a sample that "the normal use of the phrase" means "happens after a very short interval, i.e., 'soon.'"[48] This explains why the NIV and NAB translate the phrase "immediately" and Ice's favorite lexicon (Arndt-Gingrich) cites it as an example of the meaning "without delay, quickly, at once."[49] Ice's reference to Acts 22:18 illustrates the irrelevancy of his assertion. Read the passage in its context and try to understand it in Ice's sense, that is, that Christ urges Paul's *fast motion* rather than his *immediate action.* Obviously, Christ is warning Paul *immediately* (soon) to leave the city. Of course, he will do it in a hasty manner, but haste delayed will simply not fit the text. The Lord is not concerned with how fast Paul's body moves, but with *when* it begins moving. Time is of the very essence of Christ's concern for Paul. Time is of the essence in Revelation, as well (as we may sense from the urgent relevance of Revelation 1:9; 6:10).

Fourth, Ice cites Walvoord: "That which Daniel declared would occur 'in the latter days' is here described as 'shortly' (Gr., *en tachei*), that is, 'quickly or suddenly coming to pass,' indicating rapidity of execution after the beginning takes place. The idea is not that the event may occur soon, but that when it does, it will be sudden" (p. 108). But Walvoord clearly turns the passage on its head with these words. Read and compare Daniel 12:4 with Revelation 22:10:

Daniel 12:4: But you, Daniel, shut up the words, and seal the book until the time of the end; many shall run to and fro, and knowledge shall increase.

Revelation 22:10: And he said to me, "Do not seal up the words of the prophecy of this book, for the time is near."

Daniel *seals* his book because the *time* of fulfillment is in the distant future; John does *not* seal his—because "the time is *near*." What could be more clear?

Fifth, under the heading "1. The lexical use" Ice writes: "The leading Greek lexicon in our day is Bauer, Arndt, and Gingrich (BAG), which lists the following definitions for *táchos:* "speed, quickness, swiftness, haste" (p. 814)" (p. 109). But Ice's gestalt once again causes him severe elliptical failure (as in his use of Bock's comments above): he sees only what he wants to see and cites only what he wants us to know. The definition he cites derives from Homer, the Septuagint, and other sources—not the New Testament. If he were to read just a few lines further in BAG he would read the following definition based on the New Testament: *"soon, in a short time* Lk 18:8; Ro 16:20; 1 Ti 3:14 v.1; Rv 1:1; 22:6; 1 Cl 65:1."[50] In other words, the "leading Greek lexicon in our day" agrees with the preterist on Revelation 1:1 and 22:6! This explains why *all* standard English Bible versions translate *tachos* as expressing temporal nearness.

In that John is dealing with real churches (Rev. 1:4, 11) in a time of dire Tribulation (Rev. 1:9), why would he inform them that judgment will fall rapidly some two thousand years later? Such would be wholly irrelevant to their circumstances. He was *then* in "tribulation"—as were the seven churches. John's Revelation, like other letters in the New Testament, is an *occasional* letter. That is, Revelation deals with specific events occasioning the necessity of his writing. The relief must be *soon,* not amazingly fast though two thousand years (or more!) later.

Two sentences later Ice continues his error:

> The other word in the *tachos* family used in Revelation as an adverb is *tachy,* which all six times occurs with the verb *erchomai,* "to come" (2:16; 3:11; 11:14; 22:7, 12, 20). BAG gives as its meaning "quick, swift, speedy" (p. 814) and specifically classifies all six uses in Revelation as meaning "without delay, quickly, at once" (p. 815). Thus, contrary to the timing assumption of preterists like DeMar and Gentry. . . . (p. 109)

Four problems derail his argument:

(1) Despite Ice, the second lexicon definition—"without delay, quickly, at once," which he himself cites as relevant to Revelation—nicely supports the preterist viewpoint. Read either of these three nuances in the Revelation texts and the result is a matter of timing. "Without delay, quickly, at once" surely are not conducive to a two-thousand-year delay from John's day. In fact, each illustration the lexicon provides for this meaning (Matt. 5:25; 28:7; Luke 15:22) requires *immediate* action, not long-delayed action.

(2) The lexicon clearly notes *in the same sentence from which Ice draws his citation:* "it is not always poss[ible] to make a clear distinction betw[een] this mng. and the one in c below." The "c" entry reads: "in a short time, soon."[51]

(3) Even *if* we were to allow Ice's narrow rendering of the word *tachy,* note: (a) *Tachy* is *not* the explicit form found in the texts under question, which is *tachos* (Rev. 1:1; 22:6). (b) But even in the other texts in Revelation this other, related word still would not undermine the preterist notion of nearness. Rather, it would enhance it by emphasizing not only its temporal nearness but by expressing its rapid arrival.

(4) The same argumentative confusion—and worse—plagues his other points. For instance, note his statement on page 110: "For example, Isaiah 13:22 says, '. . . Her (Israel) fateful time also will *soon* come . . .' This was written around 700 B.C. foretelling the destruction of Babylon which occurred in 539 B.C." In the first place, the statement "her fateful time also will soon come" clearly speaks of *Babylon,* not Israel, as the context makes clear (Isa. 13:1, 19–22). Second, Ice contradicts himself in the very next sentence. After he notes that the fateful time refers to "Israel," he immediately states that the prophecy was "foretelling the destruction of Babylon." Third, Babylon *did* fall *soon* thereafter. According to Dallas Theological Seminary's *The Bible Knowledge Commentary:* "Isaiah was convinced that the destruction he wrote about would come quickly (**her time is at hand**). It came in 689 B.C." This was around eleven years after Isaiah wrote in about 700 B.C. Fourth, Ice is confusing separate falls of Babylon, the one here in 689 B.C. and a later one to Medo-Persia in 539 B.C. The *The Bible Knowledge Commentary* observes:

> Many interpreters, because of the mention of the fall of Babylon (v. 19), assume that Isaiah was (in vv. 17–18) prophesying Babylon's fall in 539 (cf. Dan. 5:30–31) to the Medes and Persians. However, that view has some difficulties. In the Medo-Persian takeover in 539 there was little change in the city; it was not destroyed so it continued on much as it had

been. But Isaiah 13:19–22 speaks of the *destruction* of Babylon. Also, the word "them," against whom the Medes were stirred up (v. 17), were the Assyrians (referred to in vv. 14–16), not the Babylonians. It seems better, then, to understand this section as dealing with events pertaining to the Assyrians' sack of Babylon in December 689 B.C.[52]

This type of argumentative pandemonium reigns throughout Ice's study. Unfortunately, space limitations prohibit my delving into Ice's many other miscues. Suffice it to say, he fares no better with his treatment of *engys* in Revelation 1:3. After all, when you have two very closely linked verses using two different words that *all* Bible versions translate as indicating temporal proximity, the reader should open his eyes to John's meaning and avoid Dr. Ice's. This explains Ice's difficulties with these passages, which read:

> *Revelation 1:1: The Revelation of Jesus Christ, which God gave Him to show to His bond-servants, the things which must shortly take place; and He sent and communicated it by His angel to His bond-servant John.*

> *Revelation 1:3: Blessed is he who reads and those who hear the words of the prophecy, and heed the things which are written in it; for the time is near.*

As for me and my house, we will read the translations as they appear!

Luke 21 Issues

For Dr. Ice, Luke 21 contains a key passage for understanding the relationship of A.D. 70 and the (alleged) future Great Tribulation, since it gives an "outline of history" in general (p. 95) and a "template for Israel's history" in particular (p. 97). I will interact with Ice's leading arguments by following the order of his presentation on pages 95ff. Again, space constraints forbid an analysis of each and every point, but if his *leading arguments* fail in their purpose, then his whole case is hamstrung.

Dr. Ice's presentation is characteristically misleading. For instance, on page 96 he comments:

> All three Synoptic Gospels (Matthew, Mark, and Luke) record the Olivet discourse as given by Jesus. Matthew and Mark focus exclusively upon the future events of the Tribulation, while Luke's version includes past and future elements. In

relation to Luke 21:20 Dr. Darrell Bock comments: The different emphases are most clearly indicated by what Luke
lacks. . . .

When you read this you almost certainly surmise that New Testament scholar Darrell Bock agrees with Ice's claim that "Matthew and
Mark focus *exclusively* upon the future events of the Tribulation" (emphasis mine). Yet Bock forthrightly *denies* such. While commenting
on Luke 21, Bock notes that "the other Gospels tend to focus slightly
more on the end-time, while Luke tends to stress the near future."[53]
Bock believes Matthew focuses only "slightly more" on the end time.
Indeed, he comments that "Matthew 24:6 appears to suggest that these
calamities are in the near future,"[54] rather than in the distant
eschatological tribulation.

The reader needs always to be wary of Ice's careless expressions
and use of sources. Nevertheless, Bock does hold to a futuristic view
of *some* of the verses in Matthew 24 and Luke 21 that I claim are past.
And Ice incorporates these into his own argument (though abusing
Bock's presentation and confusing his reader along the way). Due to
the significance Ice places on Bock's study, I will respond to the pieces
of Bock's analysis as presented by Ice.

Ice opens this major section of his argument with Bock's study of
the "different emphases" between portions of Luke and Matthew. These
different emphases supposedly suggest that the seeming parallels in
Matthew 24 refer to the future eschatological event, whereas their
Lucan counterparts speak of A.D. 70. Bock argues that the first-century
catastrophe and the future Great Tribulation are a "pair of related
events"[55] wherein Jerusalem's A.D. 70 "fall pictures the end."[56] Bock
writes:

> The different emphases are most clearly indicated by what
> Luke lacks: he does not mention that the Tribulation in this
> period is the most intense ever to fall on humans; he does not
> mention that no human would have survived if the Lord had
> not cut short these days; he does not note that the time should
> not be in the winter; and he does not discuss the "abomination
> of desolation," only "its desolation." Conversely, Luke alone
> mentions "the time of the Gentiles." What do these differ-
> ences mean? They indicate that Luke emphasizes a different
> element in Jesus' teaching at this point. He focuses on the
> nearer fulfillment in the judgment pattern described here, the
> fall of Jerusalem in A.D. 70, rather than the end (which he will
> introduce directly in 21:25). . . . So the instructions he offers

here are like those that appear in the description of the end in
17:23, 31. He wants to make clear that when Jerusalem falls
the first time, it is not yet the end. Nonetheless, the two falls
are related and the presence of one pictures what the ultimate
siege will be like (cited by Ice on p. 96)

To this I will respond point-by-point as follows:

Intense Tribulation

Ice's and Bock's first distinction between Matthew's (alleged) futuristic and Luke's A.D. 70 accounts is that Luke "does not mention
that the tribulation in this period is the most intense ever." The end-
time account, then, is more dreadful. But consider the following:

(1) When we place the two sections side-by-side, they seem clearly
to refer to the same phenomena, with slightly different wording based
on audience differences between Matthew and Luke:

Matthew 24:15–22

*[15] Therefore when you see the ABOMINATION OF DESO-
LATION which was spoken of through Daniel the prophet,
standing in the holy place (let the reader understand), [16]
then let those who are in Judea flee to the mountains; [17] let
him who is on the housetop not go down to get the things out
that are in his house; [18] and let him who is in the field not
turn back to get his cloak. [19] But woe to those who are with
child and to those who nurse babes in those days! [20] But
pray that your flight may not be in the winter, or on a Sabbath; [21] for then there will be a great tribulation, such as
has not occurred since the beginning of the world until now,
nor ever shall. [22] And unless those days had been cut short,
no life would have been saved; but for the sake of the elect
those days shall be cut short.*

Luke 21:20–24

*[20] But when you see Jerusalem surrounded by armies, then
recognize that her desolation is at hand. [21] Then let those
who are in Judea flee to the mountains, and let those who are
in the midst of the city depart, and let not those who are in the
country enter the city; [22] because these are days of vengeance, in order that all things which are written may be fulfilled. [23] Woe to those who are with child and to those who
nurse babes in those days; for there will be great distress upon
the land, and wrath to this people, [24] and they will fall by*

*the edge of the sword, and will be led captive into all the na-
tions; and Jerusalem will be trampled under foot by the Gentiles until the times of the Gentiles be fulfilled.*

What Matthew the Jew calls the "abomination of desolation," Luke
the Gentile explains as "Jerusalem surrounded by armies" so that the
disciples must "recognize that her desolation is at hand." See my discussion on pages 45–50 above.

(2) In my first chapter I show *in what manner* Jesus designates A.D.
70 an unparalleled/unique devastation. Again we must remember that
Matthew's record is for a *Jewish* audience, Luke's for a *Gentile* audience. Hence, Matthew emphasizes Jewish sympathies and estimations.
Elsewhere Bock allows dissimilarities between Matthew and Luke because of Luke's Gentile audience. For instance, Luke lacks Matthew's
reference to the "councils" *(synedria),* which Bock notes is "a term that
Luke does not use for his Gentile audience, since it refers to Jewish authorities."[57] I think he should recognize the same audience difference here
as well—especially in light of the very obvious parallels: for Israel this
was the worst ever tribulation (they no longer have a temple as required
by their law).

Matthew's record claims an unparalleled enormity in the events. But
remember: such claims regarding unique events or persons are common in Scripture. Is not this hyperbolic-apocalyptic statement by Jesus
like Ezekiel's prophetic analysis of the Babylonian conquest of Israel
given in the Old Testament? In Ezekiel 5:9 we read, "And because of
all your abominations, I will do among you what I have not done, and
the like of which I will never do again" (emphasis mine). According
to the dispensationalist *New Scofield Reference Bible* this section from
Ezekiel 4:1–7:27 speaks of the Babylonian conquest of Israel during
which "Ezekiel was carried to Babylon."[58] Walvoord agrees that "this
was fulfilled in the Babylonian Captivity."[59] The prophet Daniel confirms this judgment on Israel in Daniel 9:12: "Thus He has confirmed
His words which He had spoken against us and against our rulers who
ruled us, to bring on us great calamity; for under the whole heaven
there has not been done anything like what was done to Jerusalem."

Despite Ezekiel 5:9 and Daniel 9:12, in Matthew 24:21 Jesus declares the (alleged) end-times Great Tribulation unequaled. These assertions by Ezekiel, Daniel, and Jesus are not contradictory; clearly
prophetic hyperbole is at work for dramatic effect. Such bold claims
are common in ancient nonbiblical Jewish writings: Baruch 2:2;
1 Maccabees 9:27; Assumption of Moses 8:1; *Wars* proem., 1:1:4; and
5:10:5. As William Lane observes, "Emphatic affirmations of this type
are not uncommon in the OT and subsequent Jewish literature and must

not be interpreted too rigorously."[60] He even cites the Qumranian documents from near Jesus' day: "And it shall be a time of distress for all
the people redeemed by God, and among all their afflictions there will
have been nothing to equal it from its beginning until its end in final
redemption" (1QM 1:11–12).

Besides those claims regarding unparalleled suffering which I list
above (on pages 50–53 in my second chapter), consider the unique
assertions regarding Hezekiah: "He trusted in the LORD, the God of
Israel; so that *after him there was none like him* among all the kings of
Judah, nor among those who were before him" (2 Kings 18:5). Yet of
Josiah we read virtually the same estimation: "And *before him there
was no king like him* who turned to the LORD with all his heart and
with all his soul and with all his might, according to all the law of
Moses; *nor did any like him arise after him*" (2 Kings 23:25). Such
laudatory praise is not contradictory, but hyperbolic.

Isaiah 13:20 declares with a similar universal negative regarding
Babylon's Old Testament judgment: "It will never be inhabited or lived
in from generation to generation; nor will the Arab pitch his tent there,
nor will shepherds make their flocks lie down there." Yet we know
Babylon has been inhabited over the centuries since. Ice himself argues
for a "'revived' Babylon during the Tribulation" as a part of his dispensational perspective: John's Babylon in Revelation 18 must "refer to an
economic or commercial center related to the contemporary site of the
historic city of Babylon."[61] Indeed, classic and revived dispensationalists
(though not progressive dispensationalists) are fond of pointing to a future, rebuilt Babylon based on Revelation 18.[62]

And what of Tyre's judgment? Ezekiel writes in Ezekiel 26:14: "And
I will make you a bare rock; you will be a place for the spreading of
nets. You will be built no more, for I the LORD have spoken," declares
the Lord GOD." Yet Tyre was rebuilt later (1 Macc. 111:59; 2 Macc.
4:18). In fact, our Lord ministers there (Matt. 15:21–28; Mark 3:8; Luke
6:17), as do his apostles (Acts 21:3). This is not error; this is hyperbolic, poetic, dramatic, judgment talk.

All Flesh Threatened

Ice's and Bock's second distinction between Matthew's (alleged)
future-oriented and Luke's past-oriented (A.D. 70) accounts is that Luke
"does not mention that no human would have survived." But again this
appears to be hyperbolic judgment language, such as Isaiah's declaring Babylon will never be inhabited ever again (Isa. 13:20). I do not
believe Matthew's record expresses a concern for the death of the *entire world* population, but only those within the sphere and scene of
judgment in Israel. The shortening of the siege is to the advantage of

the Christians ("the elect") who under adverse circumstances flee to the mountains with only meager supplies. Therefore, God truncates the devastation, leaving many Jews alive and relieving Christian Jews from hiding any longer in the mountains.

William Lane notes of the Mark 13:20 parallel to Matthew 24:22: "according to the context, *pasa sarx* ["all flesh"] . . . must be understood of Judea and Jerusalem. Cf. Jer. 12:12 where a similar expression designates the inhabitants of Judea."[63] As Baptist exegete A. T. Robertson notes of this verse: "The siege was shortened by various historical events like the stopping of the strengthening of the walls by Herod Agrippa by orders from the Emperor, the sudden arrival of Titus, the neglect of the Jews to prepare for a long siege."[64]

Indeed, this concern for "all flesh" parallels in expression Isaiah 66:15–16: "For behold, the LORD will come in fire, and His chariots like the whirlwind, to render His anger with fury, and His rebuke with flames of fire. For the LORD will execute judgment by fire. And by His sword on all flesh, and those slain by the LORD will be many." Note that though the sword falls upon "all flesh," it results in the slaying of "many," not literally "all." As E. J. Young observes: "*All flesh* is here not to be taken in a universal sense, as, for example, Smart does, but is defined by the following verse. It stands for those of the Jewish nation, the great majority, who have abandoned the Lord for the service of idols."[65]

This usage of "all flesh" reminds us of the Pentecostal experience cited in Acts 2:16–17: "This is what was spoken of through the prophet Joel: 'And it shall be in the last days,' God says, 'That I will pour forth of my Spirit upon all mankind [lit., "all flesh"]; and your sons and your daughters shall prophesy, and your young men shall see visions, and your old men shall dream dreams." We know the Spirit was not poured out upon the entire human race at Pentecost.

Winter Warning

Ice's and Bock's third distinction between Matthew's (alleged) future-oriented and Luke's past-oriented A.D. 70 accounts is: Luke "does not note that the time should not be in the winter." Surely this cannot persuade us that the accounts are of vastly different eras. If on Bock's and Ice's analysis, Luke 21 refers to first-century events and Matthew 24 the future, it would seem that the danger of winter would be *more* pronounced—not less—in the first century than in modern times when (allegedly) the Great Tribulation breaks out. To a less technologically advanced culture in antiquity winter brings more serious complications (see Acts 27:12; 2 Tim. 4:21; Titus 3:12).[66] Ancient records show the fearsome encumbrance of winter upon war: Herod was deterred from an important battle due to winter (*Wars* 1:17:6); general Vespasian was prohibited from helping Rome during her Civil Wars due to winter (*Wars* 4:8:1; 4:10:2); troop movements were greatly affected by winter, despite important battles looming (*Wars* 4:11:1). I really do not see how Matthew's reference to winter requires a *future* great tribulation.

Abomination of Desolation

Ice's and Bock's fourth distinction between Matthew's (alleged) future-oriented and Luke's past-oriented A.D. 70 accounts is: Luke "does not discuss the 'abomination of desolation,' only 'its desolation.'" But as I note above, Luke appears to be simply rephrasing the Old Testament language for his Gentile audience. When we lay the two passages side-by-side, there appears to be a direct correlation between them (see above and my discussion on pages 188–89).

Israel's Rescue

In addition to Bock's observations, Dr. Ice comments later: "A key factor in favor of futurism and literal interpretation is that even if one takes the symbolical approach to the text, the fact that Israel is rescued—not judged—in the Olivet discourse (except Luke 21:20–24) is unavoidable and thus a *fatal* blow to preterism" (p. 98).

Unfortunately for Ice,, his "key factor" is an unprovable, anticontextual assertion. Remember my presentation of Matthew's flow (Gentry chap. 1 above), and note Luke's own context: Jesus is dealing with God's judgment on the first-century Jews and their temple for their treatment of His followers (Matt. 23:34–37; 24:1–3; Luke 21:6–7, 12, 20). The dispensationalist view requires a suppressed premise: It demands the "abomination of desolation" in a temple *other than* the first-century temple—without textual warrant. And this despite Jesus' speaking of the temple before their very eyes. How could they know he implied a *rebuilt* temple—while they were pointing to their first-century temple which stood firm, strong, and impressive?[67]

Distress Versus Tribulation

Ice makes much of the different terms Matthew and Luke employ regarding their respective catastrophes: Matthew speaks of "tribulation" (Gk., *thlipsis*); Luke of *"distress"* (Gk., *anankē*). Ice observes: "Interestingly the destruction of Jerusalem by the Romans is not called 'tribulation' but rather 'distress' in Luke. On the other hand, those passages in Matthew and Mark which futurists argue refer to the future tribulation are characterized as 'tribulation'" (p. 99).

This may be "interesting," but it is neither significant to the debate nor helpful to Ice's case. As I note in the present chapter, Luke's term for "distress" *(anankē)* appears in the Septuagint translation of Zephaniah 1:15. According to Ice's chart, this is a "tribulation" passage (p. 82). And why not? The Abbott-Smith lexicon lists the terms *anankē* and *thlipsis* as synonyms.[68]

What is more, both "great distress" (Luke 21:23) and "great tribulation" (Matt. 24:21) appear in contexts dealing with the dismantling of the first-century temple (Matt. 24:1–2; Luke 21:5–6) and confined to "this generation" (Matt. 24:34; Luke 21:32). In addition, Luke *nowhere* refers to the (alleged) future time as a "tribulation," *even though Ice says most of his material speaks of the future "tribulation."* Obviously, Luke can relate the concept of tribulation without the term *thlipsis*. In fact, *nowhere* in Luke's gospel does he even use the word *thlipsis*, "tribulation." Remarkably, the phrase *thlipsis megalē* ("great tribulation") appears in Acts 7:11 where it refers to the famine in Egypt: "Now a famine came over all Egypt and Canaan, and *great affliction* with it; and our fathers could find no food." Even the phrase "great tribulation" can refer to something other than the eschatological "Great Tribulation."

Local Versus Global

Ice presents another argument by contrasting strands in Luke 21:

> The focus of Luke 21:25–28 reveals a distinct shift from the first-century description of verses 20–24. The differences include the local focus of Jerusalem in the first-century judgment versus the global perspective of the future tribulation. The Tribulation will involve heavenly and global events that did not literally occur in A.D. 70. (p. 101)

Unfortunately, Ice's argument fails of its purpose for several reasons: (1) Luke's flow does not suggest a leap from the first century to the last century: verse 25 introduces the next section simply: "And there will be signs." This implies a continuation of the forgoing (A.D. 70) topic, not a radical change of venue. (2) Luke 21:20–21 parallels very closely Matthew 24:15–16, which Ice believes is futuristic. But *both* passages focus on *Judea,* not the world. (3) Both passages are followed by the inspired declaration that the events will occur in "this generation" (Matt. 24:32; Luke 21:32). (4) The "fainting from fear and the expectation of the things which are coming upon the *world*" (Luke 21:26) is a fear referring to events coming upon the *oikoumenē* (translated "world"). This word gives rise to our word "economy," and often refers to a local region, as in Luke 2:1 and Acts 11:28 (cp. my discussion on pp. 43–45 in my second chapter above). (5) Though Leon Morris believes the stellar catastrophe language refers to the Second

Advent (as does Ice), he admits that "such language is often used in apocalyptic to denote sudden and violent change and the emergence of a new order,"[69] as does Dallas Theological Seminary's *The Bible Knowledge Commentary* in various Old Testament passages.[70]

Unfortunately, diminishing space forbids my responding to other elements in Dr. Ice's presentation. I must move on—even if only briefly—to his comments on Revelation.

Revelation Issues

Almost certainly Ice's comments on Revelation will initially find a sympathetic ear with the reader. But I trust that the initial acceptance of his observations will be withdrawn upon further reflection. My hope is based on two reasons: (1) We have already seen the fallacious nature of Ice's arguments heretofore. These should give pause to the thoughtful reader. (2) The brief rejoinder below, along with references to additional material, should at least suggest the possibility of the preterist approach to Revelation. Obviously, time does not allow me to fully engage the book of Revelation, a large, complex, and difficult book in itself. Yet fortunately, my understanding of Revelation is now available in a thorough enough form as Chapter One in C. Marvin Pate, ed., *Four Views on the Book of Revelation* and will soon be available in more detail in my commentary *Revelation: A Tale of Two Cities*. But I will make a few observations that should be of helpful to the interested reader.

Revelational Nature

I would hope that every Christian reader would carefully ponder Dr. Ice's statement of alarm on page 104: "preterists advocate a symbolic interpretation of Revelation." If you have read Revelation you will know why we do so. As I state in my section of the *Four Views on the Book of Revelation:*

> Virtually all evangelical scholars (excluding classic dispensationalists) recognize regarding the book: *Revelation is a highly figurative book that we cannot approach with a simple straightforward literalism.* That having been stated, however, the preterist view does understand Revelation's prophecies as strongly reflecting actual historical events in John's near future—though they are set in apocalyptic drama and clothed in poetic hyperbole. As even premillennialist commentator Robert Mounce notes: "That the language of prophecy is highly figurative has nothing to do with the reality of the events predicted. Symbolism is not a denial of historicity but a matter of literary genre."[71]

Is this at all unreasonable? Should such an admission cause evangelical alarm? Please remember my presentation earlier in this chapter (pp. 172–73), which included the following elements:

Does not John himself inform us that Revelation is given "to show" (Gk., *deixai*) the message being "signified (Gk., *esēmanen*) by His angel" (Rev. 1:1 NKJV)?

Is this not the book whose major personages are a slain lamb with seven eyes (Rev. 5:6)? Locusts with faces of men (9:7–8)? A woman clothed with the moon under her feet (12:1)? A seven-headed beast (13:1)? A prostitute drunk on blood (17:3, 6)?

Taking these and my earlier observations, surely we are justified in approaching Revelation as a symbolic book. This is why *you* understand Revelation as a book of symbols. And why Dr. Ice does—when he gets down to details. In fact, does not Ice himself agree with me that *sometimes* clouds can be *symbols* of divine judgment (as in Isa. 19:1; Ps. 68:4, for example): "I do not have a problem with Gentry's understanding of these passages as they are used in their Old Testament context" (p. 106)?

Revelational Theme

Regarding Ice's concern over my interpreting Revelation 1:7 as Christ's providential judgment against Israel (like God's against Egypt in Isa. 19:1), I must refer the reader to my section of Pate's *Four Views on the Book of Revelation* for more detail. But I briefly note here:

(1) The pattern of my interpretation: I provide the basic pattern for understanding Revelation 1:7 in Chapter One above, where I explain Matthew 24:29–30 (pp. 55–65). Matthew 24:30 is thematically identical to Revelation 1:7, as well as linguistically similar, both of them being compounds of the same two Old Testament verses (Dan. 7:13 and Zech. 12:10).[72]

(2) The contextual rationale for my interpretation: The fundamental rationale for my interpretation is the two time texts preceding Revelation 1:7 by just four verses. These demand that the events must "soon come to pass" because "the time is near" (Rev. 1:1, 3). This is much like Matthew 24:34 ("this generation") controlling 24:30 (the parallel to Rev. 1:7). The reader should recall that I deal with these time texts above in this chapter.

(3) The textual justification for my interpretation: Revelation 1:7 states that this judgment will be against those who "pierced him." Those people are now long dead. The New Testament emphatically lays this guilt upon the first-century Jews (Acts 2:22–23; 3:13–15a; 5:28, 30; 7:52; 10:39; 1 Thess. 2:14–15). In fact, John declares this judgment is against "the tribes of the land [literally]," i.e., the tribes of Israel.

Conclusion

Having now reviewed Dr. Ice's argument for a future great Tribulation, I am more firmly convinced than ever of the evangelical preterist position.[73] The difficulty for the futurist in making sense of the time texts is reason enough alone at least to *appreciate* the preterist view. But when we discover the rich imagery of Old Testament prophecy and realize the dramatic nature of Israel's rejection of her Messiah (a major New Testament theme[74]), then we are *compelled,* I believe, to adopt a preterist understanding of the Great Tribulation.

As we consider the eschatological issues, let us adopt the noble Berean spirit:

> *Now these were more noble-minded than those in Thessalonica, for they received the word with great eagerness, examining the Scriptures daily, to see whether these things were so. (Acts 17:11)*

CONCLUSION

Kenneth L. Gentry Jr.

You the reader have in your hands a valuable tool for comparing two evangelical approaches to biblical prophecy. The value of our interactive presentation lies not only in its comparing, contrasting, and critiquing two evangelical options on the Great Tribulation, but also in doing so in a succinct and nontechnical format. Large and complex treatises on this subject are available, as are narrow and detailed analyses. But our book provides a condensed introduction to and overview of the basic issues.

Biblical prophecy is abused by cults, distorted by liberal theologians, confused by well-meaning enthusiasts, and debated by astute evangelical scholars. Nevertheless, it remains an important feature of the revelation of God in Scripture. As each of our chapters amply demonstrate, *numerous* Scriptures must be brought to bear upon the subject. Consequently, the *integrity* and *coherence* of God's Word is on the line. Furthermore, biblical prophecy is a significant element for framing a Christian worldview. As both of us mention in earlier chapters, one's approach to prophecy will affect his outlook for the future and thereby impact his conduct in the present. As a result, the *relevance* and *utility* of God's Word is also on the line.

By now you have read both of our presentations and our responses. If you were not aware before, you should certainly now be quite familiar with the remarkable differences between two evangelical viewpoints on the Great Tribulation. While Dr. Ice and I do agree on some important aspects of the question, many large and important issues separate us as surely as the Atlantic Ocean separates America from England.

Before I highlight a few of the key differences, though, I would like to lay down some common principles shared by both of us. Believe it or not, Dr. Ice and I agree on some important points! The reader would be wholly mistaken if he did not recognize *some* common planks shared

197

by our systems. In fact, I believe this is a vitally important contribution of our debate, namely, to alert evangelical, Bible-believing, born-again Christians that there are divergences *within* our circles on prophetic issues. Evangelicalism is not monolithic on prophecy; there are differences. But these differences are *within* the family. We stand united against all forms of rationalistic liberalism and heterodox cultism.

Our agreements include the following enormously important matters of evangelical commitment:

- We both agree that Jesus' prophecy of the Great Tribulation is a divinely inspired revelation from God, and not the ramblings of a first-century sage or mystic, as suggested by the recent liberal Jesus Seminar.
- We both believe that the prophecy involves Christ's actual perfect foreknowledge of the future beyond His day, and not a wise and perceptive guess based on developing historical forces or cultural surmises, as in the Book of Mormon's "prophecy" of the War Between the States.
- We both believe this biblical prophecy comes to concrete expression in real, historical phenomena, and is not a vague and nebulous construct applicable to any and all events, such as in the "prophecies" of Nostradamus.
- We both believe that these Tribulational events are significant factors for redemptive history, and not some inconsequential side issue stuffed away in some corner of theology, such as the debates by the Schoolmen over how many angels can dance on the head of a pin.
- We both agree that this element of prophecy does not exhaust biblical eschatology, in that we both hold to a future, glorious, public, physical return of Christ that will conclude temporal history and bring to fulfillment all remaining aspects of biblical prophecy, contrary to the liberal evolutionary view of the naturalistic heat death of the universe.

However, as you are by now well aware, our viewpoints on this great biblical theme are as opposite as can be within conservative, evangelical thinking. Consider the following:

- I hold that the Great Tribulation has *already occurred,* coming to pass in the first century.
  Dr. Ice sees it as a *still future,* fast-approaching prospect for humankind.
- I hold that these events punctuate the *end* of God's focus on and

exaltation of Israel.
Dr. Ice holds that these events introduce the *beginning* of God's renewed focus on and exaltation of Israel.

- I hold that these prophecies inaugurate the *beginning* of the Christian era in God's plan.
  Dr. Ice holds that they *conclude* the Christian era just after the church is taken from the world.
- I hold that the Tribulation is God's judgment on Israel for rejecting her Messiah.
  Dr. Ice holds that it is not God's judgment on Israel but the preparation of Israel to receive her Messiah.
- I hold that the Tribulation judgments are concentrated in local events surrounding ancient Jerusalem, though impacting to some degree other portions of the Roman empire.
  Dr. Ice believes that these judgments involve catastrophes that will literally affect the stellar universe and impact the entire planet.
- I hold that the Tribulation judgments are governed by Christ in such a way that they reflect His judgment against Israel, giving evidence that He is in heaven controlling those earthly affairs.
  Dr. Ice believes that the coming of Christ mentioned in the Tribulation passages require His public, visible, and physical presence to conclude those judgments.

Dr. Ice and I both trust and pray that you will find this presentation and interaction helpful not only to your own biblical study, but also to your spiritual growth resulting from your serious engagement of the interpretation of Scripture. We do not claim that this book presents all there is to know about this remarkable theme in eschatology. Indeed, it does not; many important issues lie beyond the page constraints of our debate. Nor do either of us claim to have all the answers ourselves. We are both constantly engaged in reading and researching in order to learn more about this biblical theme. In fact, we enjoined this debate knowing that despite our disagreements, "iron sharpens iron" (Prov. 27:17).

We trust that this book will encourage in you a truly Berean spirit, enabling you to be "more noble minded" in considering the issues. And we hope that you, as the Bereans of old, "received the word with great eagerness, examining the Scriptures daily, to see whether these things were so" (Acts 17:11). Both Dr. Ice and I lay our research and argumentation before you, urging you to open the Scriptures and evaluate the positions in the light of the God's Word. We desire that you remember that we must "let God be true" (Rom. 3:4).

RECOMMENDED RESOURCES FOR THE PRETERIST VIEW

Adams, Jay E. *The Time Is at Hand.* Nutley, NJ: Presbyterian and Reformed, 1966.

Bahnsen, Greg L. and Kenneth L. Gentry Jr. *House Divided: The Breakup of Dispensational Theology.* 2d. ed. Tyler, Tex.: Institute for Christian Economics, 1997.

———. "Tribulation or Transformation" (tape series). Texarkana, Ark.: Covenant Media Foundation, (1989).

Chilton, David. *The Days of Vengeance: An Exposition of the Book of Revelation.* Fort Worth: Dominion, 1987.

———. *The Great Tribulation.* Fort Worth: Dominion, 1987.

Clark, David S. *The Message from Patmos.* 1921. Reprint, Grand Rapids: Baker, 1989.

Davis, John Jefferson. *Christ's Victorious Reign: Postmillennialism Reconsidered.* Grand Rapids: Baker, 1986.

DeMar, Gary. *Last Days Madness: Obsession of the Modern Church.* 3d. ed. Atlanta: American Vision, 1997.

France, R. T. *The Gospel According to Matthew.* Grand Rapids: Eerdmans, 1987.

Gentry, Kenneth L. Jr. *The Beast of Revelation.* 2d ed. Tyler, Tex.: Institute for Christian Economics, 1995.

———. *Before Jerusalem Fell: Dating the Book of Revelation.* 3d ed. Atlanta: American Vision, 1999.

———. *He Shall Have Dominion: A Postmillennial Eschatology.* 2d. ed. Tyler, Tex.: Institute for Christian Economics, 1997.

———. *Perilous Times: A Study in Eschatological Evil.* Tyler, Tex.: Institute for Christian Economics, 1999.

————. *Revelation: A Tale of Two Cities*. Atlanta: American Vision, (1999).

Gregg, Steve. *Revelation: Four Views: A Parallel Commentary*. Nashville: Nelson, 1996.

Kik, J. Marcellus. *The Eschatology of Victory*. Phillipsburg, NJ: Presbyterian and Reformed, 1971.

Lightfoot, John. *Commentary on the New Testament from the Talmud and Hebraica: Matthew–1 Corinthians*. 1674. Reprint, Peabody, Mass.: Hendrickson, 1989.

Palm, David J. "The Signs of His Coming: An Examination of the Olivet Discourse from a Preterist Perspective." M. A. Thesis: Deerfield, Ill.: Trinity Evangelical Divinity School, 1993.

Pate, C. Marvin, ed. *Four Views on the Book of Revelation*. Grand Rapids: Zondervan, 1998.

Sproul, R. C. *The Last Days According to Jesus*. Grand Rapids: Baker, 1998.

Tasker, R. V. G. *The Gospel According to St. Matthew*. Tyndale New Testament Commentaries. Grand Rapids: Eerdmans, 1961.

Terry, Milton S. *Biblical Apocalyptics: A Study of the Most Notable Revelations of God and of Christ*. 1898. Reprint, Grand Rapids: Baker, 1989.

Walker, Peter W. L. *Jesus and the Holy City: New Testament Perspectives on Jerusalem*. Grand Rapids: Eerdmans, 1996.

Wright, N. T. *Jesus and the Victory of God*. Minneapolis: Fortress, 1996.

————. *The New Testament and the People of God*. Minneapolis: Fortress, 1992.

Audio and Video Resources

Christian Education Materials, P.O. Box 388, Placentia, CA 92871. KennethGentry@compuserve.com

Covenant Media Foundation, 4425 Jefferson Ave., Suite 108, Texarkana, AR 71854. tapes@cmfnow.com

Southern California Center for Christian Studies, P.O. Box 328, Placentia, CA 92871. study@scccs.org

RECOMMENDED RESOURCES FOR THE FUTURIST VIEW

Fruchtenbaum, Arnold G. *Footsteps of the Messiah: A Study of the Sequence of Prophetic Events.* Tustin, Calif.: Ariel Press, 1982.

Hoehner, Harold W. *Chronological Aspects of the Life of Christ.* Grand Rapids: Zondervan, 1977.

House, H. Wayne and Thomas Ice. *Dominion Theology: Blessing or Curse?* Portland, Ore.: Multnomah, 1988.

Ice, Thomas and Timothy Demy. *The Truth About the Antichrist and His Kingdom.* Pocket Prophecy. Eugene, Ore.: Harvest House, 1996.

———. *The Truth About the Tribulation.* Pocket Prophecy. Eugene, Ore.: Harvest House, 1996.

———. *The Truth About Jerusalem in Bible Prophecy.* Pocket Prophecy. Eugene, Ore.: Harvest House, 1996.

———, ed. *When the Trumpet Sounds: Today's Foremost Authorities Speak Out on End-Time Controversies.* Eugene, Ore.: Harvest House, 1995.

Larsen, David L. *Jews, Gentiles, and the Church: A New Perspective on History and Prophecy.* Grand Rapids: Discovery House, 1995.

McClain, Alva J. *The Greatness of the Kingdom: An Inductive Study of the Kingdom of God.* Winona Lake, Ind.: B. M. H. Books, 1959.

Pentecost, J. Dwight. *Things to Come: A Study in Biblical Eschatology.* Grand Rapids: Zondervan, 1958.

Peters, George N. H. *The Theocratic Kingdom.* 3 vols. Grand Rapids: Kregel, 1884.

Price, Randall. *Jerusalem in Prophecy.* Eugene, Ore.: Harvest House, 1998.

Ryrie, Charles C. *Basic Theology.* Wheaton, Ill.: SP Publications, 1986.
————. *Come Quickly, Lord Jesus: What You Need to Know About the Rapture.* Eugene, Ore.: Harvest House, 1996.
————. *Dispensationalism.* 1966. Reprint, Chicago: Moody, 1995.
Thomas, Robert L. *Revelation: An Exegetical Commentary.* 2 vols. Chicago: Moody, 1992, 1995.
Walvoord, John F. *Israel in Prophecy.* Grand Rapids: Zondervan, 1964.
————. *The Revelation of Jesus Christ.* Chicago: Moody, 1963.
————. *The Prophecy Knowledge Handbook.* Wheaton, Ill.: SP Publications, 1990.
————. *The Millennial Kingdom.* Findlay, Ohio: Dunham, 1959.
West, Nathaniel. *The Thousand-Year Reign of Christ: The Classic Work on the Millennium.* Grand Rapids: Kregel, 1993.
Willis, Wesley R.; John R. Master; and Charles C. Ryrie, eds. *Issues in Dispensationalism.* Chicago: Moody, 1994.

ENDNOTES

Introduction

1. Please note that throughout this book all Scripture quotations are taken from the New American Standard translation, unless otherwise indicated.
2. D. H. Kromminga, *The Millennium in the Church* (Grand Rapids: Eerdmans, 1945), 295.

Chapter 1

1. Hal Lindsey, *Planet Earth—2000: Will Mankind Survive?* (Palos Verdes, Calif.: Western Front, 1994); David Allen Lewis, *Prophecy 2000: Rushing to Armageddon* (Green Forest, Ark.: Green Leaf, 1990); Don McAlvanny et al., *Earth's Final Days* (Green Forest, Ariz.: New Leaf, 1994); and David Webber and Noah Hutchins, *Is This the Last Century?* (Nashville: Nelson, 1979).
2. Tim LaHaye, *No Fear of the Storm* (Sisters, Ore.: Multnomah, 1992), back cover copy.
3. Ibid., 49.
4. Tim LaHaye, "Twelve Reasons Why This Could Be the Terminal Generation," in *When the Trumpet Sounds,* ed. Thomas Ice and Timothy Demy (Eugene, Ore.: Harvest, 1995), chap. 21.
5. For my free, monthly Internet newsletter analyzing dispensationalism, send to: list-request@metanet.net. In the text box type: subscribe transition-list. For a web site listing some of my related articles, see http://www.cleaf.com/~covenant.
6. LaHaye, *No Fear of the Storm,* 49.
7. For a debate involving these schools and how they understand the book of Revelation, see C. Marvin Pate, *Four Views of the Book of Revelation* (Grand Rapids: Zondervan, 1997).
8. Eusebius deals with the matter at length in his famous *Ecclesiastical History,* 3:5–9, and *The Proof of the Gospel, passim.* See also Origen, *Against Celsus,* 2:13 and *Matthew* 19.
9. Josephus (A.D. 37–101) is the first-century Jewish historian who records the famous eyewitness account of the Jewish War leading to the destruction of the

temple: Flavius Josephus, *The Wars of the Jews.* A nice, compact, illustrated edition of Josephus is Paul L. Maier's, *Josephus: The Essential Works,* 2d. ed. (Grand Rapids: Kregel, 1994). The scholarly standard—complete with the Greek text, a modern English translation, and technical notes—appears in the *Loeb Classical Library,* published in ten volumes by Harvard University Press. A popular, affordable edition is the William Whiston (translated 1737) edition, *Josephus: Complete Works,* which is the version I use in my presentation.

10. H. Wayne House and Thomas Ice, *Dominion Theology: Blessing or Curse?* (Sisters, Ore.: Multnomah, 1988), chap. 13 (emphasis mine).

11. For an illustration of the confusion created by such a procedure, see Thomas Ice and Timothy Demy, *The Tribulation* (Eugene, Ore.: Harvest, 1996). See especially chapter 1, where the authors snatch verses out of context and apply them to "the Tribulation" at the end of history. Some of these clearly refer either to general Old Testament threats that may occur from time-to-time (Deut. 4:27–31) or to warnings of wrath that may actually apply to Old Testament era judgments under Assyria or Babylon. Here is my point: the unsuspecting reader cannot discover without extensive reading and research whether the authors are properly applying the passages, and this can lead to prophetic disorientation.

12. Stanley D. Toussaint, "Are the Church and the Rapture in Matthew 24?" in *When the Trumpet Sounds,* 242, 243.

13. Milton S. Terry, *Biblical Hermeneutics: A Treatise on the Interpretation of the Old and New Testaments* (1885; reprint, Grand Rapids: Zondervan, 1974).

14. See Milton S. Terry, *Biblical Apocalyptics: A Study of the Most Notable Revelations of God and of Christ* (1898; reprint, Grand Rapids: Zondervan, 1988).

15. Besides Terry, see also Louis Berkhof, *Principles of Biblical Interpretation: Sacred Hermeneutics* (Grand Rapids: Baker, 1950). For apocalyptic prophecy, see Vern S. Poythress, "Genre and Hermeneutics in Rev 20:1–6," *Journal of the Evangelical Theological Society* 36, no. 1 (March 1993): 41–54.

16. Craig A. Blaising and Darrell L. Bock, *Progressive Dispensationalism: An Up-to-Date Handbook of Contemporary Dispensational Thought* (Wheaton, Ill.: Bridgepoint, 1993), 36–37. In fact, such an attempt is evidence of "conceptual naïveté." Craig A. Blaising and Darrell L. Bock, eds., *Dispensationalism, Israel and the Church: The Search for Definition* (Grand Rapids: Zondervan, 1992), 29.

17. D. A. Carson, "Matthew," vol. 8 of *The Expositor's Bible Commentary,* ed. Frank E. Gaebelein (Grand Rapids: Zondervan, 1984), 27.

18. A. T. Robertson, *Word Pictures in the New Testament,* vol. 1 (Nashville: Broadman, 1930), 193.

19. C. Marvin Pate and Calvin B. Haines Jr., *Doomsday Delusions: What's Wrong with Predictions About the End of the World* (Downers Grove, Ill.: InterVarsity, 1995), 27.

20. Robert H. Mounce, *The Book of Revelation* (NICNT) (Grand Rapids: Eerdmans, 1977), 218.

21. William L. Lane, *Gospel According to Mark* (NICNT) (Grand Rapids: Eerdmans, 1974), 449.

22. E. J. Goodspeed, *Matthew, Apostle and Evangelist* (Philadelphia: John Winston, 1959), 21.

23. Donald Guthrie, *New Testament Introduction,* 3d. ed. (Downers Grove, Ill.: InterVarsity, 1990), 29.

24. For a brief summary of the thematic balance in Matthew along the lines of the following, see my book, *The Greatness of the Great Commission: The Christian Enterprise in a Fallen World,* 2d. ed. (Tyler, Tex.: Institute for Christian Economics, 1993), 35–39.

25. Charles C. Ryrie, *Dispensationalism* (Chicago: Moody, 1996), 20. The first edition of this work was entitled *Dispensationalism Today.*

26. See the famous statement by Papias (A.D. 60–130) as recorded in Eusebius (A.D. 260–340), *Ecclesiastical History* 3:39:16: "Matthew collected the oracles in the Hebrew language, and each interpreted them as best he could." See also Irenaeus (A.D. 130–202), *Against Heresies* 3:1:1 (cited in Eusebius, *Ecclesiastical History* 5:8:2); Tertullian (A.D. 160–220), *Against Marcion* 4:2; Origen (A.D. 185–254, cited in Eusebius 6:25:3–6); Eusebius (*E. H.* 3:24:5–6); and Jerome (A.D. 340–420), *Lives of Illustrious Men,* 3.

27. For example: "Now all this took place that what was spoken by the Lord through the prophet might be fulfilled" (Matt. 1:22). See similar statements in Matthew 2:15, 17, 23; 4:14; 8:17; 12:17; 13:14, 35; 21:4; 26:54, 56; 27:9.

28. Carson, "Matthew," 35.

29. P. W. L. Walker, *Jesus and the Holy City: New Testament Perspectives on Jerusalem* (Grand Rapids: Eerdmans, 1996), 26.

30. Anthony J. Saldarini, "Understanding Matthew's Vitriol," *Bible Review,* April 1997. See other studies of this phenomenon in Matthew: S. McKnight, "A Loyal Critic: Matthew's Polemic with Judaism in Theological Perspective," in *Anti-Semitism and Early Christianity: Issues of Polemic and Faith,* ed. C. A. Evans and D. A. Hagner (Minneapolis: Fortress, 1993), 55–79; George Stanton, "The Origin and Purpose of Matthew's Gospel: Matthean Scholarship from 1945–1980," in *Aufstieg und Niedergang der römischen Welt,* ed. H. Temporini and Walter Haase (Berlin: de Gruyter, 1985), 253, 280.

31. Liberal "Christians" and modern Jews declare as anti-Semitic the evangelical proclamation that there is no salvation outside of Christ. For example: "Rabbi A. James Rudin notes that 'whenever he hears the claim that "there is only one way to God,"' he hears an echo of totalitarianism." Tony Carnes, "Is Jewish-Christian a Contradiction in Terms?" *Christianity Today* 41, no. 4 (April 7, 1997): 50. Jews today view the New Testament itself as anti-Semitic. Jewish theologian Dan Cohn-Sherbok writes: "This animosity [toward Jews] was fueled by the Gospel writers who described Jesus attacking the leaders of the nation, whom he accused of hypocrisy and iniquity. . . . The New Testament thus laid the foundation for the theological negation of Judaism and the vilification of the Jewish people." Don Cohn-Sherbok, *The Crucified Jew: Twenty Centuries of Christian Anti-Semitism* (Grand Rapids: Eerdmans, 1992), 12. He comments on John's record of Christ's rejection during His trial (John 19:6–7): "Not surprisingly, such a diatribe against the Jews and the Jewish faith has served as a basis for Christian persecution of the Jews through the centuries." Ibid., 13.

32. See my book, *He Shall Have Dominion: A Postmillennial Eschatology,* 2d. ed. (Tyler, Tex.: Institute for Christian Economics, 1997).

33. Jerusalem seems to share *with* Herod this fear of the newborn king. D. A. Hagner, *Matthew* (Dallas: Word, 1993), 28.

34. Norval Geldenhuys, *The Gospel of Luke, New International Commentary on the New Testament* (Grand Rapids: Eerdmans, 1951), 139. See also John Lightfoot, *Commentary on the New Testament from the Talmud and Hebraica* (1859; reprint, Peabody, Mass.: Hendrickson, 1989), 77–78.

35. Luke records a parable portraying Christ's ministry in Israel as a man who plants a fig tree but receives no fruit after three years, ending in his cutting down and burning the tree (Luke 13:6–9).

36. W. R. Telford, *The Barren Temple and the Withered Tree,* Journal of the Study of New Testament Studies Series 1 (Sheffield, England: JSOT Press, 1980), 193ff.

37. Carson, "Matthew," 469.

38. Ibid., 470.

39. Ibid.

40. Eusebius, *The Proof of the Gospel,* ed. and trans. W. J. Ferrar (Grand Rapids: Baker, 1981), 2:120. See also Justin Martyr, *Dialogue with Trypho the Jew,* translated and edited by R. P. C. Hanson (New York: Association Press, 1964), 17: "For other nations have not inflicted on us [that is, Christians] and on Christ this wrong to such an extent as you have."

41. R. T. France, *The Gospel According to Matthew* (Grand Rapids: Eerdmans, 1987), 330. As Lightfoot puts it: "As if all the guilt of the blood of righteous men, that had been shed from the beginning of the world, had flowed together upon that generation." Lightfoot, *Commentary on the New Testament from the Talmud and Hebraica,* 305.

42. For a few samples, see Eusebius, *The Proof of the Gospel,* edited and translated by W. J. Ferrar (Grand Rapids: Baker, 1981): 1:110, 114, 210; 2:13–14, 26–27, 140, 146, 152. For observations on important statements in Matthew 23 and 24, see: 1:157, 2:120, 137–38.

43. France, *Matthew,* 212.

44. R. V. G. Tasker, *The Gospel According to St. Matthew: An Introduction and Commentary* (London: Tyndale, 1961), 206.

45. Carson, "Matthew," 487.

46. Jesus also includes a judgment-taunt against Israel: "For I say to you, you shall see Me no more till you say, 'Blessed is He who comes in the name of the LORD!'" (Matt. 24:39). Given the present context, this indicates that they will not see Him again, for they do not so proclaim Him. The words "until you say" are in the subjunctive mode, suggesting an indefinite possibility. The phrase functions as an equivalent to "unless." See France, *Matthew,* 332; C. C. Allison, *Journal for the Study of the New Testament* 8 (1983): 75–84; D. C. Allison, "Matt. 23:39=Luke 13:35b as a Conditional Prophecy," *Journal for the Study of the New Testament* 18 (1983): 75–84. After all, Matthew's gospel leaves Jerusalem empty and destroyed, rather than with a lingering hope (Matt. 12:45; 21:41; 23:38; 24:3–31). It closes in Galilee, rather than Jerusalem, with a commission to the nations (Matt. 28:18–20). Luke's writings take a slightly different approach. Luke's gospel has a famous section where Jesus "sets His

face" toward Jerusalem (Luke 9:51, 55; 13:22, 33; 18:31; 19:28) and ends with Jesus in Jerusalem. Acts picks up in Jerusalem and then spreads out and away from Jerusalem, ending up in Rome (Acts 1:8; 19:21; 28:14, 16).

47. Robertson, *Word Pictures,* 1:187.

48. Walker, *Jesus and the Holy City,* 7.

49. Frederic W. Farrar, *The Life of Christ* (New York: Burt, n.d.), 409. "In the Judaism of their day there were three interconnected entities (the Land, Jerusalem, and the temple) which formed, as it were , a concentric pattern of geographical *realia* which are theologically significant." Walker, *Jesus and the Holy City,* xii. The rabbis spoke of the ten degrees of holiness that narrowed down to the holy of holies. See the Mishnah: *Kelim* 1:6–9; Josephus, *Wars* 1:1:10; 5:227; 5:5:6; and *Against Apion* 2:2:8.

50. For ancient Jewish love for Jerusalem see the following: Ezekiel 38:12; the Apocrypha: Jub. 8:12, 19; 1 Enoch 26. I highly recommend reading the extremely important study on Jesus and Jerusalem: Walker, *Jesus and the Holy City.*

51. Ibid., xi.

52. E. P. Sanders, *The Historical Figure of Jesus* (London: Penguin, 1993), 262. For important studies on the significance of the temple, see Walker, *Jesus and the Holy City;* and R. J. Bauckham, "The Parting of the Ways: What Happened and Why," *Studia Theologica* 47 (1993): 135–51.

53. Walker, *Jesus and the Holy City,* 13.

54. Josephus, *Antiquities* 15:11:3, 5; *Wars* 5:5. *Middoth* 1:1–5:4 in Herbert Danby, trans., *The Mishnah* (New York: Oxford University Press, 1933), 589–97.

55. Philo, *The Special Laws: I,* 1:72–73.

56. Tacitus, *Fragments of the Histories* 2; and *History* 5:8.

57. William Hendriksen, *Matthew* (NTC) (Grand Rapids: Baker, 1973), 289–90.

58. Alfred Marshall, *The Interlinear Greek-English New Testament* (Grand Rapids: Zondervan, 1959), 108.

59. Robertson, *Word Pictures,* 1:194.

60. France, *Matthew,* 212–13.

61. House and Ice, *Dominion Theology,* 293–94. Apparently, he has not changed his position, see: Thomas Ice and Timothy Demy, *The Truth About the Tribulation* (Eugene, Ore.: Harvest, 1996), 12–13. See also: Paul D. Feinberg, "Dispensational Theology and the Rapture," in *Issues in Dispensationalism,* ed. Wesley R. Willis and John R. Master (Chicago: Moody, 1994), 241. See also John F. Walvoord, *The Prophecy Knowledge Handbook* (Wheaton, Ill.: Victor, 1990), 381, 386; and J. Dwight Pentecost, "Matthew," in *The Bible Knowledge Commentary: New Testament,* ed. John F. Walvoord and Roy B. Zuck (Wheaton, Ill.: Victor Books, 1985), 76.

62. This prophecy is not *ex eventu,* otherwise it: (1) would have mentioned the fires so prominent in the temple's destruction; (2) would not urge flight from the city had it already occurred; and (3) would have "corrected" Jesus' exhortation to flee to the mountains of Judea in light of the actual Christian flight to Pella in the foothills of the mountains.

Chapter 2

1. P. W. L. Walker, *Jesus and the Holy City: New Testament Perspectives on Jerusalem* (Grand Rapids: Eerdmans, 1996), 19.
2. "Many apocalypses were produced by unknown Jewish authors between 200 B.C. and A.D. 100 in imitation of the book of Daniel." G. E. Ladd, "Apocalyptic," in Walter A. Elwell, *Evangelical Dictionary of Theology* (Grand Rapids: Baker, 1984), 63. For a collection of such works, see James H. Charlesworth, ed., *The Old Testament Pseudepigrapha*, vol. 1, *Apocalyptic Literature and Testaments* (Garden City, NY: Doubleday, 1983).
3. See Josephus, *Wars* 4:3:9; 4:5:1; 7:8:1 and Tacitus, *Histories* 4:1–13. Regarding this "rising tide of Jewish nationalism," see F. F. Bruce, *New Testament History* (Garden City, N.Y.: Doubleday, 1969), 338–339; Walker, *Jesus and the Holy City,* 128; and R. Jewett, "Agitators and the Galatian Congregation," *New Testament Studies,* 17 (1970–71), 198–212.
4. Other texts suggest a militaristic kingdom concern: 2 Corinthians 5:16 may allude to the Jewish longing for a "fleshly" militaristic Messiah. N. T. Wright, *The Climax of the Covenant* (Edinburgh: T & T Clark, 1991), 408. John 18:33–35 indicates Jesus' concern that Pilate was believing the political charges against Him. See also John 19:12 and Acts 17:6–7.
5. William L. Lane, *The Gospel According to Mark, New International Commentary on the New Testament* (Grand Rapids: Eerdmans, 1974), 457.
6. Friedrich Büschel, *"anti,"* in *Theological Dictionary of the New Testament,* 10 vols., ed. Gerhard Kittel and trans. Geoffrey W. Bromiley (Grand Rapids: Eerdmans, 1964), 1:372.
7. A. T. Robertson, *Word Pictures in the New Testament* (Nashville: Broadman, 1930), 6:215.
8. Tim LaHaye, "Twelve Reasons Why This Could Be the Terminal Generation," in *When the Trumpet Sounds,* ed. Thomas Ice and Timothy Demy (Eugene, Ore.: Harvest, 1995), 432.
9. D. A. Carson, "Matthew," vol. 4 of *The Expositor's Bible Commentary,* ed. Frank E. Gaebelein (Grand Rapids: Zondervan, 1984), 498. See also C. Marvin Pate and Calvin B. Haines Jr., *Doomsday Delusions: What's Wrong with Predictions About the End of the World* (Grand Rapids: Zondervan, 1995), 36.
10. John F. Walvoord, *The Prophecy Knowledge Handbook* (Wheaton, Ill.: Victor, 1990), 383.
11. Thomas Ice and Timothy Demy, *The Truth About the Tribulation* (Eugene, Ore.: Harvest, 1996), 21.
12. G. W. Bowersock, *Fiction as History: Nero to Julian* (Berkeley, Calif.: University of California Press, 1994), 29.
13. Bo Reicke, *The New Testament Era: The World of the Bible from 500 B.C. to A.D. 100* (Philadelphia: Fortress, 1968), 110 (emphasis mine).
14. For implications of this for the Book of Revelation, see Kenneth L. Gentry Jr., *Before Jerusalem Fell: Dating the Book of Revelation,* 3d. ed. (Atlanta: American Vision, 1999); and Gentry, "The Preterist View of Revelation," in *Four Views on the Book of Revelation,* ed. C. Marvin Pate (Grand Rapids: Zondervan, 1998).

15. F. F. Bruce, *New Testament History* (Garden City, N.Y.: Doubleday, 1969), 338–339. See also R. Jewett, "Agitation of the Galatian Congregation," *New Testament Studies* 17 (1970–71): 198–212.

16. See also *Wars* 2:17:10; 4:3:2; and Philo *Letter to Caius* 30.

17. For example: Josephus, *Wars* 3:1:3; 3:4:4; *Ant.* 20:5:3; 20:8:6–10; and Tacitus, *Histories* 1:2–3.

18. *Annals* 12:43. See also Suetonius *Claudius* 18:2; Dio Cassius, *Roman History* 9:11; Orosius, *History* 7:6; Josephus, *Antiquities* 20:51, 101; and K. S. Gapp, "The Universal Famine Under Claudius," *Harvard Theological Review* 18 (1935): 261.

19. See Roman historians Tacitus, *Annals* 2:47; 12:43, 58 14:27; 15:22; Pliny, *Natural History* 2:86; Seneca, *Epistles* 91:9; Philostratus, *Life of Apollonius* 4:11, 4:34; Zonaras, *Annals* 11:10; and Suetonius, *Nero* 48; *Galba* 18. See also Orosius, *History* 7:7.

20. W. J. Coneybeare and J. S. Howson, *The Life and Epistles of St. Paul,* 2 vols. (New York: Charles Scribner's, 1894), 1:126.

21. Charles John Ellicott, ed., *Ellicott's Commentary on the Whole Bible,* 8 vols. (Grand Rapids: Zondervan, n.d.), 6:146. See D. H. K. Amiran, "A Revised Earthquake Catalouge of Palestine," *Israel Exploration Journal* 1 (1950–51): 223–24; and vol. 2 (1952): 48–62.

22. For information on the presence of the messianic kingdom see my book, *He Shall Have Dominion: A Postmillennial Eschatology,* 2d. ed. (Tyler, Tex.: Institute for Christian Economics, 1997), Part III; and my section in Darrell L. Bock, ed., *Three Views of the End of History* (Grand Rapids: Zondervan, forthcoming).

23. For example, see: Acts 4:1–3; 5:17–18, 27–33, 40; 6:12; 7:54–60; 8:1ff.; 9:1–4, 13, 23; 11:19; 12:1–3; 13:45–50; 14:2–5, 19; 16:23; 17:5, 13; 18:6, 12–18; 20:3, 19; 21:11, 27–32, 36; 22:3–5, 22–23, 30; 23:12, 20–21, 27, 30; 24:5–9, 27; 25:2–15, 24; 26:21. See also 2 Cor. 11:24; 2 Thess. 2:14–15; Heb. 10:32–34; Rev. 2:9; 3:9.

24. Walker, *Jesus and the Holy City,* 90.

25. The Neronic persecution is the first and most grievous Roman persecution. It lasted for forty-two months, from around November, A.D. 64, to the death of Nero, June 8, A.D. 68. See discussion in my book, *Before Jerusalem Fell: Dating the Book of Revelation,* 2d. ed. (Bethesda, MD: Christian Universities Press, 1997), chap. 5.

26. Orosius, *The Seven Books of History Against the Pagans,* 7:7. See Roy Joseph Deferrari, ed., *The Fathers of the Church,* vol. 50 (Washington, D.C.: Catholic University of America Press, 1964), 298–99.

27. W. H. C. Frend, *The Rise of Christianity* (Philadelphia: Fortress, 1984), 109.

28. Suetonius, *Claudius* 25:4. See Dio Cassius, *History* 60:6; Josephus, *Ant.* 19:5:2ff.; and Orosius, *History* 8:6:15ff. See also Acts 18:1–3.

29. Acts 20:28–30; Rom. 16:17–18; 1 Cor. 15:12; 2 Cor. 11:3–4; Gal. 1:6–9; 2:5, 11–21; 3:1, 5; Phil. 3:18–19; Col. 2:8, 18–23; 1 Tim. 1:3–7, 19–20; 4:1–3; 6:20–21; 2 Tim. 2:18; 4:2–5, 10–16; 2 Peter 2:1–3, 10–22; Jude 4, 8, 10–13, 16.

30. The name *Loukas* is Greek, not Hebrew. In Colossians 4:11, 14 Paul distinguishes his name from the names of those of the "circumcision." In Acts 1:19, Luke speaks about the Jews' language as "*their* proper tongue." These indicate he is a non-Jew.

31. Neh. 11:1, 18; Isa. 48:2; 52:1; 66:20; Dan. 9:16, 24; Joel 3:17.

32. For Jewish references to Israel as the "holy land," see 2 Baruch 63:10; 4 Ezra 13:48; 2 Maccabees 1:7.

33. Walker points out that in Mark's account, the flight from the temple (Mark 13:14) intentionally contrasts with the "gathering of the elect" (Mark 13:27). God intends the temple to be a "house of prayer for all nations" (Mark 11:17), but Israel becomes ingrown and self-centered. In the temple's demise, the elect will be scattered away from Jerusalem and the temple so that the Lord may "gather" the nations into the kingdom.

34. See the Mishnah: *Maaser Sheni* 1:5; *Pesahim* 10:3; and *Rosh ha-Shanah* 4:1.

35. A. D. Nock, "The Roman Army and the Roman Religious Year," *Harvard Theological Review* 45 (1952): 239; and C. Roth, "An Ordinance Against Images in Jerusalem, A.D. 66," *Harvard Theological Review* 49 (1956): 169–177. Tertullian (A.D. 160–220) writes concerning the Roman ensigns: "The camp religion of the Romans is all through a worship of the standards, a setting the standards above all gods" (*Apology* 16).

36. Josephus: "Now the Jews, after they had beaten Cestius, were so much elevated with their unexpected success, that they could not govern their zeal, but, like people blown up into a flame by their good fortune, carried the war to remoter places" (*Wars* 3:2:1).

37. Josephus comments that "had he, at that particular moment, decided to force his way through the walls, he would have capture the city forthwith, and the war would have been over. . . . Hence it came about that the war was so long protracted and the Jews drained the cup of irretrievable disaster" (*Wars* 2:19:4).

38. We should note that the Gentiles overrunning the land, city, and temple are ceremonially unclean (Acts 10:15; 11:19); they defile the temple (Acts 21:28).

39. "The eagle was adopted as the standard of the legion, and was carried by the first maniple of the first cohort." Sir Paul Harvey, *The Oxford Companion to Classical Literature* (Oxford: Clarendon, 1937), 49.

40. Josephus, *Wars* 7:1:1.

41. Lane, *Mark*, 471.

42. Walvoord, *The Prophecy Knowledge Handbook,* 160. J. Dwight Pentecost, *Thy Kingdom Come* (Wheaton, Ill.: Victor, 1990), 180; and Charles Dyer, "Ezekiel," in *The Bible Knowledge Commentary: Old Testament,* ed. John F. Walvoord and Roy B. Zuck (Wheaton, Ill.: Victor, 1985), 1236.

43. The Jewish War is limited to three and one-half years: Spring A.D. 67–August–September A.D. 70. See my book, *The Beast of Revelation* (Tyler, Tex.: Institute for Christian Economics, 1989), chap. 5.

44. John A. Martin, "Isaiah," in *The Bible Knowledge Commentary: Old Testament,* 1065–66.

45. The eastern area around Jericho is the last place Vespasian conquers in preparing for the direct siege of Jerusalem (*Wars* 4:8:1; 4:9:1).

46. 2 Sam. 22:15; Job 36:32; Pss. 18:14; 140:6; Ezek. 21:10; Zech. 9:14; Rev. 11:19; 16:18.

47. Charles H. Dyer, "Jeremiah," in *The Bible Knowledge Commentary: Old Testament,* 1135.

48. Milton S. Terry, *Biblical Apocalyptics: A Study of the Most Notable Revelations of God and of Christ* (1898; reprint, Grand Rapids: Baker, 1988), 280. Terry is widely cited by dispensationalist futurists as an authority on hermeneutics. For instance, see J. Dwight Pentecost, *Things to Come: A Study in Biblical Eschatology* (Grand Rapids: Zondervan, 1958), 5, 38–39, 42, 50, 54, and so on. As I show in my first chapter above, Terry is a strong advocate of preterism, which is evident in both his *Biblical Apocalyptics* and his hermeneutics manual, *Biblical Hermeneutics: A Treatise on the Interpretation of the Old and New Testaments* (reprint, Grand Rapids: Zondervan, 1974).

49. Walvoord and Zuck, eds., *The Bible Knowledge Commentary,* 843, 1059–60, 1066, 1416–17, 1477–78.

50. *Phaino* ("appear") may indicate "perceive, recognize," and not just "visibly" or "personally appear." See 2 Corinthians 13:7; Luke 24:11.

51. Interestingly, though, both the Jewish historian Josephus and the Roman historian Tacitus report several remarkable prodigies during the Jewish War. Tacitus: "In the sky appeared a vision of armies in conflict, of glittering armor. A sudden lightning flash from the clouds lit up the temple . . . . A superhuman voice was heard to declare that the gods were leaving it, and in the same instant came the rushing tumult of their departure." *Histories,* 5:13. See Josephus, *Wars* 6:5:3; Eusebius, *Eccl. Hist.* 3:8:2–3.

52. Alfred Edersheim, *Sketches of Jewish Social Life* (Grand Rapids: Eerdmans, 1972 [1876]), 14. See Mishnah tractates: *Orlah* 3:9; *Gittim* 1:2; *Abodah Zarah* 1:8; and *Mikwaoth* 8:1. *Kelim* 1:6 notes that "there are ten degrees of holiness. The Land of Israel is holier than any other land."

53. Alfred Edersheim, *The Life and Times of Jesus the Messiah* (1883; reprint, Grand Rapids: Eerdmans, n.d.), bk. 1, chap. 7.

54. Gen. 49:28; Exod. 24:4; Ezek. 47:13; Matt. 19:28; Luke 22:30; Acts 26:7; Rev. 21:12.

55. Christian Maurer, *"phule,"* in *Theological Dictionary of the New Testament,* 10 vols., ed. Gerhard Kittel and Gerhard Friedreich, and trans. Geoffrey W. Bromiley (Grand Rapids: Eerdmans, 1985), 9:246.

56. Robert L. Thomas, *Revelation 1–7: An Exegetical Commentary* (Chicago: Moody, 1992), 1:334.

57. See Gentry, *He Shall Have Dominion,* 321ff.; and Gary North, *Leviticus: An Economic Commentary* (Tyler, Tex.: Institute for Christian Economics, 1995), chap. 25.

58. This cannot refer to the transfiguration, which occurs only six days later. Jesus' statement expects that only "some standing here" will live to see it.

59. For a whole biblical-theological analysis of this redemptive reality see Walker, *Jesus and the Holy City.* See also David E. Holwerda, *Jesus and Israel: One Covenant or Two?* (Grand Rapids: Eerdmans, 1995).

60. The clarion call to salvation or the strong word of God may be expressed as a "voice like a trumpet." See Isa. 58:1; Jer. 6:17; Hos. 8:1; cp. Rev. 1:10; 4:1.

61. See also the Septuagint (the Greek translation of the Old Testament): 2 Chron. 36:15–16; Hag. 1:13; Mal. 2:7. And probably the "seven angels" of the "seven churches" in Revelation 2–3.
62. France, *Matthew,* 345. This is perhaps the best commentary for studying the Olivet Discourse.
63. For more information see my book, *Before Jerusalem Fell,* chaps. 8, 13; and Walker, *Jesus and the Holy City,* passim.
64. In the Old Testament, the Jews were often gathered into public assembly by the literal sound of the trumpet (Exod. 19:13, 16, 19; Lev. 23:24; Num. 29:1; Ps. 81:3–5; Joel 2:15).
65. Pentecost, *Thy Kingdom Come,* 255.

Chapter 3

1. Greg L. Bahnsen, "The Great Tribulation—Part 2," audio cassette recording #01298 (Auburn, Calif.: Covenant Tape Ministry, n.d.), side 1.
2. Arnold Fruchtenbaum, *Israelology: The Missing Link in Systematic Theology* (Tustin, Calif.: Ariel Ministries, 1989, 1992), 570.
3. Ibid., 574–75.
4. Ibid., 575.
5. John F. Walvoord, *Israel in Prophecy* (Grand Rapids: Zondervan, 1962), 44–45.
6. George M. Harton, "Fulfillment of Deuteronomy 28–30 in History and in Eschatology" (Th.D. diss., Dallas Theological Seminary, August 1981), 16.
7. Ibid., 17–18.
8. Ibid., 18.
9. Ibid., 20.
10. Ibid., 21.
11. Ibid., 22.
12. Ibid., 24.
13. Ibid., 24.
14. David Larsen, *Jews, Gentiles, and the Church* (Grand Rapids: Discovery House, 1995), 23.
15. Ibid., 23–24.
16. Harton, "Fulfillment," 233.
17. J. Randall Price, "Old Testament Tribulation Terms," in *When the Trumpet Sounds,* ed. Thomas Ice and Timothy Demy (Eugene, Ore.: Harvest House, 1995), 61. The Hebrew terms, as provided in Dr. Price's chart, have been removed.
18. Paul Benware, *Understanding End Times Prophecy* (Chicago: Moody, 1995), 244.
19. One of the most readable and extensive discussions on the chronology of the 70 weeks is found in Harold H. Hoehner, *Chronological Aspects of the Life of Christ* (Grand Rapids: Zondervan, 1977), 115–39. A more popular presentation is Herb Vander Lugt, *The Daniel Papers* (Grand Rapids: Radio Bible Class, 1994).
20. Hoehner, *Chronological,* 139.
21. J. Randall Price, "Prophetic Postponement in Daniel 9 and Other Texts," in

     Issues in Dispensationalism, ed. Wesley R. Willis and John R. Master (Chicago: Moody, 1994), 152–53.

22. Ibid., 156.
23. David Chilton, *The Days of Vengeance: An Exposition of the Book of Revelation* (Fort Worth: Dominion, 1987), 385–86.
24. Ibid., 66.
25. Eugene H. Merrill, *An Exegetical Commentary: Haggai, Zechariah, Malachi* (Chicago: Moody, 1994), 328.
26. Kenneth L. Gentry Jr., *He Shall Have Dominion: A Postmillennial Eschatology* (Tyler, Tex.: Institute for Christian Economics, 1992), 471.

Chapter 4

1. J. Randall Price, "The Desecration and Restoration of the temple as an Eschatological Motif in the Tanach, Jewish Apocalyptic Literature, and the New Testament" (Ph.D. diss., University of Texas at Austin, 1993).
2. Darrell L. Bock, *Luke 9:51–24:53* (Grand Rapids: Baker, 1996), 1675.
3. Ibid., 1676.
4. Kenneth L. Gentry Jr., *Before Jerusalem Fell: Dating the Book of Revelation* (Tyler, Tex.: Institute for Christian Economics, 1989), 176.
5. Bock, *Luke 9:51–24:53,* 1679–80.
6. Ibid., 1680–81.
7. Kenneth L. Gentry Jr., *He Shall Have Dominion: A Postmillennial Eschatology* (Tyler, Tex.: Institute for Christian Economics, 1992), 206.
8. Ibid., 275.
9. I. Howard Marshall, *Commentary on Luke* (Grand Rapids: Eerdmans, 1978), 776.
10. Ibid., 776–77.
11. Gary DeMar, *Last Days Madness* (Atlanta: American Vision, 1994), 169.
12. Gentry, *He Shall Have Dominion,* 339.
13. H. Wayne House and Thomas Ice, *Dominion Theology: Blessing or Curse?* (Portland: Multnomah, 1988), 286.
14. Bock, *Luke 9:51–24:53,* 1691–92.
15. Robert L. Thomas, *Revelation 1–7: An Exegetical Commentary* (Chicago: Moody, 1992), 32.
16. David Chilton, *The Days of Vengeance: An Exposition of the Book of Revelation* (Ft. Worth: Dominion, 1987), 43.
17. Gentry, *He Shall Have Dominion,* 273.
18. Ibid., 273–74.
19. Ibid., 274.
20. Ibid., 273.
21. For a summary of the Shechinah glory in the Bible, see Thomas Ice and Timothy Demy, *Fast Facts on Bible Prophecy* (Eugene, Ore.: Harvest House, 1997), 193–96.
22. Tremper Longman III and Daniel G. Reid, *God Is a Warrior* (Grand Rapids: Zondervan, 1995), 181.
23. Gentry, *Before Jerusalem Fell,* 133.

24. DeMar, *Last Days Madness,* 20.
25. John F. Walvoord, *The Revelation of Jesus Christ* (Chicago: Moody, 1966), 35.
26. Gentry, *Before Jerusalem Fell,* 138.
27. Walter Bauer, *A Greek-English Lexicon of the New Testament and Other Early Christian Literature,* trans. and adapt. William F. Arndt and F. Wilbur Gingrich (Chicago: University of Chicago Press, 1957).
28. Spiros Zodhiates, *The Complete Word Study Dictionary New Testament* (Chattanooga, Tenn.: AMG, 1992), s.v. 5034, 1369.
29. G. H. Lang, *The Revelation of Jesus Christ: Selected Studies* (1945; reprint, Miami Springs, Fla.: Conley & Schoettle, 1985), 387–88.
30. F. Blass and A. Debrunner, *A Greek Grammar of the New Testament and Other Early Christian Literature,* trans. and rev. Robert W. Funk (Chicago: University of Chicago Press, 1961).
31. Nigel Turner, *A Grammar of New Testament Greek,* ed. James H. Moulton, vol. 3, *Syntax* (Edinburgh: T & T Clark, 1963), 252.
32. Mal Couch, unpublished notes on Revelation, n.d., s.v. Rev. 1:1.
33. Gentry, *Before Jerusalem Fell,* 138.
34. Kurt Aland, *A History of Christianity,* vol. 1, *From the Beginnings to the Threshold of the Reformation,* trans. James L. Schaaf (Philadelphia: Fortress, 1985), 88.
35. Ibid.
36. Ibid., 87.
37. Ibid., 92.
38. Gentry, *He Shall Have Dominion,* 254, 276, 418.
39. DeMar, *Last Days Madness,* 285.
40. Ibid., 296.
41. Ibid., 289.
42. Ibid., 289–90.
43. Ibid., 290.
44. Couch, unpublished notes on Revelation.
45. J. Barton Payne, *The Imminent Appearing of Christ* (Grand Rapids: Eerdmans, 1962), 86.
46. Gentry, *Before Jerusalem Fell,* 141.
47. Philip Edgcumbe Hughes, *The Book of the Revelation* (Grand Rapids: Eerdmans, 1990), 237.
48. William R. Newell, *Revelation: A Complete Commentary* (1935; reprint, Grand Rapids: Baker, 1987), 362.
49. Gentry, *Before Jerusalem Fell,* 140.
50. Stanley D. Toussaint, "The Contingency of the Coming of the Kingdom," in *Integrity of Heart, Skillfulness of Hands: Biblical and Leadership Studies in Honor of Donald K. Campbell,* ed. Charles H. Dyer and Roy B. Zuck (Grand Rapids: Baker, 1994), 232–33.
51. F. C. Jennings, *Studies in Revelation* (New York: Publication Office "Our Hope," n.d.), 22.
52. Walvoord, *The Revelation of Jesus Christ,* 37, 334.
53. John F. Walvoord, *Israel in Prophecy* (Grand Rapids: Zondervan, 1962), 26.

Chapter 5

1. Gary DeMar, *Last Days Madness: Obsession of the Modern Church* (Atlanta: American Vision, 1997), 72.
2. Greg L Bahnsen and Kenneth L. Gentry Jr., *House Divided: The Break-Up of Dispensational Theology* (Tyler, Tex.: Institute for Christian Economics, 1989), 266–67.
3. Kenneth L. Gentry Jr., *He Shall Have Dominion* (Tyler, Tex.: Institute for Christian Economics, 1992), 162–63.
4. J. Randall Price, *Jerusalem in Prophecy: God's Stage for the Final Drama* (Eugene, Ore.: Harvest House, 1998), 251–55.
5. Ibid., 250–51.
6. Ibid., 251.
7. Ibid.
8. D. A. Carson, "Matthew," in *The Expositor's Bible Commentary,* vol. 8, ed. Frank E. Gaebelein (Grand Rapids: Zondervan, 1984), 497.
9. Stanley D. Toussaint, *Behold the King: A Study of Matthew* (Portland: Multnomah, 1980), 270.
10. James Barr, *The Semantics of Biblical Languages* (London: Oxford University Press, 1961), 218.
11. Arnold Fruchtenbaum, *The Footsteps of the Messiah: A Study of the Sequence of Prophetic Events* (San Antonio: Ariel Press, 1982), 446.
12. William F. Arndt and F. W. Gingrich, *A Greek-English Lexicon of the New Testament* (Chicago: University of Chicago Press, 1957), 563.
13. *New Geneva Study Bible* (Nashville: Nelson, 1995), 1766.
14. Daniel B. Wallace, *Greek Grammar Beyond the Basics* (Grand Rapids: Zondervan, 1996), 153.
15. James R. Gray, *Prophecy on the Mount* (Chandler, Ariz.: Berean Advocate Ministries, 1991), 62.
16. Kenneth L. Gentry Jr., *The Greatness of the Great Commission* (Tyler, Tex.: Institute for Christian Economics, 1990).
17. Robert H. Gundry, *Matthew: A Commentary on His Literary and Theological Art* (Grand Rapids: Eerdmans, 1982), 480.
18. James Morison, *A Practical Commentary on the Gospel According to St. Matthew* (London: Hodder and Stoughton, 1883), 463.
19. John F. Walvoord, "Christ's Olivet Discourse on the Time of the End: Signs of the End of the Age." *Bibliotheca Sacra* 128, no. 512 (October–December 1971): 318–19.
20. Ibid., 319.
21. Ibid.
22. D. A. Carson, "Matthew," *The Expositor's Bible Commentary,* vol. 8 (Grand Rapids: Zondervan, 1984), 500.
23. See David Chilton, *Paradise Restored: An Eschatology of Dominion* (Tyler, Tex.: Reconstruction Press, 1985), 274–6.
24. Stanley D. Toussaint, "A Critique of the Preterist View of the Olivet Discourse" (an unpublished paper presented to the Pre-Trib Study Group, Dallas, Texas, 1996).
25. Walvoord, "Christ's Olivet Discourse on the Time of the End," 317.

26. J. Randall Price, *Charting the Future* (San Marcos, Tex.: privately published charts, n.d.).

27. Arnold Fruchtenbaum, personal letter to Thomas Ice, dated September 16, 1994.

28. Toussaint, "Critique of the Preterist View of the Olivet Discourse."

29. Arndt and Gingrich, *Greek-English Lexicon,* 635.

30. Gerhard Kittel and Gerhard Friedrich, eds., *Theological Dictionary of the New Testament,* 10 vols. (Grand Rapids: Eerdmans, 1967), 5:859.

31. Ibid., 5:865.

32. Toussaint, "Critique of the Preterist View of the Olivet Discourse."

33. Ibid.

34. D. D. Buck, *Our Lord's Great Prophecy* (Nashville: South-Western Publishing House, 1857), 229.

35. Richard Cunningham Shimeall, *Christ's Second Coming: Is It Pre-Millennial or Post-Millennial?* (New York: John F. Trow and Richard Brinkerhoff, 1866), 157–59.

36. Henry George Liddell and Robert Scott, *A Greek-English Lexicon* (Oxford, England: Oxford Press, 1968), s.v. "aster," 261.

37. Gundry, *Matthew,* 487.

38. Randolph O. Yeager, *The Renaissance New Testament* (Bowling Green: Renaissance Press, 1978), 3:312.

39. Nigel Turner, *A Grammar of New Testament Greek,* vol. 3, *Syntax* (Edinburgh: T & T Clark, 1963), 214.

40. Arndt and Gingrich, *Greek-English Lexicon,* 598–600.

41. Ibid., 599.

42. Buck, *Our Lord's Great Prophecy,* 292.

43. Shimeall, *Christ's Second Coming,* 159–60.

44. For a biblical overview of the Shechinah glory, see Thomas Ice and Timothy Demy, *Fast Facts on Bible Prophecy* (Eugene, Ore.: Harvest House, 1997), 193–96.

45. Fruchtenbaum, *Footsteps,* 443.

46. Gentry, *He Shall Have Dominion,* 275.

47. C. F. Keil and F. Delitzsch, *Commentary on the Old Testament,* 10 vols., *Commentary on the Book of Daniel,* (Grand Rapids: Eerdmans, 1975), 235–36.

48. Toussaint, "Critique of the Preterist View of the Olivet Discourse," n.

49. See page 131 in this chapter.

50. Arnold Fruchtenbaum, *Israelology: The Missing Link in Systematic Theology,* rev. ed. (Tustin, Calif.: Ariel Ministries Press, 1992), 798–99.

51. Bahnsen and Gentry, *House Divided,* 276–83.

52. Ibid., 283.

53. Kenneth L. Gentry Jr., "A Preterist View of Revelation" in *Four Views on the Book of Revelation,* ed. C. Marvin Pate (Grand Rapids: Zondervan, 1998), 86–89.

54. Ibid.

55. Kenneth L. Gentry Jr., "A Brief Theological Analysis of Hyper-Preterism," *The Counsel of Chalcedon* 17, no. 1 (March 1995): 20.

Chapter 6

1. For a presentation and debate on Revelation see C. Marvin Pate, ed., *Four Views on the Book of Revelation* (Grand Rapids: Zondervan, 1998). I am the preterist contributor in that volume. For a helpful summary of the major viewpoints, see also Steve Gregg, *Revelation: Four Views: A Parallel Commentary* (Nashville: Nelson, 1996). For a thorough presentation of my preteristic understanding of Revelation, see my doctoral dissertation published as *Before Jerusalem Fell: Dating the Book of Revelation,* 3d ed. (Atlanta: American Vision, 1999).

2. For my preteristic analysis of several important passages often thought to relate to our future (e.g., Dan. 9:24–27; 2 Thess. 2:1–10; and others), see Kenneth L. Gentry Jr., *Perilous Times: A Study in Eschatological Evil* (Tyler, Tex.: Institute for Christian Economics, 1999).

3. David L. Turner, "The Structure and Sequence of Matthew 24:1–41: Interaction with Evangelical Treatments," *Grace Theological Journal* 10, no. 1 (Spring 1989): 7.

4. Ibid., 10.

5. P. C. Craigie, *The Book of Deuteronomy* (NICOT) (Grand Rapids: Eerdmans, 1976), 141 n. 9.

6. Ibid.

7. J. A. Thompson, *Deuteronomy: An Introduction and Commentary,* Tyndale (Downers Grove, Ill.: InterVarsity, 1974), 108; J. Ridderbos, *Deuteronomy,* Bible Student's Commentary, trans. Ed M. van der Maas (Grand Rapids: Regency, 1984), 90; A. D. H. Mayes, *Deuteronomy,* New Century Bible Commentary (Grand Rapids: Eerdmans, 1981), 156–157; C. F. Keil and F. Delitzsch, *Commentary on the Old Testament,* vol. 3, *The Pentateuch,* trans. James Martin (reprint, Grand Rapids: Eerdmans, 1975), 313; and W. L. Alexander, *Deuteronomy,* vol. 3 of *The Pulpit Commentary,* ed. H. D. M. Spence and Joseph S. Exell (reprint, Grand Rapids: Eerdmans, 1950), 74.

8. Walvoord applied this passage to past history without any mention of a future, eschatological reference: "*Deuteronomy 4:25–31.* Israel was warned not to make idols or sin morally because God would judge them and drive them out of the land. They were promised restoration if they return to the Lord. This was fulfilled in history." John F. Walvoord, *The Prophecy Knowledge Handbook* (Wheaton, Ill.: Victor, 1990), 38. Earlier, he noted that this passage "seems to be a reference to events which are yet future." John F. Walvoord, *The Nations, Israel, and the Church in Prophecy* (reprint, Grand Rapids: Zondervan, 1988), 104.

9. See G. T. Manley, "Deuteronomy," in *New Bible Commentary,* ed. Francis Davidson (Grand Rapids: Eerdmans, 1954), 218; J. A. Thompson, *Deuteronomy* (TOTC) (Downers Grove, Ill.: InterVarsity, 1974), 268; Raymond B. Dillard and Tremper Longman III, *An Introduction to the Old Testament* (Grand Rapids: Zondervan, 1994), 165; Roland Kenneth Harrison, *Introduction to the Old Testament* (Grand Rapids: Eerdmans, 1969), 658; and Willem VanGemeren, *Interpreting the Prophetic Word* (Grand Rapids: Zondervan, 1990), 79

10. John S. Deere, "Deuteronomy," in *The Bible Knowledge Commentary: Old Testament,* ed. John F. Walvoord and Roy B. Zuck (Wheaton, Ill.: Victor Books, 1985), 313.

11. "This happened when Samaria was besieged by the Arameans, 2 Kings 6:28–29, and when Jerusalem was besieged by the Chaldeans, Lam. 2:20; 4:10, and by the Romans." Ridderbos, *Deuteronomy*, 260. "This description no doubt applies to the Chaldeans . . . , but it applies to other enemies of Israel beside these, namely to the great imperial powers generally, the Assyrians, Chaldeans, and Romans." Keil and Delitzsch, *Pentateuch*, 442. "The gruesome scenes here predicted (vv. 52–57) were accomplished in the sieges of Samaria (2 Ki. 6:28) and Jerusalem (La. 2:19–33). . . . These prophetic words have been fulfilled several times in Jewish history from 722 B.C. onwards, and not least in the present century. . . . At the destruction of Jerusalem the Romans consigned many Jews into slavery, transporting a large number to Egypt by ship." R. K. Harrison, "Deuteronomy," in *The Eerdmans Bible Commentary*, ed. Donald Guthrie and J. A. Motyer, 3d. ed. (Grand Rapids: Eerdmans, 1970), 225. See also Darrell L. Bock, *Luke 9:51–24:53* (Grand Rapids: Baker, 1994), 1656; Manley, "Deuteronomy," 218; and Earl S. Kalland, "Deuteronomy," in *Expositor's Bible Commentary*, ed. Frank E. Gaebelein (Grand Rapids: Zondervan, 1992), 174.

12. Sunukjian, "Amos," in *The Bible Knowledge Commentary: Old Testament*, 1436, 1437.

13. Ice's plain and simple approach to Scripture is often little more than loud bravado. I challenge the reader to take Ice's test: Ask your "schoolchild" to outline "the elements in the history of Israel" (p. 77).

14. Feinberg, "Systems of Discontinuity," *Continuity and Discontinuity*, 73.

15. Craig A. Blaising, "Development of Dispensationalism," *Bibliotheca Sacra* 579: 272.

16. Craig A. Blaising and Darrell L. Bock, eds., *Dispensationalism, Israel and the Church: The Search for Definition* (Grand Rapids: Zondervan, 1992), 378.

17. Ibid., 29.

18. William L. Lane, *Gospel According to Mark* (NICNT) (Grand Rapids: Eerdmans, 1974), 449.

19. Bock, *Luke 9:51–24:53*, 1680.

20. Thomas Ice, "Dispensational Hermeneutics," in Wesley R. Willis and John Masters, eds., *Issues in Dispensationalism* (Chicago: Moody, 1994), chap. 2.

21. Merrill F. Unger, *Introductory Guide to the Old Testament* (Grand Rapids: Zondervan, 1951), 329.

22. Since composing my original presentation, I have come across a fine summary of the various messianic-political movements and revolts in the first century prior to A.D. 70: N. T. Wright, *The New Testament and the People of God* (Minneapolis: Fortress, 1992), 170–181. Wright summarily states the first-century situation (p. 176): "This brief list of movements of revolt in the years preceding the war gives, I think, sufficient indication of the mood of the country as a whole. . . . This broad base of revolutionary activity is particularly the case in the main Jewish War itself (A.D. 66–73)." He mentions "two would-be messianic movements" and other movements led by "messianic or quasi-messianic figures" (p. 173). This fits perfectly the warning of Christ in Matthew 24:4–7.

23. A. T. Robertson, *Word Pictures in the New Testament* (Nashville: Broadman, 1933), 284.

24. Walvoord, *The Prophecy Knowledge Handbook,* 15.

25. John F. Walvoord, *The Revelation of Jesus Christ* (Chicago: Moody, 1966), 35.

26. See Robert L. Thomas, *Revelation 1–7: An Exegetical Commentary* (Chicago: Moody, 1992), 455; and idem, *Revelation 8–22* (Chicago: Moody, 1995), 30, 46, 49, 90, 264, 360, 386, 467.

27. See Walvoord, *The Prophecy Knowledge Handbook,* 332.

28. I would like to offer a couple of asides here. (1) Earlier, Ice says the A.D. 70 judgment on Israel was the "ultimate curse." Yet here, he argues that the future great tribulation will witness her "greatest distress." If the future tribulation is her *"greatest* distress" what becomes of the *"ultimate* curse" in A.D. 70? Surely, then, it is not really "ultimate," since the greatest is to come! (2) Ice sees the Babylonian assault (586 B.C.) and the later Roman conquest (A.D. 70) as fulfilling the Deuteronomy 28:49–68 passage (p. 79). Yet Deuteronomy 28 contains the judgments to befall the Gentiles in the future great tribulation: "Within Deuteronomy 28–30 we see a specific reference to the Tribulation when it says, 'And the LORD your God will inflict all these curses [Deut. 28] on your enemies and on those who hate you, who persecuted you' (Deut. 30:7)." "Moses tells us that the time of tribulation will include in its purposes a time of retribution to the Gentiles for their ill treatment of the Jews" (p. 78). But Ice says the future Great Tribulation is unparalleled (based on Matt. 24:21)— even though Scripture defines it in the same terms as the A.D. 70 holocaust. Ice seems confused here.

29. The Greek version of the Old Testament which was used by Christ and the apostles.

30. We should translate the word "earth" in verse 18 as "land," as does the New King James Version.

31. Walvoord, *The Prophecy Knowledge Handbook,* 310.

32. John D. Hannah, "Zephaniah," in *The Bible Knowledge Commentary: Old Testament,* 1525.

33. Walvoord, *The Prophecy Knowledge Handbook,* 169.

34. J. Dwight Pentecost, *Thy Kingdom Come* (Wheaton, Ill.: Victor, 1990), 123.

35. In fact, preterists may be either postmillennial (J. M. Kik, *The Eschatology of Victory* [Phillipsburg, N.J.: Presbyterian and Reformed, 1971]), amillennial (Jay Adams, *The Time Is at Hand* [Phillipsburg, N.J.: Presbyterian and Reformed, 1970]), or premillennial (David L. Turner, "The Structure and Sequence of Matthew 24:1– 41").

36. Indeed "it is possible as well that chronological speculations, based on the prophetic literature, and in particular the hope of release after seventy years of 'exile' (Dan. 9:2, 24; Jer. 25:12; 29:10; 2 Chron. 36:21f.; cp. Ant. 10:267; 11:1) may have fueled hopes of sudden deliverance" in the first century. N. T. Wright, *The New Testament and the People of God* (Minneapolis: Fortress, 1992), 173n.

37. For greater detail see Gentry, *Perilous Times,* chap. 1.

38. Lewis Sperry Chafer, *Major Bible Themes,* rev. John F. Walvoord (Grand Rapids: Zondervan, 1974), 306 (emphasis mine). See also Richard L. Niswonger, *New Testament History* (Grand Rapids: Zondervan, 1988), 168, rebuts Hoehner.

Aune has a date of A.D. 29: David E. Aune, *The New Testament in Its Literary Environment* (Philadelphia: Westminster, 1987), 11.

39. Space prohibits my analysis of Daniel 9, but I refer the reader to Gentry, *Perilous Times,* 31–40.

40. J. Barton Payne, "The Goal of Daniel's Seventy Weeks," *Journal of the Evangelical Theological Society* 21, no. 2 (June 1978): 97–116.

41. Turner, "The Structure and Sequence of Matthew 24:1–41," 7. D. A. Carson, "Matthew," in *Expositor's Bible Commentary,* ed. Frank E. Gaebelein (Grand Rapids: Zondervan, 1984), 8:507.

42. J. Dwight Pentecost, *Things to Come: A Study in Biblical Eschatology* (Grand Rapids: Zondervan, 1958), 281.

43. Pentecost, *Thy Kingdom Come,* 255–56.

44. Bock, *Luke 9:51–24:53,* 1692.

45. Only in Revelation 20 does John glance beyond his declared time frame of "near" or "shortly." Though Ice thinks this incorporates a contradiction in my view (p. 112), it most certainly does *not.* How could a time frame—even symbolically designated—of one thousand years in length be fulfilled "soon"? John specifically stretches out the events of this section beyond his overriding time constraints.

46. This will undoubtedly surprise the reader who has been shielded from nondispensational interpretations. For those interested in a succinct overview of Revelation with supporting evidence for this viewpoint, I recommend reading my chapter in Pate, *Four Views on the Book of Revelation,* 35–92. Also see closer scrutiny of Revelation 13 (on the Beast) and 17 (on the Harlot) in Gentry, *Perilous Times,* chaps. 4 and 5. For more information, see my commentary: *Revelation: A Tale of Two Cities* (Atlanta: American Vision, 1999).

47. See, for example, the following versions: *King James Version, New King James Version, New International Version, American Standard Version, New American Standard Version, Revised Standard Version, New Revised Standard Version, New American Bible, Today's English Version, New Testament in Modern English, Amplified Bible, New English Bible, New Jerusalem Bible, New Testament in the Language of the People, New Testament in the Language of Today, Contemporary English Version.*

48. I. Howard Marshall, *The Gospel of Luke* (NIGTC) (Grand Rapids: Eerdmans, 1978), 676.

49. Arndt and Gingrich, *Lexicon,* 807.

50. Marshall cites Revelation 1:1 and 22:6 as evidence that the "normal use of the phrase *en tachei* suggest[s] that 'soon' is the meaning." Marshall, *The Gospel of Luke,* 676.

51. The coming of Christ here is not his Second Coming at the end of history, but his judgment coming upon Jerusalem (see discussion of Matthew 24:27).

52. John A. Martin, "Isaiah," in *The Bible Knowledge Commentary: Old Testament,* 1060. See also Seth Erlandsson, *The Burden of Babylon: A Study of Isaiah 13:2–14:23* (Lund, Sweden: C. W. K. Glerrup, 1970), 91–92.

53. Martin, "Isaiah," 1657.

54. Bock, *Luke 9:51–24:53,* 1664.

55. Ibid., 1650.

56. Ibid., 1656.

57. Ibid., 1669.

58. *New Scofield Reference Bible* (New York: Oxford University Press, 1967), 841 n. 3

59. Walvoord, *The Prophecy Knowledge Handbook,* 160, 161, 162.

60. Lane, *Mark,* 471.

61. Thomas Ice and Timothy Dean, *The Truth About Jerusalem in Bible Prophecy* (Eugene, Ore.: Harvest, 1996), 27, 28.

62. Thomas, *Revelation 8–22,* 317. See also Charles H. Dyer, *The Rise of Babylon: Sign of the End Times* (Wheaton: Tyndale, 1991); and Hal Lindsey and Chuck Missler, "The Rise of Babylon and the Persian Gulf Crisis: A Special Report"(Palos Verdes, Calif.: Hal Lindsey Ministries, 1991). Though Walvoord disagrees, John F. Walvoord, *The Revelation of Jesus Christ,* 246–47.

63. Lane, *Mark,* 471 n. 82.

64. Robertson, *Word Pictures,* 1:191.

65. Edward J. Young, *The Book of Isaiah,* vol. 3 (Grand Rapids: Eerdmans, 1972), 530.

66. Regarding Paul's comments on Timothy's coming before winter, Hendriksen writes: "Then navigation ceased, or if attempted at all, became very danger-ous, as Paul knew by experience (read Acts 27)." William Hendriksen, *Expo-sition of the Pastoral Epistles* (Grand Rapids: Baker, 1957), 332.

67. For additional documentation on the majesty and fame of the New Testament temple, see Bock, *Luke 9:51–24:53,* 1660–63.

68. G. Abbott-Smith, *Manual Greek Lexicon of the New Testament* (Edinburgh: T & T Clark, 1937), 28, 208

69. Leon Morris, *The Gospel According to Luke,* Tyndale New Testament Com-mentaries (Grand Rapids: Eerdmans, 1974), 300.

70. See my discussion on pages 55–57.

71. Ibid., 38. Citing Robert H. Mounce, *The Book of Revelation* (NICNT) (Grand Rapids: Eerdmans, 1977), 218. For a helpful, succinct discussion of apoca-lyptic hermeneutics, see: Vern S. Poythress, "Genre and Hermeneutics in Rev 20:1–6," *Journal of the Evangelical Theological Society* 36 (March 1993): 41–54.

72. Most commentators agree that Matthew 24:30 and Revelation 1:7 speak to the same issue, even dispensationalists such as Robert Thomas (*Revelation 1–7,* 76) and John Walvoord (*Revelation,* 39). Various older commentators apply both texts to A.D. 70. For example, see John Lightfoot: "The vengeance of Christ upon that nation is described as his 'coming,' John xxi.22; Heb. x.37: his 'com-ing in the clouds,' Revelation I.7: 'in glory with the angels,' Matt. xxiv.30, &c." Lightfoot, *Commentary on the New Testament from the Talmud and Hebraica: Matthew–1 Corinthians* (1658; reprint, Peabody, Mass.: Hendrickson, 1989), 2:422, cp. 319. See also Adam Clarke, *Clarke's Commentary* (1832; reprint, Nashville: Abingdon, n.d.), 6:971.

73. Two other preterist approaches exist, both of which I resist: (1) Liberal preterism, which basically interprets Revelation as an *ex eventu* editorial revision.

(2) Hyperpreterism, which views *all* prophecy as fulfilled in A.D. 70. I stand against both abuses of preterism just as Dr. Ice stands against all cultic forms of premillennialism (e.g., Mormonism, Jehovah's Witnesses, Seventh-Day Adventists, Worldwide Church of God).

74. See especially Peter W. L. Walker, *Jesus and the Holy City: New Testament Perspectives on Jerusalem* (Grand Rapids: Eerdmans, 1996); David E. Holwerda, *Jesus and Israel: One Covenant or Two?* (Grand Rapids: Eerdmans, 1995); and Gentry, *Perilous Times*.